D1301485

Richard Harton

UNDER THE HAMMER

St. Martin's Press
New York

UNDER THE HAMMER. Copyright © 1991 by Richard Harton. All rights reserved. Printed in the United States of America. No part of this book may be used or reproduced in any manner whatsoever without written permission except in the case of brief quotations embodied in critical articles or reviews. For information, address St. Martin's Press, 175 Fifth Avenue, New York, N.Y. 10010.

Library of Congress Cataloging-in-Publication Data

Harton, Richard.
    Under the hammer / Richard Harton.
        p.   cm.
    ISBN 0-312-05981-7
    1. Harton, Richard.   2. Auctioneers—Biography.   I. Title.
HF5476.H37A3   1991
381'.17'092—dc20
[B]   90-27509
                                                                        CIP

First published in Great Britain by Macdonald & Co. (Publishers) Limited.

First U.S. Edition: July 1991
10 9 8 7 6 5 4 3 2 1

Chapter 1

'It's a biscuit barrel,' I said.

'Aye, it's Cromwellian,' Mr Barthorpe replied with all the authority of a born and bred Yorkshireman. Clearly his many years in Sussex had done little to undermine his inbred native self-confidence.

'Er, well . . .' I hesitated as I decided how best to break the truth, 'actually, I'm afraid it's late nineteenth-century.'

'Aye, that's what I said young man, it's Cromwellian.'

It had not been a good morning and it appeared to be getting worse. It was also getting hotter; at least I was. I felt a fresh trickle of perspiration dribble down the back of my neck until it was eventually absorbed by my shirt collar. Mr Barthorpe, with his luxuriant grey walrus moustache, was probably somewhere in his mid-eighties, and seemed as oblivious to the heat as he was to the true historical period of Oliver Cromwell. The kitchen of the Barthorpe bungalow, where we stood, had every window closed tight and an Aga going flat out. Despite this the old man wore a white shirt with a stiff collar, a woollen tie, a coarse tweed three-piece suit and highly polished black boots. Finally, just in case that lot wasn't a match for anything the elements might throw at him, he had taken the added precaution of putting on a thin pullover under his waistcoat. All this might have been regarded as nothing other than prudent in a normal English summer, but this was not a normal English summer. It was the summer of 1976, when week after week of temperatures in the seventies and eighties had turned the rivers into meandering strips of hard-baked clay and the roads into ribands of oozing black glue.

I mopped my brow and the back of my neck with an

1

already soggy handkerchief and tried again.

'No, Mr Barthorpe, it's not Cromwellian. Cromwell was seventeenth-century; this biscuit barrel is nineteenth-century; that makes it Victorian.'

'Why?'

The question was tossed down like a gauntlet.

'Why what?'

'Why d'ye keep saying it's not Cromwellian when it is?'

'Mr Barthorpe,' as I spoke I could feel my self-restraint beginning to melt away in the heat, 'I keep saying it's not Cromwellian because it's not Cromwellian. It's Victorian. They didn't even have biscuit barrels like this in the seventeenth century!'

Mr Barthorpe eyed me sullenly in silence, then his mouth slowly twisted into an expression which fell somewhere between a grotesque smile and a sneer. Whatever it was, the muscular contractions involved had a dramatic effect on his previously immobile moustache: it rose up like a stage curtain. For the first time a set of huge brilliant-white dentures loomed into view. They seemed to be out of scale with the rest of his face and their overall appearance was so dramatic that I was momentarily paralysed by a sort of dreadful fascination.

'So *you* say,' Mr Barthorpe hissed in a voice laden with contempt and distrust, 'so *you* say.'

The curtain descended again and the dentures vanished as suddenly as they had appeared.

'Right! Look at this,' I said, recovering some of my composure and pointing to a diamond-shaped mark on the bottom of the disputed piece. 'Do you know what that is?'

Mr Barthorpe made no reply. Instead he reached into his jacket pocket and withdrew a battered spectacles case. Slowly, and with some sense of ceremony he opened the case and took out a set of National Health glasses. He closed the case, put it back in his pocket and very deliberately entwined the flexible arms of the glasses around the backs of his elephantine ears. Having completed this somewhat theatrical performance he stepped forward and stooped so that his face was no more than a few inches from the biscuit barrel.

'Well,' he said, peering at the mark and then glaring up at me, 'you're s'posed to be t'bloody expert, you tell me.'

'Certainly. It's a registration mark which shows that this design was recorded with the Registration of Designs office. The important thing about that is that these marks were only used between 1842 and 1883, so that proves beyond any doubt that this piece is Victorian.'

Without saying a word Mr Barthorpe reached out and took his discredited treasure from me. He stood staring at the mark for some moments and then looked up again.

'No more to be said then,' he muttered. 'I'll show you out young man.'

Despite myself, I began to feel sorry for the old man as he led me from the kitchen into the cool dark little entrance hall. All too often I had to destroy long held illusions about precious family heirlooms. I never found it easy and usually tried to side-step doing it if possible, but on that occasion I consoled myself with the fact that I hadn't been given a choice.

Mr Barthorpe, who just a few minutes earlier had been about as friendly as a cornered polecat, now opened the door for me with almost deferential courtesy. As I stepped into the sunshine he looked again at the tell-tale mark on his biscuit barrel.

'Before you go, Mr 'arton – and I'm sorry to 'ave dragged you all this way for nothin' – these two letters in this 'ere mark – the L and M – what d'they mean?'

'One of them is the code letter for the year of registration,' I said, only too happy to have been given the opportunity to end our encounter on a friendly note, 'and the other is the code for the month.'

'I see, I see. So what month and year do these two actually stand for then?'

As he spoke, his pink face, shot with tiny blue veins, was a picture of child-like innocence and curiosity.

'The L is for 1882 but I'm afraid I haven't a clue which month the M stands for. I've never really committed those particular date letters to memory,' I said, apologetically. 'I'd have to look it up.'

Mr Barthorpe gave a long sniff and once more lifted his

gaze from the biscuit barrel to me. Gone was the innocence. In its place was a steely glare and those extraordinary teeth again. With all the speed, ferocity and, when it came to bridgework, a fair amount of the physical appearance of a great white shark, he swept in for the kill.

'You know booger-all!' he said, and firmly closed the door.

As I drove back to Kington it crossed my mind that my morning had not been particularly representative of the popular idea of what a fine art auctioneer does with his time. Usually envisaged draped languidly over his rostrum, gavel in hand, selling things for prices that sound like long distance telephone numbers, it's a picture in which the Mr Barthorpes of this world tend not to feature very often, if at all. In fact, in real life, they play all too large a part.

That particular morning I had seen half a dozen would-be clients. In the course of those visits I had seen a Persian rug which was little more than half its original size and therefore a lot less than half its original value; a Chippendale chair which (rather predictably) wasn't Chippendale; a Queen Anne table which was Queen Anne but was still only worth about a fifth of what the owner thought it should make; a clock which appeared to have been made from spare bits left over from about twenty other clocks; a 'Stradivarius' violin which, along with several thousand others, had begun life in nineteenth-century Prussia rather than seventeenth- or eighteenth-century Italy; a 'Regency' table which was all of five years old; and, of course, Mr Barthorpe's biscuit barrel.

It had been a *bad* morning, and on top of that I had some very serious thinking to do. So, not for the first time that summer, I parked my car high on the Sussex Downs overlooking Kington and sat down on the scorched brown wiry grass. It was almost one o'clock and the temperature was obviously in the eighties again. There was no breeze at all, so the air hung heavy with a shimmering heat haze which seemed to smother every sound except the busy chirruping of the invisible army of grasshoppers that surrounded me.

Below me, the old market town, still dominated by the Conqueror's fortress, lay spread out like the open pages of

4

an atlas. All the narrow streets and lanes appeared to radiate from the castle like the spokes of a wheel from its hub. Then they tumbled away downhill making a mellow patchwork of brick, stone, stucco, flint and tile. There was very little sign of pedestrian life; only the most dedicated or desperate shopper was going to endure the inferno of the High Street that near noon.

Kington had presented a different face to me on a day ten years earlier when, at the age of seventeen, I had splashed through those same streets on a cold wet morning in February. I was on my way to an interview for a job with Charles Wilson and Company, Fine Art Auctioneers and Valuers, who according to their letterhead were located at 23 Waterloo Street. I was to meet a partner – a Mr Parkes – at ten o'clock. Beyond that, all I knew about the firm, the partner, or indeed fine art could have been perfectly adequately summarised on the back of the return bus ticket in my mackintosh pocket. As a result of this, I was less than confident about my coming interview. Nor were my butterflies helped by my first sight of Waterloo Street. I had never seen, let alone set foot in an auction gallery, but I had a mental picture of what one would look like. Although I don't recall the detail of the image, it certainly involved a combination of Portland stone, oak panelled doors, marble steps and iron railings. What actually confronted me in Waterloo Street was a scene of almost total devastation. Just three buildings remained; immediately on my right, a single cottage stood defiantly in an ocean of mud and brick rubble, whilst further down on the other side of the road another cottage leaned like a drunkard against what appeared to be some sort of tatty warehouse. A bulldozer grubbed away noisily in the mud, heaping up rubble and soil, while several bonfires, piled high with old timbers, blazed and crackled at various points down the street sending great plumes of sparks high into the black rain-sodden sky.

If I had given any thought at all to what I was doing I would have turned around and gone straight home. As it was, like some automaton, I picked my way along the broken red brick pavement to the far cottage. Blackened brass numbers on the door confirmed that it was number twenty-one. It didn't take a Sherlock Holmes to deduce that, no matter how unlikely or unpalatable it might be, the old warehouse next door had to be number twenty-three.

Charles Wilson's auction galleries were built of the sort of glazed brick often seen in Victorian institutional buildings. The double doors and all the windows at street level were fitted with similarly institutional frosted green safety glass – the type with wire mesh running through it. The only acknowledgment of the building's current status was a peeling sign suspended with the aid of some electrical cable from a metal bracket over the door. It confirmed that this was indeed 'The Auction Galleries' and went on to explain in copperplate script that 'Charles Wilson & Co' held 'Regular Sales of Period Furniture, Silver, Jewellery, Pictures, Objects D'art, Libraries of Books, etc'.

I tried the door but it was locked, so I pressed the bell and waited. Nothing happened. The problem with doorbells in big buildings is that you never know whether the things are broken or if they are jangling away like fire alarms somewhere in the bowels of the place, so I hammered on the door for good measure. Just as I stepped back to see if there was any sign of life in the first floor windows, the door was thrown open.

'Yes, can I help you? We're not on view I'm afraid.' The speaker was a tall, good looking, athletically built man in his mid-fifties. His grey hair was swept back and his clear blue eyes looked at me over a pair of gold framed half-moon spectacles which were perched on the end of his nose. He wore a heavy overcoat, and was carrying a clipboard on which he balanced a box of manila tags, a roll of Sellotape and a pen. As he spoke, the pen rolled off the board and fell to the floor. Stooping to recover it he dropped the Sellotape and the tags, and in a desperate attempt to save them he let go the clipboard. On hitting the floor, the hand-written notes it held came free and spread themselves over the doorstep and muddy pavement.

'Oh, sod it!' he said.

I helped him gather up the soiled sheets of paper. 'I have an appointment with Mr Parkes.'

He looked blank. 'My name's Richard Harton – the

6

appointment is for ten o'clock – I've got a letter from Mr Parkes confirming it.'

'Oh, of course, of course! Come in Ronald. I'm Duncan Parkes. It's good to meet you.' He shook me by the hand enthusiastically.

'Er, Richard,' I ventured.

'Sorry?'

'Richard – my name – it's Richard.'

'Course it is. What did I say? Memory like the proverbial sieve you know. Come this way.'

With this, he turned and loped off into a maze of furniture.

I closed the door behind me and pursued Duncan Parkes into the cavernous interior of 23 Waterloo Street. It seemed, on first sight, to be one big room which rose from a bare concrete floor to a high pitched roof. The roof itself was punctuated by sky-lights which apparently let in more than light, since galvanised buckets were strategically placed below two of them. The full extent of the decoration throughout looked to comprise peeling pale grey emulsion and chipped off-white gloss. Some two feet above our heads, at intervals around the walls, a few gas heaters of uncertain vintage hissed and flickered with very little conviction. If they were producing any heat at all, and their appearance suggested otherwise, it must have been going straight up into the roof void since the temperature at ground level was definitely icy.

The furniture was piled everywhere. Chests of drawers stood three high; towers of chairs teetered precariously beside stacks of tables; a row of grandfather clocks, some with their works on the floor next to them, lined one wall, and, littered throughout, stacks of gilt-framed pictures were propped against any available objects. The overall impression was one of complete and unqualified chaos.

Every now and then, as Duncan Parkes zig-zagged through this obstacle course, he would stop and point out pieces to me.

'Look at that *bonheur du jour* Richard. What a little beauty!'

'Yes.'

7

'Now look at that, have you ever seen a more exquisite *petite commode*?'

'No.'

'And what about that? One of the most magnificent *armoires* I've ever seen!'

'Oh, yes, magnificent.'

I had no idea what he was talking about. More to the point, on most occasions, I wasn't even sure which thing I was supposed to be looking at, so I just admired in the general direction indicated and tried to make the right noises.

'This main room,' he went on, 'is Gallery One, and there are three more galleries – one through that door, another through that one, and one up the stairs there. Bigger than it looks from outside, isn't it?'

'Yes.'

'Not what you were expecting I bet!'

'No,' I said, 'no, it's not.'

'This is my office. Come on in, Richard.'

He opened a door marked PRIVATE and I followed him into a small dingy room dominated by a very large desk. A smaller desk stood in a corner, and a low bookcase with glass doors occupied one wall. There were four chairs, each apparently originating from a different set.

I have said that the overall impression given by Gallery One was that of chaos. Duncan Parkes's office now made it appear to be a model of order and efficiency. Every horizontal surface, including almost all the floor space, was piled high with files, papers, china, glass, unidentifiable bits of wood and metal and a number of rolled-up rugs. A grey blanket of dust lay over everything.

'Take a seat, old chap.' He gestured towards a chair already fully occupied by six or seven small grubby pictures.

'Just pass those over to me – I'll stick them here for now.' He piled them carelessly on top of a heap of files on one of the other chairs.

'Hold on,' he said, 'don't sit down yet. Let's dust that chair or your suit will get filthy.'

Delving into one of the drawers in his desk, he produced a grubby yellow cloth which he flicked energetically at the chair seat causing a cloud of dust to spiral into the air. We both sat down.

'Well, Richard, I've asked Tom Jeffreys, our chief cashier, to join us. He's only just joined the firm and he feels –.' He was interrupted by a knock at the door which opened simultaneously to admit a small bustling man of about sixty who seemed to be almost entombed in a large sheepskin coat.

'Ah, right on cue,' Duncan Parkes said. 'This is Mr Jeffreys, our chief cashier . . .'

'Chief accountant,' corrected the newcomer.

'Er, yes, quite, chief accountant,' confirmed Duncan Parkes, though sounding less than comfortable with the revised title.

'Anyway, take a seat, Mr Jeffreys.'

'Delighted DP. Where do you suggest?'

'Good point,' Parkes replied as he glanced around the office. 'Just hand those pictures over to me and then pass the files to Roland who can . . .'

'Richard,' I said, a little impetuously.

'What?'

'Richard . . . not Roland . . . my name . . . Richard . . .' I tailed off, wishing I hadn't bothered to mention it.

'Yes! Absolutely! Richard! So pass the files to Richard and then he can put them over on the desk in the corner.'

The pictures which I had passed, one by one, to Duncan Parkes were now passed, one by one, back to him by Tom Jeffreys. This time he stacked them on top of the bookcase next to some sort of crudely carved wooden figure. Tom Jeffreys pointed at it.

'What is that ugly little thing?' he asked.

'That? Oh, it's a Songe wood fetish figure.'

'Well, silly me, I should have guessed. Not worth anything is it?'

'Could make a hundred pounds.'

'Good God,' Tom Jeffreys looked at it with complete disgust, 'I wouldn't give you the time of day for it!'

I finished piling the files on the desk and sat down as Duncan Parkes slid back into his own seat.

'As I was saying –'

9

'I'm sorry to interrupt, DP, but this chair is covered in filth.' Jeffreys picked up a greasy cobweb between finger and thumb to illustrate his point.

'You're right!' Parkes sprang to his feet. 'Hold on.' Again he sidled along the narrow strip of unencumbered floor between his desk and the bookcase and, armed with his yellow duster, attacked the chair with considerable ferocity. Once again the air filled with dust.

'Leave it, leave it, for Christ's sake, leave it!' Tom Jeffreys staggered back, his hand clamped over his mouth and nose. 'I'd rather sit on it than inhale the damned stuff.'

Duncan Parkes renegotiated the tortuous route back to his chair and sat down. 'Sorry about the current state of chaos, Richard, but we're in the middle of cataloguing a big sale and everything else just has to take a back seat.'

He trawled through the rubbish on his desk and came up with a packet of cigarettes and a gold lighter.

'Normally you'd find this place all ship-shape and Bristol fashion, so don't think we're always like this.'

He smiled broadly as he lit a cigarette, but away on his left and unseen by him, Tom Jeffreys looked at me and slowly shook his head.

'But as I was saying,' Duncan Parkes continued, 'Mr Jeffreys feels that he will be fully occupied looking after the estate agency side of the business, so I thought this might be an ideal opportunity for you. You said in your letter that you wanted to get out of accountancy and into auctioneering, and this would be a good way to do the one by making use of your experience in the other. What do you think?'

'Well, if it would help me to get started in the business . . .'

'Excellent! I felt sure you'd agree. Mr Jeffreys and I think it will take about a third of your time to handle the accounts for the auction galleries and the rest of your time could then be spent on the fine art side. Of course, as you become more experienced at cataloguing and valuing we can get a junior to handle the book-keeping donkey-work. To start with you'd spend the majority of your time portering, but that's the best way there is to get to know your way around this business – and it'll keep you fit. Look at me!' He slapped an undeniably slim waistline with both hands to underline his point. Tom Jeffreys looked bored. Duncan Parkes turned to him. 'Were there any questions you wanted to ask Richard, Mr Jeffreys?'

'Yes. How long have you been articled to these chartered accountants you're working for?'

'Eight months – since I left school,' I said.

'And when did you decide you didn't want to be a chartered accountant?'

'About ten minutes after I started working there.'

'Par for the course I would have thought,' said Duncan Parkes who had started picking through the letters on his desk.

'And you're used to doing bank reconciliations and trial balances?' Tom Jeffreys continued.

'Yes.'

'And you've kept a set of double entry books and maintained a separate clients' account?'

'Well, er –'

'Of course he has,' Duncan Parkes cut in before I could tell the truth. 'Now just how much do you get paid at the moment?'

'Five pounds a week,' I said, far too young and inexperienced to realise that it was essential to add a minimum of fifty per cent when answering that particular question.

'Really?' Once again a broad smile swept over Duncan Parkes's face as he spoke. 'I'm sure we can improve upon that – so let's say we'll start you on seven pounds ten shillings and then review it after six months. Okay?'

'Yes,' I said.

'Excellent. Now, when can you start Robert?'

Back in the ruins of Waterloo Street I mused over the fact that I had just stumbled into a job in the fine art world. The interview, over which I had lost so much sleep, had lasted barely ten minutes, and most of that had been spent playing pass-the-oil-painting. I hadn't managed to ask a single question; I hadn't learned anything about Charles Wilson and Company; instead I'd just allowed myself to be swept along by the whirlwind that was Duncan Parkes.

'Want a lift?' It was Tom Jeffreys in an aged but immaculate Ford.

11

'I'm only going to the bus station.'

'Get in.'

I have said that Tom Jeffreys was a small man, and like so many people of small stature he seemed to compensate for his lack of height with an inexhaustible supply of energy. His quick nervous movements and sharp features gave him an air of vulpine aggression; something at its most exaggerated – as I was about to discover – when he was behind the wheel of a car.

The journey to the bus station was barely a quarter of a mile, but that didn't prevent it from being subject to three near misses and an almost ceaseless torrent of abuse from Tom regarding the general incompetence of his fellow road users. In the all too brief pauses between expletives he explained that he had worked for many years as the chief cashier for a large UK engineering group in the Far East – presumably where he'd polished his driving skills. On his recent retirement he and his wife had returned to England where he had decided to take the job with Wilson's to supplement his pension and keep boredom at bay. He made no bones about the fact that he found the change from large multi-national public company to small provincial partnership more than a little frustrating.

'The important thing is, Richard,' he said, completely disregarding the road ahead, 'don't let the buggers take themselves too seriously.'

He surprised me considerably by swerving round a pedestrian I was quite certain he hadn't seen.

'Now take DP back there,' he continued, 'he's okay, a nice bloke really and, so I'm told, one of the best auctioneers around. Not that I'd know anything about that of course. Bloody silly if you ask me, all those people paying hundreds of quid for filthy dirty old stuff that I wouldn't allow in the garden shed let alone the house.'

We overtook an orderly queue of five cars waiting at a set of traffic-lights, cut back in front of the first in the line and drove on while the signals were still on red and amber.

'Just look at that thing on the bookcase. What did he say it was?'

'A fetish figure I think,' I said.

12

'Yes, that's it! Well, the mind boggles at what they used to get up to with that – doesn't bear thinking about. But I ask you, a hundred pounds! That's three months salary for you, Richard. And by the way, you should have asked for more money – I can see I'm going to have to teach you a few of the facts of life my boy.' Somehow we just missed the cyclist for whose safe deliverance I'd been praying for the previous twenty or thirty seconds.

'And that's what I'm getting at,' he went on, as we stopped abruptly outside the bus station, half on the road and half on the pavement, 'they're all right – DP and Mr Anthony . . .'

'Mr Anthony?'

'Anthony Wilson – he's the senior partner, in charge of the estate agency side of things, doesn't have much to do with the auction galleries. He's my problem. But as I was saying, they're all right but both of them are so tight I'm surprised they don't squeak when they walk. Just look at that building: freezing cold; running with water; falling down about their ears; most of the street demolished around them, and there they sit. Won't spend any money on it, won't move out either – no bloody idea! Anyway, see you in a couple of months' time, Richard.'

I had barely closed the car door when, without any obvious warning and to a cacophony of car horns and squealing tyres, Tom Jeffreys pulled straight back into the moving stream of traffic and accelerated away. His only act in recognition of the mayhem for which he was responsible was a two-fingered salute to the unfortunate motorists in his wake.

It was already apparent to me that my newly chosen career was going to be very different to the stagnant calm of the chartered accountant's office.

13

Chapter 2

Looking back, if my first week at Wilson's was like a bad dream then the first day was an absolute nightmare. I was tossed about on a sea of meaningless terms and incomprehensible instructions while everyone else worked like precisely engineered cogs in a finely tuned machine. It's bad enough starting a new job when you know what you're doing, but starting as a complete novice is really heavy going. To make matters even worse, the week I had chosen to embark on my new career just happened to be the week of Wilson's April sale.

Being the possessor of neither car nor licence, my journey to work on the first morning (and for many to come) was by a lumbering green double-decker bus. It was a pretty standard example of its type. Each body panel rattled or vibrated, sometimes in unison with its fellows, sometimes independently of them. The seats, dampened by the residual April showers on the raincoats of the passengers, gave off an aroma of stale cigarette smoke which, when combined with the bouquet of the odd three-day-old shirt and the occasional case of halitosis, produced a pungent and heady cocktail. As the vehicle lurched, swayed and shuddered on its way, the driver regularly crashed the gears sending the small group of standing passengers tottering, first three or four steps forwards then, just as they had regained their balance, three or four steps backwards again.

I must say that being in close company with fifty or sixty damp, expectorating fellow human beings has never really been my idea of fun – certainly not before nine o'clock in the morning anyway. On that occasion, however, I would happily have chosen to stay with them rather than get off at Kington. Nevertheless, off I got.

Waterloo Street hadn't improved much since my earlier visit, although the bulldozer had gone and the bonfires had long since turned to wet piles of fine white ash. The early spring sunshine, flashing back off the glistening brick pavement and the smooth slate roof of the Auction Galleries, was trying valiantly to make the place look a little more cheerful. It was an uphill task.

If the rest of the street hadn't changed, Wilson's certainly had. There were a dozen or so cars parked outside. The front doors were wide open, and assorted people were coming and going. I took a deep breath in a futile attempt to quell my butterflies and entered the building.

The place had been transformed. The chaos and dirt were gone and in their place was a wonderful display of beautifully arranged furniture. The walls were hung with hundreds of pictures, and brightly coloured rugs and carpets covered the floor. I stood for a few moments staring at the place.

'Looks better than the last time you were here, doesn't it, Richard!'

Unnoticed by me, Duncan Parkes had followed me into the building and was standing just behind me, a bulging briefcase in one hand and a thick file of papers under the other arm.

'Here, grab hold of this,' he said, handing the file to me. 'Don't drop it, it's all the reserves for this sale.'

I would have liked to have asked what reserves were but I didn't get a chance. Duncan had already set off in the direction of his office.

'Did I mention to you that we'd be selling this week?' he asked over his shoulder as we almost ran through the gallery.

'No.'

'Oh, well, never mind, as good a time to start as any – mind you, I expect you'll find it a bit hectic to begin with.'

This was to prove the understatement of the week.

'Morning, boys. Not overdoing things I hope?'

Duncan's remark was addressed to a group of four or five

15

lads slumped on pieces of furniture at the far end of the gallery. They made up an extraordinary selection of shapes and sizes; the only thing they seemed to have in common, apart from their youth, was that they all wore blue aprons emblazoned with the name WILSON'S.

'Nah, jus' 'avin' a cup a char, Mr Parkes – we've bin at it since eight this mornin'.'

'Yes, Philip, but at what? That's the question – at what?' Duncan grinned at them as he spoke and strode on.

On arriving in his office I felt quite relieved to find it was just as much a mess as when I'd first seen it. In fact, if anything, it was worse. He took the file from me and dumped it on his desk along with his briefcase.

'Now, where's Margaret?' he asked, as if I would automatically know who he was talking about.

'Here,' said a voice from just outside the half-open door. The door then received a spirited kick and in response opened fully to allow a petite, dark-haired woman in her mid-thirties to enter. She wore a business-like dark grey suit and despite her slight stature, carried a huge pile of files, letters and sale catalogues.

'Give those to me, Margaret,' Parkes said, stepping forward to take the load.

'Okay. Thanks, but please don't muddle them up again, DP, it took me most of last night to sort them out.'

He didn't seem to hear, and lumped everything down next to the file and briefcase on the desk. 'Now Margaret, this is our new boy, Richard Harton,' Duncan said. 'Richard, this is Margaret Graham, my secretary and personal assistant. Margaret's the one who really runs the place.' He beamed benignly at Margaret Graham. Over the next few years, the truth of his words was to become evident to me. Margaret Graham was the only one who could control Duncan's enthusiasm and productively channel his bursts of energy. She usually managed it by the simple but skilful expedient of convincing Duncan that he was the one who'd actually suggested whatever it was she wanted him to do. An old technique I know, but no less accomplished for that.

'Right then, Richard,' Duncan continued, 'let's get you started. It's going to be a three-day sale – about fifteen

16

hundred lots in all. We sell furniture, clocks, rugs and pictures tomorrow; porcelain, metalware and miscellaneous on Wednesday; silver on Thursday – only about three hundred lots that day, nice and easy!' He smiled at me as he searched through his jacket pockets. 'Margaret, where are my cigarettes?'

'How should I know, you've only just arrived. I expect you've left them in the car again.'

'Never mind,' he said, 'I'll get them later.'

'No, no,' she said, 'I'll get them for you now, otherwise you'll smoke mine all morning. Where are the keys?'

'Where was I?' Duncan said as Margaret left the office. 'Oh yes: we're selling tomorrow, Wednesday and Thursday, so today is stacking-back day. That's when all the lots that have been on view to the general public for the last few days are lined up out at the back so they can be brought forward to the front to be shown when they're sold; then they're taken back out to the back again . . . simple really!' I must have looked very vague. 'Yes . . . well . . . anyway . . . Henry will explain it all to you. He's the lanky one out there in the gallery. Go and have a word with him, ask him to give you an apron, and say I've told you to work with him today. Good luck!'

With that, Duncan Parkes opened the door and ushered me out of his office.

Really, he was quite right about stacking-back being simple. It is, as long as you know what you're doing or have somebody with infinite patience to teach you. I didn't get somebody with infinite patience, I got Henry Dodds.

Henry was an Old Etonian who had failed signally to capitalise on the head start that parental wealth and influence had given him. Three and a half years after bidding farewell to his Alma Mater (and a less than distinguished academic record) his career in fine art seemed permanently stalled at the none too dizzy height of head porter at Wilson's. Frustration at his lack of upward mobility probably made Henry more mean-spirited than he otherwise might have been. It certainly aggravated a tendency to regard any newcomer – no matter how inept – as a potential threat. At any rate, my arrival was greeted with a marked lack of enthusiasm.

17

Among the motley group at the far end of the gallery, Henry Dodds was easily identifiable. He must have been at least six feet four or five inches tall, but he was so thin that his entire frame looked as though it was in imminent danger of collapse. This resulted in a stoop which brought him down to a more manageable six feet one or two. His lank blonde hair hung down in a drooping blinker over his right eye. As I approached, he examined me coolly with the other eye.

'Yes?'

'My name's Richard Harton. Mr Parkes said I was to find Henry Dodds and . . .'

'Well, you've found him,' Henry drawled, 'but what do you want, a medal?'

He turned to his colleagues, apparently inviting some celebration of his rapier-like wit. None came. Two of them slowly chewed gum, as another delicately peeled his hand-rolled cigarette from where it had stuck to his upper lip. All four looked bored.

'. . . he told me,' I continued, 'to say that I was to work with you today.'

'Oh, well, that's fine then. Mr Parkes wants him to work with me today.' Henry turned again to the other four, 'we needn't worry about the stacking-back with wonder-boy here. We can all relax and go home early.'

'Do give it a rest, Henery,' said one of the other porters. He was easily the most striking in appearance after Henry Dodds; almost cubic in build, with forearms the size of my thighs, and a dense thatch of blonde hair.

'Yeah,' chipped in another, 'what's the problem, 'Eners? Don't tell me Caroline's gorn an' wivdrawn yer conjugular rights again!'

'Ooh, let's hope not,' the cubic one went on, 'he's always impossible when that happens, ain't you, Henery?'

'Shut up you lot,' Henry snapped. 'I'm going to see Parkes about this – just dumping some idiot, who hasn't got a clue what he's doing, on me on a day like this; and without a word of warning. I'm not putting up with it. It's him or me this time!' And with that, Henry Dodds stormed off towards Duncan Parkes's office.

One of the porters who hadn't contributed to the

18

proceedings, but had watched everything with a detached air of boredom, slid from his perch on a tall chest of drawers and wandered over to me as Henry flounced off.

'Don't worry, Sunshine,' he said, a pair of smiling brown eyes peering out from below a thick dark fringe. 'Henry's like that with everyone. He can't help it – too much inbreeding I expect. He'll be back in a minute – he won't get any change out of DP.' He smiled broadly and stubbed out the cigarette which Henry had left burning in a nearby ashtray.

'Filthy habit,' he said, 'but practically every silly sod in this place does it. Can't abide it myself.'

It didn't seem the right time to mention that I smoked a pipe.

'I'm Jim Watson by the way,' he went on, 'and Mr Universe over there is my little brother Patrick. The other two yobs are Phil Dixon and Colin Jones. They both work for us at Watson's Removals – the family firm you know!'

'You don't all work for Wilson's then?' I said.

'No, mate. We just help out over sales and do most of the removals DP has to arrange. Mind you, Pat and me both did our apprenticeships here before we started working for Dad, so we know as much about it as young Henery.'

'Talk of the devil,' said Patrick, 'here comes Petal now. Sorted DP out then, dear?'

Henry Dodds ignored the taunt and walked straight past us, disappearing into a cupboard beneath the wide staircase that dominated the gallery. He re-appeared in a moment with a blue apron which he tossed at me.

'Get your jacket off and put that on,' he ordered. I obeyed. The apron touched the floor. With a lot of hitching up and folding at the waist I managed to adjust it so it was clear of the ground, although the resulting bulge in the midriff made me look as though I was pregnant.

Henry stood in silence watching the operation with obvious distaste. His expression suggested that a slow and agonising death would be too easy for me.

'What a cross-patch he is today, Pat,' observed Jim Watson.

'Always the same at sale time,' his brother replied. 'Brings on his old problem – allergy to work.'

19

'Now that's unfair, Pat, I won't stand by and listen to that,' Jim went on. 'You can't be sure he's allergic to work – we ain't seen him do none yet!'

'Well give him a chance for Chrissake, Jim, we've only known him for about four years.'

'Oh, do shut up, you two.' Henry was plainly not amused. 'We can always use another removal firm you know. We don't have to use bloody Watsons. You're hardly la crême de la bloody crême!'

'What'd he say, Jim?'

'Not sure, but I think you've gone and hurt his feelings again, Patrick – you will always go too far!'

'Sorry, Jim – I always forget what a sensitive little flower he is.'

'Right,' Henry barked, obviously deciding to re-establish his authority without delay. 'Jim and Patrick, get out to Gallery Three and sort out the line – *now!*'

'Yessir,' they shouted in unison, Jim snapping to attention and saluting while Patrick clicked his heels. As they sprinted, giggling, from the gallery Henry turned to the rest of us.

'Okay, you lot, we're going to line the furniture in Gallery One.'

Colin Jones and Philip Dixon appeared wholly unexcited by the prospect, and I just looked blank.

'Right, Harton,' Henry concentrated his attention on me, 'it's quite simple, we're going to stack-back the furniture in Gallery . . .'

'But you said we was goin' to line it,' interrupted Colin.

'It's the same thing, as you well know,' snarled Henry.

'Yeah, I know it, an' Phil knows it, an' Jim an' Pat know it, but I don't 'spect bleedin' what'sis name does, do 'e?' Colin persisted, quite obviously genuinely concerned about the confusing nature of the instruction I was receiving, and seemingly oblivious to Henry's rising colour.

'Well, he does now.'

'Yeah, but 'e wouldn't 'ave done if I 'adn't said nuffin', would 'e?' Colin insisted.

'That's right 'Enery, fair's fair,' Phil contributed helpfully. 'You've got to explain it proper to 'im or the poor sod won't know what's 'appenin', will 'e?'

'Oh, give me strength,' Henry muttered, and cast his eyes heavenwards.

'Now listen, Harton, because I intend to say this once and only once. We are going to stack-back the furniture in Gallery One – here, you'll need this.' He pushed a dog-eared sale catalogue at me.

'I'll shout out a lot number and say what the piece is,' he went on, 'and you can find it. Once you've got it, shout out so that I can tick it off in my catalogue, and then take it out to Jim and Patrick who'll be putting the stuff in line out in Gallery Three. Right?'

'Right,' I said.

'And remember, we always work backwards through the lots,' Henry said, gathering speed, 'so the first lot number, which will be our last, will end up at the front not the back so that it'll be the first tomorrow. Clear?'

'Er . . .'

'Right, let's go! Lot four hundred and thirty-six – a Victorian burr-walnut Sutherland table on turned underframe.'

The description was shouted by Henry even faster than the instructions he had just gabbled at me. As he started bawling, the near moribund Colin and Phil both seemed to undergo a dramatic change. Suddenly coming to life, they began to rush about the gallery in search of the piece. I stood rooted to the spot. What was a Sutherland table? What did burr-walnut look like? What was a turned underframe?

'Well, don't just stand there, Harton,' shrieked Henry. I leapt involuntarily in amongst the furniture, snatching at and examining every lot ticket on every table I could see.

'Got it,' shouted Colin.

'Lot four hundred and thirty-five,' bellowed Henry, 'a set of six Regency rosewood dining chairs, two with arms.'

'Got 'em,' shouted Phil, almost immediately.

'Right, one carver and one standard in line, the rest in seating,' shouted Henry, who now might just as well have been talking in code as far as I was concerned.

'Lot four hundred and thirty-four – a Georgian mahogany chest of drawers.'

''Gainst the wall on the left,' shouted Colin.

'Lot four hundred and thirty-three – a Venetian giltwood . . .'

And so it went on throughout the morning, at the same breakneck pace with Henry Dodds screaming himself hoarse without pause. Each time a new description was shouted out, I ran about pretending to know what it was I was looking for, when in fact, most of the time, I was just trying to stay out of the way of the others. I tried to envisage what teapoys, *prie-dieux* and loo tables looked like, but I never managed to identify any of them before Colin or Phil, so I just continued dashing around without result, like a demented spaniel. Henry was so engrossed he didn't seem to notice my general lack of input, or at least, he didn't notice it until we got to lot seventy-three.

'Lot seventy-three,' croaked Henry, 'a Georgian mahogany framed wing chair upholstered in green velvet.'

I set off into the midst of the now dwindling collection of furniture in Gallery One.

'Where the bloody hell do you think you're going now?' he screamed. 'You're standing next to the sodding thing. For God's sake just bring it here!'

He was right. Standing just a couple of feet away on my right was a large comfortable looking high backed armchair. I checked the lot ticket sewn to one of the arms – LOT 73. I folded my catalogue in half, stuffed it in the back pocket of my trousers and wondered momentarily about the best way of going about lifting the thing. Somehow, it looked rather awkward.

'Harton! . . .'

The shriek from Henry galvanised me into action. I bent down, grasped the underside of the chair and lifted. I immediately encountered my first serious problem. Although I had succeeded in raising it above ground level without injury to either the piece or myself, its back was now half an inch away from my nose, completely blocking the view in front of me. I juggled it a little, trying to tilt it to the left slightly, hoping that I'd be able to peer round the right hand side of the thing. Unfortunately, it became obvious that I would have needed a neck like a flamingo for that to work.

'For God's sake, Harton! . . .'

Henry had pleaded for divine intervention so many times that morning, I was suddenly inspired to put some trust in The Lord myself. So, in desperation, I adjusted my load once more and lurched forward into the unknown. As has usually been my experience, The Almighty was otherwise engaged at that particular moment when I needed his undivided attention. No sooner had I taken my first faltering step than the loose seat cushion slipped from the chair to the floor and wrapped itself around my right foot. It didn't actually trip me, but it did throw me off balance, causing my right thigh to make intimate contact with, what I later discovered to be, the carved corner of a large dining table. The result of the collision was that I immediately lost all sense of feeling in my leg. Hopping now, I ricocheted sideways off the dining table, and smashed into a large chest of drawers. It was probably fortunate that at that point I caught my left shin an eye-watering blow on an oak stool. Lot 73 and I crashed to the floor, my face buried in the seat of the chair.

'*No! No! No! No!*'

Just what I wanted – advice from Henry. It was only when I staggered to my feet that I became aware of the size of my audience. My re-emergence from the upholstery was greeted with a spontaneous round of applause from not only Colin and Phil, but also Jim and Patrick who had been enticed back from Gallery Three by the general commotion.

'More! More!'

My humiliation was complete.

Henry Dodds bore down on me. He was scarlet. 'You bloody idiot. Have you any idea how much damage you could have done?' Not waiting for a reply, he pushed me aside. 'That's not the way to carry a wing chair – this is the way to carry a wing chair.'

So saying, he spun the chair round to face him, seized hold of the arms and swung the piece up and over in one sweeping movement, so that lot 73 ended upside-down on his head: the legs pointing up to the ceiling, the back pointing down to the floor behind him, leaving an uninterrupted view ahead. It was a very impressive feat of athletics – especially for someone of Henry's unathletic build – and I would have been even more impressed, had it not been for the chandelier.

I can't pretend that I knew a great deal about chandeliers at that stage in my career but it had looked all right to me. I glanced at the catalogue that evening when I got home and it was described as 'large' and 'impressive' with 'scrolled branches' and 'faceted glass drops'. There was certainly at least one undeniable fact about the thing, and that was its whereabouts at the moment Henry so effortlessly tossed the chair over his head – it was suspended immediately above him.

The gallery about us was suddenly a blizzard of refracted light as hundreds of glass droplets exploded into the air. Like all worthwhile disasters it happened in slow motion. The crashing and tinkling of fragmenting lustres, biting into polished wood and shattering on bare concrete seemed to go on for ages. In reality, I suppose it was over in seconds.

Finally there was silence, broken only by the sound of the metal skeletal remains of the chandelier, still hung with a few tenacious ribbons of glass, squeaking pathetically to and fro on its hook. I turned my attention from the chandelier to Henry who, still wearing the chair on his head and having bent low to disentangle himself from the overhead obstruction, conjured up a picture of a tortoise with rickets. His eyes were fixed on something or someone somewhere behind me, and as I looked around at my other companions I saw they too were looking in the same direction. Duncan Parkes had appeared on the scene. A scene he was surveying with an expression which suggested no excuse, no matter how imaginative, would be good enough.

'Would somebody like to explain,' he asked in a soft, menacing voice, 'just what the hell is going on?'

'I . . . I . . . I . . .' stuttered an almost puce Henry, as a fresh cascade of droplets slid from their temporary resting place on the upturned chair and drizzled noisily to the floor. He struggled to disentangle himself from lot 73 without doing further damage to either his surroundings or his reputation. For a moment there was silence again, then Jim Watson spoke:

'Nothing to worry about, Mr Parkes, it's only Henry teaching Richard how us professionals carry wing chairs.'

24

I never really got to know Henry because he left Wilson's a few months later. He was off sick for a while and his mother, a formidable lady, came in to tell Duncan Parkes that Henry was suffering from nervous exhaustion brought on by overwork. Duncan had looked terribly concerned for a few moments and then asked how long Henry had had a second job. When Mrs Dodds asked him what he meant, Duncan explained that he assumed from what she'd said that Henry must have a second job since he'd never noticed him overworking at Wilson's. The interview just seemed to go downhill from there and I never saw Henry again.

Chapter 3

'I don't know what you're making such a fuss about, Margaret, it's really perfectly straightforward,' Duncan said, as he paced up and down the gallery.

'Perhaps it is,' Margaret Graham persisted, 'but I still can't see what harm it would do to take Richard with you. He could act as a back-up, and it would be good experience for him. After all, he's been working here for three months now, and he hasn't been out on a valuation with you yet.'

Duncan stopped pacing and looked thoughtful. 'Now that's something I've been meaning to mention to you,' he said. 'I was only thinking that the other evening. The lad will never learn if he doesn't get practical experience.' He threw down his cigarette and screwed it into the concrete floor with the sole of one of his polished black brogues.

'I know,' Margaret said, 'it's been worrying me too. I think you're absolutely right.'

'Good. That's decided then,' he continued, 'Richard will come out with me today.'

Margaret Graham had done it again. It had taken her fifteen minutes of bulldog-like tenacity involving both gentle cajoling and straightforward stubbornness, but, in the end, she'd got her way. What was more, not only had she convinced Duncan that I should go with him on his calls that day, she'd also convinced him that he was the one who'd thought of it.

Margaret's insistence that I should spend the day with Duncan was not entirely due to her selfless interest in the furtherance of my career. The main reason was DP's latest love affair with a piece of gadgetry. I say his latest because, even in the short time I'd been at Wilson's, I'd witnessed the

26

appearance and subsequent disappearance of a good dozen or so bits of apparatus. He would produce whatever it was with a great flourish and hail it as the thing destined to change our working or domestic lives or, on the odd unnerving occasion, both. The least impressive item had been a sort of angle-bracket affair designed to be clamped to the receiver of a telephone. The idea was that the bracket rested on your shoulder keeping the telephone in place next to your ear, thereby leaving your hands free to take notes, stir your tea, etc. There was really nothing wrong with the thing itself, but, unfortunately, Duncan insisted on trying to wedge the telephone against his left ear when the bracket was clearly designed exclusively for the right. The bracket broke, along with the telephone, the second time it hit the floor. The most spectacular failure was undoubtedly an early pump-action cork remover. Duncan had been exceptionally excited about that and had only lost interest in it when, the first time he used it, he blew the bottom out of a bottle and emptied the claret it had contained down a new pair of light grey flannels.

As each item fell from grace it was tossed onto the bookcase in his office where it was left to gather dust. The faintest suggestion that we might actually throw away whatever it was was always greeted with a storm of protest. Duncan would maintain that he was going to start using it again just as soon as he'd got some new batteries, or found the instruction book, or got hold of the right sort of glue.

His latest attachment had been formed to a piece of equipment which Margaret Graham had quite rightly identified as being potentially even more catastrophic than the pump-action cork remover: it was a portable tape recorder. A pretty bulky thing by today's miniaturised standards, it was then the latest thing in lightweight office equipment. You fixed the main part of it to your belt and spoke into a hand-held microphone which was fitted with all the necessary controls.

Duncan had bought it the previous afternoon and hadn't stopped enthusing about it. It was going to revolutionise valuation work. The tedious business of writing down the description and price of every single item in a house was a thing of the past. No more lost notebooks; no more mislaid pens; another triumph for twentieth-century technology over nineteenth-century drudgery. Duncan Parkes was ecstatic. Margaret Graham was deeply concerned. The thing about Margaret was that she knew Duncan better than he knew himself. She knew, for instance, that he was incapable of reading more than the first couple of pages of an instruction book before boredom set in. Once that had happened, trial and error took over, usually with the greater emphasis on error. She also knew that he was essentially a creature of habit and that, despite his enthusiasm for the new, he was really only comfortable with the old. Finally, she knew that he would go to almost any lengths to prove her wrong. So it was that I was despatched with Duncan that morning, armed with notebook and pen.

'Of course I don't mind Richard taking notes, Margaret, but it really isn't necessary,' Duncan had continued to protest as we left the galleries.

'I know, but it'll be good experience for him,' Margaret replied as she saw us off.

'Yes, well, of course, there is that to it.'

There was just the odd powder-puff cloud in the otherwise clear July sky as we hummed along the winding downland road in Duncan's Jaguar. Our first appointment involved a probate valuation in Oakbourne, one of the many tiny villages hidden away in the folds of the South Downs.

'Do you know what we do when we make a probate valuation?' Duncan asked as we drove along.

'Not really.'

'Well, we make a list of all the things in the house belonging to the person who has just died – in this case, an old retired major – and we put a value on each one. In most cases the lowest value we think we can get away with.'

'Get away with?'

'Yes. The valuation will be used to assess death duties on the estate, and if the Inland Revenue establish that the values are too low they'll challenge the whole thing, then we'll be in the soup.'

'How can you be sure of getting it right?' I asked.

'Well, sometimes it doesn't matter anyway; for instance, if

28

a picture when Jones said "The major is still in
dence," ' Duncan mimicked the butler's sonorous tones.
st couldn't resist it!'

allowed myself the luxury of a faint forgiving smile.

Ah well,' he went on, 'let's get on with the job.'

He opened his briefcase and took out his tape recorder
the notebook Margaret had forced on us. He tossed the
k across to me.

Margaret's adamant that you should take notes just in
e something goes wrong with the recording,' he said as he
ped the equipment to his belt. 'I think it's a lot of
sense but I suppose it can't do any harm.' He plugged in
microphone and peered at the controls. 'Right then,
ks simple enough, all I've got to do is press "Forward"
d "Record" and we're in business. We'll start over here.'

Duncan made his way back to the door and stood in front
a small side table made of a dark honey-coloured wood
th a tight curly grain.

'A George I,' Duncan began 'burr walnut side table fitted
ree drawers above a shaped apron . . .'

It was there that he seemed to come across his first
oblem. He went to pull out one of the drawers to have a
k at it. Unfortunately, it needed two hands, so he had to
t the microphone down on the table. He turned towards
e light with the drawer and then walked over to the
indow to get a better look. The microphone, still attached
his belt, and still switched on, slid across the table top,
ropped to the floor and bounced along behind him like a
ithful puppy. Duncan turned and looked at it, obviously
urprised to find he was being followed. He picked it up,
alked back to the table and replaced the drawer.

'Where had I got to?' he asked.

'A George I burr walnut side table fitted three drawers
bove a shaped apron,' I read back from the notes I had
aken.

'Oh, yes . . . raised on cabriole legs terminating in pad
eet; width – two feet eight inches; value – two hundred
ounds.' He fumbled with the microphone and turned it off.
Now,' he said, 'let's play it back to make sure it's working
properly.'

the whole lot's going to be sold, the eventual sale price is the
figure they work on. It gets complicated when the executors
or beneficiaries decide to sell some of the pieces and to keep
others.'

'Why?'

'Let's suppose they sell a quarter of the things and keep
the other three quarters. If the bits they sell *all* make twice
as much as we valued them at, the Inland Revenue will
simply re-assess the value of all the things they kept as well –
say we'd valued them at £15,000, the Revenue would
re-assess them at £30,000. They'd just multiply our figure by
two. See what I mean?'

'Yes,' I said, 'so how do you stop that happening?'

'Simple! Every now and then I overvalue something.
Then, although ninety per cent of the stuff that's sold still
makes twice as much as I said it was worth, ten per cent
makes less. The revenue can't claim everything was
undervalued.'

'Does that do the trick then?'

'Every time.' Duncan looked smug. 'They'd have to
contest the valuation piece by piece if they wanted to
challenge it and they soon got tired of that.'

'But aren't we almost defrauding the Inland Revenue?'

'Certainly not! Mind you, if they were paying my fees, I'd
start putting on higher values,' he winked as he spoke. 'Here
we are.'

We had drawn up in a narrow lane alongside a high, neatly
clipped yew hedge. A small oak gate, green with lichen and
age, opened into an immaculate garden with precisely
manicured lawns, and borders which were laid out with
more than a suggestion of military order and symmetry. The
house itself was whitewashed with tiny windows peering out
from below a high-pitched thatch roof.

'The only person here is the butler,' Duncan said.
'Apparently he served with the major in the army and stayed
with him in civvy street. I gather the old boy looked after
him pretty well in the will.'

Duncan gave the wrought iron bell-pull a tug and we stood
waiting outside the nail-studded blackened front door. The
door was opened by a man straight out of Wodehouse – tall

with a starched white shirt, black jacket, grey waistcoat and grey striped trousers. His general aura was as smooth and slick as his Bryl-creamed hair. He oozed quiet, calm, authority.

'Mr Parkes?'

'Yes, that's right,' Duncan replied, 'and this is my assistant, Richard Harton.'

'Good morning to you both. Do come in. I am Jones,' the butler intoned as he closed the door behind us. 'I think you will find everything ready for you, but if you need anything, please let me know. I believe the solicitors have informed you that the silver is no longer here, Mr Parkes.'

'Yes, they have,' Duncan said. 'I'm going to see it at the bank tomorrow.'

'Oh good. Then I'll leave you gentlemen to it.' He turned to go, then hesitated. 'I almost forgot,' he said, turning back to us, 'did the solicitors also mention that the major is still in residence?'

'Yes, I believe they did,' Duncan said, in what I thought was the most extraordinarily matter-of-fact way.

'Oh good. He's in the drawing room – it was always his favourite room.'

'I quite understand. We won't need to disturb him.'

'Excellent, but should you need him moved, let me know and I'll put him in another room.'

As Jones glided silently away, my blood ran cold. The thought of his late employer stretched out, lying in state in the drawing room, let alone being humped around the house like a sack of potatoes, was an idea which didn't appeal. The expression on my face must have given away the horrors going through my mind.

'Do close your mouth,' Duncan said, 'you look as though you've seen a ghost.'

'It's hardly surprising,' I said. 'You didn't tell me the major was still in the house.'

'Didn't seem important.'

I was staggered. There we were discussing nothing less than a cadaver in the drawing room, and Duncan seemed to consider it about as remarkable as coming across a dead wasp on a window sill. I had no idea he could be that callous.

'Oh, come on,' he said in a bored
viewing over with and pay our respects,
you're never going to concentrate on wor

He opened one of the oak planked doc
entrance hall. 'I think this is the drawing

I remained rooted to the spot. 'Do co
Duncan said with some impatience, 'we h

I followed him into a low, oak-beam
streamed through the little diamond-pane
and splashed onto the plain white walls.
room and I could understand why it had
favourite. But where was he? I glanced
was no sign of the deceased.

Duncan strolled over to the huge in
which effectively took up an entire wall at
room. Set in front of it was a solitary wing
that stood a low table. He pointed to a rec
box which stood on the table.

'The major!' he announced with a sweepi
hand. I walked over and looked at it. It
casket and on the lid was a brass plaque insci

Major Harold Arthur George Fra
Born 1881 – Died 1966
RIP

'He was . . . he was cremated three week
gasped as he fought to control his laughter. 'J
has got to scatter ashes . . . in the West Cou
the old boy . . . the old boy wanted . . .' It w
gave up the effort of trying to speak, and gri
of the wing chair so tightly that his knuckles tu
bent almost double trying to keep down the
unseemly outburst. I was pretty unamused,
face turned red and tears rolled down his chee
seized by a coughing fit, I felt very little sympat

'Heee . . . heeee . . . heeeeee . . .' he w
regained some sort of control. 'Where's y
humour, Richard?' Slowly he dried his eyes an
apologetic grin.

'Sorry, it was a bit unkind, but it was your

After pressing most of the available buttons Duncan eventually succeeded in rewinding the tape. He pressed 'Play'.

'A George I,' his disembodied voice said from somewhere near his trouser fly, 'burr walnut side table fitted three drawers above a shaped apron . . . thud . . . rumble . . . rumble . . . BANG . . . bang . . . bang . . . bang . . . bang . . . clunk . . . rumble . . . Where had I got to? . . . Murmur . . . murmur . . . Oh yes . . . Raised on cabriole legs terminating in pad feet; width – two feet eight inches; value – two hundred pounds . . .' Duncan stood looking down at the now silent tape recorder. His face was a portrait of confusion as he stared in disbelief at the machine.

'What the hell was that?' he asked.

'What?' I replied, as innocently as I could, not really wanting to get involved in a detailed explanation.

'That noise; all that bloody noise; all that crashing and banging. There's something wrong with the thing!'

'I think that's when you pulled the microphone off the table and dragged it across the room.'

'When I what?' snapped Duncan.

'When the microphone fell off the table,' I said, deciding on the spot to put a softer focus on events.

'But it was switched off.'

'Er, I don't think so.'

'Yes it was,' Duncan insisted, 'but perhaps it switched itself on again when it fell off the table.'

'Yes, perhaps it did,' I said quickly, very relieved to have been presented with the escape route.

'Anyway,' Duncan went on as he ran the tape back again, 'it's no good with all that background noise. You'd better dictate the description into it from your notes.

I did as I was told, then Duncan took the microphone again and headed for the next piece of furniture.

'A Charles II oval oak gateleg table, fitted single frieze drawer, raised on baluster-turned supports . . . I'd better just have a look under here.'

He got down on his hands and knees and briefly peered at the underside of the table top. Unfortunately, when he went to stand up again he mis-timed it by a fraction of a second.

His head cracked against the table causing the whole piece of furniture momentarily to jump from the ground.

'Ow . . . bugger it . . .' he said as he reeled sideways clutching his wound. A few more colourful expressions followed before he regained his composure.

'Where had I got to?' he asked, still rubbing his head.

'. . . raised on baluster-turned supports,' I replied.

'Oh yes . . . Width – four feet; value – one hundred pounds,' he concluded.

'I think you'd better play that back,' I suggested.

'What?'

'I think you'd better play it back.'

'Why?'

'I just think you should.'

'Oh, very well.'

After a lot of rewinding, fast forwarding and more rewinding he got to his description of the table. He listened, grave faced, to every word and winced visibly when the tape replicated the noise of his head striking the three hundred year-old table. He was only halfway through the torrent of expletives that followed when he switched it off.

'Shall I dictate it from the notes?' I asked.

'Yes please,' came the curt reply.

Duncan struggled on manfully with four more pieces of furniture before he abandoned the experiment. He just suddenly tossed the tape recorder and microphone back into his briefcase and, without a word of explanation, continued dictating to me as though nothing had happened. He didn't need to say anything; I knew it was just another gadget destined for the top of the bookcase.

'Where are we going now?' I asked as we drove away from the major's.

'We'll have a pint and a sandwich, then on to Ashley Park. I've got to look at a few things for William Grigson.'

Shortly after half-past one we drove through the arched lodge gate of Ashley Park. Although I'd never met him, Bill Grigson was a local legend. It was said he had started his business life as a boy on a barrow in London's East End, repairing radios and other household appliances. By the

34

time he bought Ashley Park in the mid-fifties he was a multi-millionaire.

As we rounded a clump of three cedars the mansion came into view; it was hideous. A Gothic horror fantasy of castellated turrets and lancet windows.

'Awful looking place isn't it?' Duncan commented.

'Terrible,' I replied.

'Don't let William hear you say that, though, he thinks it's wonderful.'

The car crunched to a halt on the gravel outside the mansion's main door. As we got out, the stocky figure of a gardener came shambling towards us. He wore baggy old corduroy trousers, a green cardigan with holes at the elbows, and a particularly disreputable looking pork pie hat. On closer examination, the only thing that didn't seem to fit his otherwise horticultural image was what appeared to be the stub of a havana cigar clenched between his teeth.

'Dunky my son, 'ow are yer?'

I had never before heard anyone address Duncan Parkes, Fine Arts Auctioneer and Valuer, as 'Dunky', let alone 'my son'.

'Very well thank you, William, and how are you?'

So this was no gardener. This was the fabled Bill Grigson.

'Can't complain, Dunk, can't complain, but then it don't do no good if yer do, does it?'

'Certainly not in my experience anyway,' Duncan said as he took his briefcase from the back of the Jaguar. 'William, this is my new assistant – Richard Harton. I'm sure he'd be fascinated to see some of your collection if you have the time to give him a bit of a tour.'

'Course I will – no problem. I'll just show yer the stuff I want yer to look at. It's in the coach 'ouse. Then I'll give the boy the grand tour.'

Bill Grigson led us towards a large, square, red brick stable block topped by a clock tower.

'What'd 'e say yer name was, son?' he asked as we walked.

'Harton, Richard Harton.'

'Okay, Dick, ever bin in a Roller?'

'A Rolls Royce? No never.'

'Well, now's yer chance.'

As we entered the courtyard, around which the stable block was arranged, a brand new maroon Rolls Royce stood parked on the cobbles in the middle of the yard.

'Not another one!' Duncan laughed. 'How many does this make, William, three or four?'

'Jus' the free now, Dunk. I can't 'elp it – they're me only vice.'

Grigson polished the Spirit of Ecstacy emblem with a corner of his cardigan.

'D'yer like the colour? I 'ad it done special.'

'Very classy,' Duncan said as he walked round the car admiring it, 'very classy indeed.'

Bill Grigson seemed physically to puff-up with pride. 'Well, if you give it the fumbs-up, Maestro,' he said, 'it must be all right.'

I was told to make myself comfortable in the Rolls while Bill Grigson showed Duncan the things to be valued. Grigson was back in a few moments, sliding into the driving seat and starting the car without saying a word. We floated effortlessly out of the stable yard and along a wide gravel carriageway which led into the eighteenth-century parkland.

'What d'yer fink, Dick? All right, ain't she?'

'Magnificent,' I said.

We drove for some fifteen minutes, through mature shaded woodland, around lakes and over stone bridges. At one point we stopped by a small pond where a dozen huge carp appeared at the water's edge from nowhere and took pieces of bread from their owner's hand. The bread had appeared from Bill Grigson's cardigan almost as miraculously as the fish had appeared from the depths of the pond. Eventually, we ended up back in front of the mansion.

'What're yer interested in most, Dick; furniture, pictures, books, arms an' armour . . .?'

'I don't really know, Mr Grigson,' I replied, overwhelmed by the choice. 'Furniture, I suppose, but I like arms and armour as well.'

'Quite right too. So do I, an' for Gawd's sake don't call me Mr Grigson, the name's Bill – an' none of this "William" stuff eiver. Yer boss only does it to annoy me cos I call 'im Dunky!' Bill Grigson gave a throaty chuckle as we went into his home.

It was far more attractive inside than out. The rooms were large and light. The tall Gothic windows, despite their forbidding appearance from the outside, poured the afternoon sunlight into every corner. Each room was named after its style of furnishing and decoration. Bill Grigson recited them as we went from room to room. 'Chippendale . . . 'Epplewhite . . . Regency . . . Chinoiserie . . .'

'Look at that,' he pointed to a red laquered bureau bookcase, 'I bought that at Christies free years ago. Took on all the trade an' beat 'em. In the end it was just me an' Malletts. Was they sick? Yer should 'ave seen their faces.'

He talked of his pieces as a big game hunter would speak of the trophy heads hanging on his study wall. It obviously meant a great deal to him that he was able to outbid major international dealers like Malletts.

'This is the library. Got some good stuff in 'ere. Bought most of it by the yard back in the fifties. Got some really good gear like that – well, yer could in them days.'

He stood in the middle of his impressive collection, looking up at the bookcases which towered above us and lined each wall.

'What do you mean when you say you bought them by the yard?' I asked.

'Oh, that's when yer buy books jus' for their fancy leather bindin's. Might be twenty, fifty, a 'undred books in a lot – nobody cares what they are, jus' what their bindin's look like. Like I said, I got some good stuff buying like that.'

The tour went on: Dining Room . . . Sheraton Room . . . Billiard Room. Eventually, we stopped at a green baize-covered door. Bill dragged a formidable bunch of keys from his sagging trouser pocket, but on trying the door found it was already unlocked.

'Mario must be in 'ere,' he said, 'otherwise it'd be locked. It's me Arms an' Armour Museum.'

The rooms we went into had apparently been the original kitchens and foodstores for the house. Now they were packed with display case after display case full of muskets, swords, armour, pistols, daggers and every other imaginable weapon. To call it a museum was no wishful overstatement.

At the far end of the main room, on a high stool, sat a

strange, swarthy, spider-like figure dressed in a blue boiler suit and a black beret. He was cleaning a small pistol which he stared at intently through a pair of pebble-lensed glasses.

'What yer up to in 'ere, Mario?'

'Chrise! What I uppa to? What I uppa to? I uppa to what you say I shoulda be uppa to! You say "Cleana da Scoddisha stuff, Mario," so I cleana da Scoddisha stuff an' den you say what I uppa to?'

The words poured out in a semi-intelligible torrent. Bill Grigson appeared unmoved. 'Yeah, yeah, keep yer bleedin' 'air on, son,' he said. 'Jus' pop out to the coach 'ouse an' see if Mr Parkes 'as finished. 'E might need an 'and shiftin' some of the big stuff.'

'Oh, sure, sure, goa to da coacha 'ouse; no problem!' Mario clambered down from his stool and, complaining passionately, made for the door. 'Cleana da Scoddisha stuff; no problem! Don'a cleana da Scoddisha stuff; no problem! Wake-a-up itsa two o'clock in da mornin'; no problem! Lettsa move roun' alla da Chippenwhite an' 'Eppendale; no problem! Letsa put it alla back agayn; no problem!'

Bill Grigson grinned as Mario's protests faded away. ''E's a good lad really. Came over 'ere as an Italian POW 'an never went back. Nazis killed all his family – lost a few of me own to them sods of course.' He picked up the pistol Mario had been cleaning. 'Know what that is, Dick?' he asked.

'Eighteenth-century Scottish, isn't it?'

'Yeah, that's right – mid-eighteenth-century Scottish all-steel pistol with ram's horn butt. D'yer know why the Scots made their pistols entirely from steel?'

I confessed I had no idea.

'Well, it was all down to the way they used to fight, see. They'd run towards the enemy, fire their muskets an' drop 'em while they was runnin; then when they was about fifty feet away from the enemy ranks they'd fire these pistols; then what d'yer fink they did?'

'No idea.'

'They frew the bleedin' fings at 'em – just chucked 'em straight at the enemy. Then it was all 'and to 'and combat.' Bill Grigson stood looking pensively at the pistol in his hand. 'This might just be old enough to 'ave been used at

Culloden, yer know. Fousands of 'ighlanders got killed up there on Drummosie Moor, an' for what? Jus' money an' power, Dick. Don't let nobody tell yer they're important, boy – they're not what they're cracked up to be.'

'Well, what did you make of William?' Duncan asked, as we drove back to Kington.

'I liked him,' I said, 'but he's certainly an extraordinary man.'

'You can say that again; and don't get taken in by his simple cockney costermonger act. He's got a mind like a razor, and not just for business either. He's well read and self-educated to a far higher level than he'd have you believe. He has to practise hard to keep that cockney accent.'

'What about his collection,' I asked. 'Did he build it up himself?'

'Every bit. He takes advice on specific pieces now and then, but when he was buying most of his pieces – back in the late fifties and early sixties – he was single-handed.'

'Did he know what he was doing?'

'Not really, but he didn't make many mistakes and he never made the same one twice. He's just got a natural instinct for what's good. Did he show you his arms collection?'

'Yes, it seemed very impressive,' I said.

'Probably the best private collection in the country, and what you've seen is just a quarter of it; most of it's tucked away in cupboards.'

Duncan talked on about the complex Bill Grigson; about his painfully shy wife, Elizabeth, and the tiny flat they shared in one of the attics in Ashley Park; about the fact that he only needed two hours sleep each night and, as a consequence, did indeed often wake the hapless Mario at two in the morning to try out a new room arrangement; and finally, about his passion for snooker.

'Do you play?' Duncan asked.

'Yes, but not very well,' I said.

'You sound perfectly qualified,' Duncan smiled as he spoke.

'Why do you say that?'

'Oh, no reason, no reason at all . . .'

Chapter 4

The springs on Colin Burrell's L-plated Mini seemed to sigh with relief as he got out and walked round to the passenger door. Colin was a good six feet tall and must have tipped the scales at about fifteen stone. He gathered himself up and once again insinuated his bulk into the tortured, creaking little vehicle. Although I'd watched him execute the same manoeuvre on a dozen other occasions, on its completion I was still faintly surprised to find there was enough room left for me to take the wheel.

'OK? Nice and relaxed?' he asked.

'No,' I said.

'Nothing to worry about you know,' he went on. 'I wouldn't be letting you take the test if I didn't think you were going to pass.' With a screwed-up red and white handkerchief, he dabbed at the beads of perspiration on his forehead and chin. The first time I'd seen him do it, I'd assumed the perspiration was a symptom of otherwise concealed panic, generated by one of my more exotic pieces of driving. But, as the lessons had gone on, I'd realised there was no obvious connection between his discomfort and my performance. 'We'll just drive into Langton and wander round for half an hour,' he continued, 'then it'll be about time for the test.'

It had been obvious from my first days at Wilson's that it was essential that I got my driving licence as quickly as possible. Not just because I'd need to be able to drive to do the job properly, but also to put an end to the brain-numbing bus journey at either end of the day. Somehow, the Downland Bus Company had contrived to turn a trip which took twenty minutes by car, into forty-five minutes in the

40

morning, and no less than an hour and a half in the evening. Admittedly, three quarters of an hour of the homeward trip was spent in The Bell at Markfield, but only because I had to wait when I changed buses there. The only thing that had stopped me from taking my test earlier was the cost of the lessons – one pound five shillings per hour; recommended full course, eighteen pounds fifteen shillings. That was two and a half weeks' wages before tax, and it had taken me the better part of a year to get the money together.

Colin Burrell put me through my paces in the maze of suburban roads that formed the northern reaches of Langton-on-Sea. Langton had been a tiny fishing village until it was caught up in the Victorian boom for seaside resorts. As the railway made it possible for the masses to travel, they flocked from London to the south coast, and Langton was one of the places they flocked to. Miraculously, the core of the old village with its stooping cottages and narrow winding streets had survived largely intact. But now it was cut off from the sea by a solid rank of pompous Victorian hotels, each one standing like an over-iced wedding cake trying to out-do its equally overdressed neighbours in the battle for business.

On the other three sides, old Langton had been surrounded by miles of shops, homes and factories. It was in those roads that I'd spent two lunchtimes a week for the past seven weeks. There I had supposedly perfected my hill start and emergency stop, and learned how to reverse round corners without backing into lamp-posts.

'No! No! Do you know what you just did?'

Colin's outburst was uncharacteristic and came like a lightning bolt out of a clear blue sky.

'What? What? What'd I do?'

I was thrown completely. I'd just pulled out of a T-junction without mishap, and there wasn't another car in sight. What on earth had I done wrong?

'That was a HALT sign and you treated it like a GIVE WAY sign. If you do that in your test you've had it. They'll fail you and that will be the end of it.'

Until then my stomach had been the temporary home of a handful of fluttering butterflies. Now it churned like a cement mixer. The palms of my hands were cold and clammy, and my heart raced like an engine out of gear. All self-confidence had melted away in a moment. By the time we reached the test centre, just minutes later, I was the next best thing to a gibbering idiot.

Inside the centre, Colin Burrell examined a large display board, mopped his brow and frowned.

'You've got Arthur Preston,' he said.

'Is that bad?' I asked.

'Well, he's the Chief Examiner and a bit of a stickler. He's fair enough really, but he's a bit dour.'

A broken man, I went back to the car and waited alone for Mr Arthur Preston's unwelcome arrival. Examiners, all identically dressed in their long dark raincoats, were coming and going the whole time, but immediately he stepped out of the building, I recognised my man. Tall, thin, with close-cropped grey hair and steel-rimmed spectacles, he looked like a member of the Waffen SS. He walked straight to the car and got in.

'Good morning. Read the number of the white Ford over there please,' he said without looking at me.

I did as I was told. He silently made a note on the clipboard he carried. 'Drive out of the gate and turn left.'

I did.

'When you get to the junction at the bottom of the road, turn left.'

I did, and just as I did, Mr Preston, Chief Examiner for all Langton-on-Sea, gave a sigh of exasperation which told me I was lost. As if to ensure he got his message over without any misunderstanding, he sighed loudly once more and started drumming his fingers on his clipboard. I'd done something wrong, but what? Then it dawned on me, the terrible truth: I'd done it again. I'd GIVEN WAY when I should have HALTED. So that was it. I'd failed the test in the first two minutes. The rest was just a waste of time, a formality. What was the point? I couldn't believe my own stupidity. I didn't care anymore. I just wanted to get it over with. Three-point-turn, hill start, emergency stop, all executed with kamikaze flair. Back at the test centre came the superfluous questions on the highway code.

'What does this road sign mean?' he asked, finally.

'Don't know,' I replied, looking out of the window.

'Well, look at it again,' he persisted.

'No good,' I said, by then in a full-blooded, foot-stamping sulk, 'I dunno.'

'Young man, you could cause a very serious accident by being unfamiliar with this road sign,' he went on, his voice cold enough to ice over the inside of the windscreen, 'furthermore, you are currently wasting both your time and mine, which is curious since you are paying for both.'

'No overtaking,' I snarled.

'Oh, congratulations,' he said, sarcastically.

We sat in silence for some time as he slowly and meticulously completed the failure slip. At last, he tore it very slowly from its pad and handed it to me.

'You have just passed the most elementary of driving tests. Good morning,' he said, and was gone.

I sat there, staring at the pass slip. 'Thank you,' I croaked, eventually, long after Arthur Preston was well on his way back to the building.

'I've heard he does that: sighs and drums his fingers and so on,' Colin Burrell said, as we drove back to Kington, 'I think it's because he likes to see how people behave under pressure. You obviously didn't have any problems, anyway.'

It was about a week later that I received a telephone call from Anthony Wilson. He was always known as 'Mr Anthony'. Apparently, this had begun when his father, Charles, was still in charge of the firm and it was considered confusing to have two Mr Wilsons in the same office. Despite the fact that Charles Wilson had been dead for over ten years, the habit continued and Anthony Wilson was still 'Mr Anthony' to all the staff. A round, bouncy little man in his late fifties, he was invariably dressed in highly polished brown brogues and tweed suit, complete with yellow silk handkerchief cascading foppishly from the top pocket. He looked more like a gentleman farmer than an estate agent, with his ruddy complexion, pepper and salt hair, moustache and bushy eyebrows all suggesting an outdoor man. In fact, the closest Mr Anthony ever got to the great outdoors was

43

when he crossed the road from his office to the Devonshire Arms Hotel – a journey he made with some regularity. His other trademark was that he talked in duplicate.

'Yes, yes,' or 'no, no,' or, perhaps most often of all: 'Really! Really!'

Mr Anthony's relationship with Duncan was a curious one. Neither seemed entirely comfortable in the company of the other although, outwardly, they were always friendly enough. It was probably just that they were such different characters there was no meeting of minds. The area where this inability to communicate proved most exasperating was that of money. It wasn't, as Tom Jeffreys maintained, really that they were mean; as it happened, they were both capable of spontaneous acts of great personal generosity. The problem was they could never agree on anything and, as a result, any bright idea or suggestion which involved parting with a few pennies, was discussed over and over again before it was eventually shelved. Consequently, The Galleries' roof leaked, the paintwork peeled and staff salaries remained index-linked to that of the average Third World paddy-field coolie. It therefore came as a complete surprise when I got the call from Mr Anthony.

'Hello, hello, dear boy. Congratulations on passing your test. First class, first class,' he wittered, 'any plans for getting a motor?'

I said I hadn't. The cost was out of the question for the foreseeable future.

'As I thought, as I thought. Just what I told Mr Parkes, just what I told him. We had a chat about it yesterday and we agreed you should have a company car. Not a new one you understand, just a little runabout.'

'That would be marvellous, marvellous,' I said, picking up his habit as if it were contagious.

'Mr Parkes was going to keep his eyes open for one,' he continued, 'but as luck would have it, I picked up a real little snip myself today. Real stroke of luck, stroke of luck.'

'Wonderful, wonderful,' I said before I could stop myself. It really did seem to be catching.

'Yes, yes,' Mr Anthony went on, 'not new of course, not new, but a real little goer. See you all right for two or three years if you look after her.'

'Tremendous, tremendous,' I heard myself say, as my mouth began to work completely independently of my brain.

'Good, good. Jeffreys has got the keys, log book, all that sort of stuff. Collect it all from him and he'll tell you where it's parked. Well done, old boy. Well done.'

Fortunately his telephone went down before I could say anything else.

Tom Jeffreys sat behind a huge oak table in his eyrie in the attic of Wilson's Kington estate office. As usual everything about him was in perfect order: books and files neatly labelled, pens in one pot, pencils in another, not a paperclip out of place. It was hardly surprising that Tom loathed the Auction Galleries. They were dirty, often noisy, frequently disorganised, and they suffered from a sense of impermanence caused by the constant coming and going of pieces for sale. That feeling was heightened by our habit of commandeering bits of furniture for use as temporary office equipment. On top of that, in between sales, the offices frequently spilled out of their approved, cramped quarters and took over areas of the galleries themselves. This was all pure hell to Tom, who would complain bitterly when he came to help us at sale time, always escaping back to the order and calm of his garret as quickly as possible.

'Did he tell you what it was?' he asked. 'And I don't use the past tense lightly.'

'No, I didn't get a chance to ask.'

'Well, take a look at that, young Richard, and all will be revealed.'

Tom tossed an elderly looking green log book across the table towards me. I picked it up and read the details inside. 'A 1956 Ford Prefect!'

'Got it in one.'

'I know he said it wasn't new,' I said, 'but *1956* – that makes it eleven years old.'

'Good to see your mental arithmetic's as sharp as ever,' Tom smirked.

'But, *1956*!' I couldn't believe it. I hadn't expected anything smart. Perhaps a Mini or something like that, four or five years old. But a 1956 Ford Prefect! It hadn't crossed my mind that even DP and Mr Anthony could have dreamed that one up.

'Oh, DP doesn't know anything about it,' Tom said, 'he just agreed in principle that you should have a car. You know him – that means you would have been drawing your pension before you actually got one. No, no, this is all Mr Anthony's own work. God knows what DP will say when he sees it.'

'What's it look like?' I asked.

'Just like an eleven year old Ford Prefect with a hundred thousand miles on the clock would look like: tired!'

'Where is it?'

'Parked in Castle Street, if it hasn't been mistaken for an abandoned vehicle and towed away. Come on, I'll show you.'

Even from a distance – and my initial sighting was from the opposite end of Castle Street – my first ever company car obviously possessed certain unique qualities. To begin with there was a marked list to one side. This meant that the driver's side of the car stood about two inches higher than the passenger side. Tom Jeffreys and I stood, heads involuntarily tilted, looking at the deformed little machine.

'What's wrong with it?' I asked.

'Springs seem to be shot on one side,' he said, 'I understand the previous owner was a little old man whose wife weighed in at eighteen stone.'

'You're joking!'

'No, poor little blighter must have spent most of his life driving round in circles.'

Another idiosyncrasy was the colour. To all effects and purposes it was white, only I kept getting the uncomfortable feeling it wasn't. The closer I got, the less white it became, but the real colour wasn't one you could actually put your finger on. You certainly couldn't have gone to a colour chart and pointed to one of those little rectangles and said, 'That is the colour of my car.' It was altogether too enigmatic for that.

'What colour do you reckon it is, Tom?' I asked, keen on a second opinion.

'White!' he replied, full of conviction. Then he hesitated

and said, 'White-ish . . .' and finally, '. . . blue-ish-white . . .?'

'Mmmm, that's what I thought,' I said. 'Strange, isn't it?'

'Yes, it must have been re-sprayed at some stage and now the top coat's been rubbed thin and the old blue paintwork's showing through. Distinctive though!'

'Very,' I said.

'Well, let's take it for a spin and see if anything important falls off.' He threw me the keys and I opened the driver's door. A heavy, damp, fungal smell rose from the upholstery as soon as we got in. Tom Jeffreys wrinkled his nose. 'Mr Anthony said the previous owner had died,' he muttered, as he cranked open his window, 'but he didn't mention he'd done it in here.'

My window complained loudly as I struggled to wind it down. It eventually stopped moving completely at the half-way point.

'Don't worry about that, Richard. Start her up. Let's go.'

I put the key in the ignition, pulled out the choke and pulled the starter. Without a moment's hesitation, and much to the surprise of both Tom and myself, the engine came to life. Like a good, newly-qualified driver, I checked my rear-view mirror.

'Blimey,' I said, 'look at that.'

Behind us, Castle Street had all but disappeared in a dense pall of oily black smoke.

'Too much choke,' Tom shouted, as he fought to get his window up again. 'Put the bloody choke in!'

I did, and although it certainly helped to the extent that we could see the houses on the other side of the street again, it couldn't be said to have cured the problem.

'Get moving, Rich, for God's sake, before somebody calls the fire brigade.'

I put the car into gear and we took off down the street in a series of spirited leaps and bounds.

'You're a graduate of the Kangaroo-Clutch School of Motoring I see,' my companion observed, acidly.

'Not used to the car, that's all,' I muttered as I went through the gears. Second . . . third . . . fourth? There I came across yet another little idiosyncrasy: there was no

47

fourth gear. I stirred away with the gear stick, trying to find it, as we cruised sedately down Castle Street in neutral, still making enough smoke for an Atlantic convoy.

'I think you'll find there's only three forward gears on this model,' Tom remarked, obviously thoroughly enjoying himself.

'Thanks for letting me know,' I said, as we drifted to a stop at the junction with the High Street.

'Let's go along the High Street, past St Peter's, then we can come back up Memorial Hill,' he suggested.

It was on Memorial Hill that the real trouble began. There was the usual queue of lorries and cars on the steep incline, waiting for the lights to change, so we pulled up behind them. Following approved driving procedure to the letter, I depressed both brake and clutch, pulled on the handbrake, changed into neutral and took both feet off the pedals. I suppose we were surprised at the sheer speed at which the shops on either side of Memorial Hill started to pass us as we careered backwards down the street. It was certainly a couple of seconds before we both snatched, simultaneously, at the handbrake and effectively ended up holding hands. It was to no avail anyway, the brake was already fully on.

'BRAKE! BRAKE!' Tom screamed, helpfully.

I stamped down on the footbrake as hard as I could and we slewed to a halt. Fortunately there had been nothing behind us.

'Bloody handbrake's useless,' Tom gasped.

'Yes,' I said, still trembling.

'You'll have to hold it on the footbrake and clutch,' he said. 'Do you know how to do that?'

'I think so,' I replied, not at all certain that I did. Suddenly, a tremendous incentive for me to succeed appeared on the scene. It was about fifty feet long, foreign, articulated, and I was in its way. The driver of the lorry put his hand on his klaxon horn and almost sent Tom Jeffreys and me through the fragile, vibrating roof of the Ford. I stamped on the accelerator and let out the clutch. We screamed up Memorial Hill, leaving two parallel black streaks of smoking rubber on the road behind us, and squirted through the lights as they changed to red. This was the sort of driving Tom was used to.

'How much did he pay for this death-trap?' I asked, as Tom disembarked hastily just outside the estate office.

'A hundred quid, but don't tell DP.'

'A hundred pounds! A hundred pounds!' Duncan repeated the figure as though there was a chance it might sound less the second time around. 'He must have had a brainstorm.' He paced around the car clockwise and then paced around it again in the opposite direction. 'It looks lop-sided,' he said.

'It is,' I replied.

'And it's a weird colour.'

'Yes.'

He stuck his head through the half-open driver's window and sniffed. 'I think it smells,' he said.

'It does.'

'Oh, well, if he's bought it I suppose that's it,' he said, looking resentfully at the partnership's latest capital asset. 'Just one thing though . . .'

'What's that?'

'Get the wretched thing fully serviced before you drive it anywhere, otherwise it'll probably have brake-failure the first time you take it out.'

Chapter 5

'But Dun-can, eet ees so 'evy. You must not leeft eet on your own!' Antoinette Porter protested.

She had just opened the boot of her car to reveal a large bronze group of two horses. 'Eet took two men to put eet een the car.'

'Well, I think it will only take one man to get it out again,' Duncan said. He bent his knees, gripped hold of the bronze, and straightened up again, lifting the heavy metal casting clear of the car.

'Oh, Dun-can, 'ow strong you are!'

DP quickly made his way into Gallery One, leaning backwards to counter-balance the weight of the piece. He put it down gently on a big oak refectory table in the middle of the gallery.

Jim and Patrick Watson and I had been watching Duncan's virtuoso performance from the staircase. As Duncan put the bronze down, Patrick looked at us both, then at DP.

'Oh, Meester Parkes,' he said in a husky imitation of Duncan's French client, 'what a big strong boy you are!'

Duncan looked up and winked, then he immediately turned his attention back to Antoinette Porter as she entered the building.

With all male members of staff, Mrs Porter was consistently the most popular of Wilson's clients. It wasn't just that she was beautiful, although she was certainly that. Born and brought up in the south of France, she had the dark hair and eyes and olive skin of a native of the Mediterranean. Now in her mid-thirties, her looks and willowy figure made her as alluring in a pair of faded jeans and a sloppy sweater as in a silk ball gown, but that wasn't her secret. It was simply that she had that rare gift of making everybody she spoke to feel, temporarily at least, as though they were the most important person in the world. No matter whether it was some crusty old county brigadier or a tongue-tied spotty porter at Wilson's; each was flattered, beguiled, and finally left with a warm after-glow.

Her husband, Alan, ten years her senior, was a successful and wealthy financier. He was only an occasional visitor to Wilson's, and when he did accompany his wife, he always seemed uncomfortable and diffident. According to Duncan, Alan Porter had met Antoinette at a Parisian cocktail party; it was on a Monday. The following weekend they were on their honeymoon. It was firmly believed by those who knew both protagonists that it was Antoinette who had decided to marry Alan, rather than the other way round. He was just not the sort of man to sweep a woman off her feet. This left all devotees of Antoinette with an uncomfortable thought: the suspicion that she had married Alan Porter for his money.

The strong possibility that Antoinette was, or at least had been, a gold-digger was dealt with simply and expediently by her fans. It was regarded as an isolated flaw in an otherwise brilliant jewel and, as such, was overlooked.

Over the previous few weeks we had seen quite a lot of Antoinette Porter. An elderly aunt of her husband's had died, and Mrs Porter was busy fulfilling her spouse's role as the old lady's executor. This was good news for us since the entire contents of Aunty's house was going to be sold through Wilson's. The bronze horses were an early arrival.

'So everytheeng else weel be collected tomorrow?' she said.

'Yes,' Duncan replied, 'Watson's Removals will be at the house by nine thirty, and we'll be there at eight o'clock to list everything.'

'Eight o'clock. Right. Weel you be coming yourself, Dun-can?'

'Unfortunately, no. I have to be elsewhere tomorrow, so Richard will take over for me, and Jim and Patrick will both be on the vans of course.' He looked at the three of us, still standing on the stairs. 'What a team!' he said.

51

'Oh, yes, I could not weesh to be in better 'ands,' she said, smiling, and then turned back to Duncan. 'But when are you going to 'ave lunch weeth me again, Duncan? Eet 'as been a very long time.'

'It has, too long,' he said. 'How about one day next week; Tuesday, say?'

'I theenk that weel be fine, but I weel check my diary when I get 'ome, and call you. You must come to the farm and I weel cook you sometheeng very special. *Au revoir.*' She and Duncan kissed on both cheeks, then she looked up at us. '*Au revoir*, boys, see you tomorrow.'

She blew a kiss and was gone.

'Well, I think it's bleeding disgusting, if you ask me,' Jim said loudly to nobody in particular, 'an old geezer like Mr Parkes acting up to a young bit of stuff like that.'

'Old! Old!' Duncan said. 'I'll show you who's old.' And with that, he promptly did a handstand in the middle of the gallery – something that might have been considered eccentric in any other fifty-six-year-old fine arts auctioneer, but in Duncan was quite normal. The contents of his jacket pocket – wallet, cheque book, pen, small change – dropped to the floor around him, but he still held the position rock-solid, toes pointing to the ceiling, arms locked rigid. Eventually, he lowered his feet back to the floor and stood up straight again all in one slow, controlled movement. 'Now,' he said, his face only slightly flushed, 'a little less of the old if you don't mind. I'll have ten bob on none of you three whipper-snappers being able to do that!'

None of us showed any more inclination to take up the challenge than we had on earlier occasions. 'As I thought,' Duncan said, as he stooped to pick up his belongings.

'I don't think you should do them handstands like that, Mr Parkes,' Jim said, gravely. 'It's not fair. It might have been highly embarrassing for us three.'

'Embarrassing for you – how?'

'Well, where would we have looked if your pension book had dropped out of your pocket then?'

The Ford Prefect wheezed and rattled its way through the October fog as I crossed Ashdown Forest. A forest in name only; really open moorland dotted with clumps of pine and birch, it's best known as the haunt of Winnie-the-Pooh. Coincidentally, Alan Porter's aunt's cottage was close by A.A. Milne's old house – Cotchford Farm.

By the sixties, Cotchford was again famous (some thought infamous), this time as the home of Brian Jones, the Rolling Stone. In due course, the locals were thoroughly scandalised when the new incumbent was found floating dead in his own swimming pool.

As my protesting vehicle rocked, rolled and splashed its way down the muddy, potholed track past the farm, I wondered what Milne would have made of it all. I decided, on balance, he would not have approved one little bit.

Antoinette Porter greeted me at the cottage gate. Her hands were filthy and she pushed her dark hair back from her forehead with the back of her hand.

'Ello, Reechard, I am so glad to see you, I don't know what to do next. Eet ees all such a mess.'

It was. She had started emptying cupboards, and wrapping china in newspaper. There was china and newspaper everywhere.

'I think the best we can do is clean this lot up and then leave the rest of the packing to Watson's,' I said.

'That's just fine by me, but what can I do to 'elp, then? Apart from make tea, that ees – I know I 'ave to make lots and lots of tea. I know that every Breeteesh workman needs lots and lots of tea.'

'Well, you could help me,' I said.

'But of course. What must I do?'

I explained that I had to make a list of everything we were taking for sale. A code number was written against each item on the list. The same number then had to be written on a ticket which was either tied or stuck on the piece concerned.

'It's so that when we catalogue the piece back at the Galleries, we'll know who it belongs to,' I said. 'It would be a great help if you could write out the tickets and tie them on for me.'

'Sure I weel, Reechard. Where do we start?'

'We'd better start with your smalls,' I said, 'they're the first things Watson's will want to handle.'

53

It was one of those sentences with a life-force of its own. It came from nowhere and had its own destiny. I realised, as I spoke the first few words, that it was going to be a disaster but I was powerless to stop it. It just kept coming, and as it came it got worse.

Antoinette Porter first laughed, then feigned shock. 'Why, Reechard! They always say that the Englishman is so quiet and retiring, but eet ees not true.'

I could feel myself blushing to the roots of my hair.

'Now I 'ave embarrassed you,' she said, 'I did not mean to. Never mind, eet weel be our leetle secret. I take eet that "smalls" ees one of those English words with more than one meaning.'

'Yes,' I said, loosening my tie a little as my temperature and colour slowly returned to normal. 'I was actually talking about the china and glass and decorative things.'

'Okay! Let's get started weeth the "smalls"!' she said. 'Mind you, nothing you might say about the Watsons' preferences would surprise me – especially Arther. 'E should not be allowed out weethout a muzzle!'

We were working upstairs by the time I heard the Watson convoy crashing down the track. I looked out of the bedroom window at the ill-matched vehicles as they made their uneven way towards the cottage.

Watson's could not be, indeed never had been, described as a prestigious firm of carriers. Their men didn't wear smart aprons or overalls bearing the company logo (there wasn't a company logo anyway), nor were their lorries decorated in a corporate livery. In fact, the lorries didn't even display the Watson name, although on the side of one of the trucks you could just make out the name of the previous owner. Watson's attraction was quite simply that they were good at what they did. They turned out at short notice, arrived on time, didn't get hysterical at last minute changes of plan, and charged half what their more aloof rivals did. They were certainly as valuable to Wilson's as Wilson's were to them, frills or no frills.

That day the convoy comprised three trucks – two of them were reasonably respectable Fords, but leading the procession was an ancient blue Bedford van. The windscreen was cracked from top to bottom, and the bodywork was covered in dents and raw fibre-glass. It was Arthur Watson's favourite vehicle – probably because he could identify with its disreputable appearance – and Arthur himself was at the wheel.

Arthur was the doyen of the family firm. He wasn't particularly tall, but otherwise he was larger than life in every way. His age was difficult to determine because although he had a full head of hair, along with his untidy moustache, it was almost white. He also tended to get short of breath, but that was probably due to the Woodbines he chain-smoked rather than the natural march of time. Although a good two stone overweight, with most of the unwanted poundage concentrated in an impressive beer gut, he was still able, when inclined, to outwork anybody on his team, with the possible exception of his younger son, Patrick. In the end, however, it was Arthur's sheer loudness which was his most remarkable feature. Even the most confidential confidence would be communicated, usually across a crowded room, with all the restraint of a public address system on full volume.

Since, after beer, Arthur's only serious passions were women and dirty jokes, he could be a dangerous man to be with in the presence of clients – especially elderly lady clients. As soon as he boomed the words, ''Ere, did I tell yer the one about . . .?' the only sensible thing to do was to try to propel him bodily into the garden, or street or anywhere the client wasn't.

'Gor blimey, boys, what'd I tell yer? The dirty little stoat's upstairs wiv 'er already an' they ain't bin 'ere more than a couple of hours,' Arthur's voice bellowed in the hallway below. Antoinette Porter walked to the bannister rail and looked down on him sternly.

'Arther Watson, be'ave yourself.'

''Ello, Mrs Porter,' Arthur leered up at her, quite unabashed. 'I always be'ave meself, you know that. Any chance of a little kiss before I start work.'

'Absolutely not, or you weel never start work, I know you. All you weel get today ees tea – and I shall make some now.' She bounced downstairs and patted Arthur on the cheek as she passed him. 'Any trouble from you today, Arther, and I shall report you to Meeses Watson next time I see 'er.'

'Okay, Mrs P, I give in,' he said, 'but remember, I like me tea like me women – hot, strong an' sweet!'

As Arthur chuckled, coughed and snorted down the hall, Patrick climbed the stairs. 'How's it going, mate?'

'Okay,' I said. 'I'll be finished by midday.'

'Good. Any chance of a lift back to Kington when you go? I want to give them a hand to get started here, but there's some stuff I should sort out back at the store for tomorrow; then I'll pop down to The Galleries and help them unload. Shouldn't think they'll be back much before three.'

'No problem.'

'And don't worry about the old man and Mrs Porter,' he went on, 'she's used to him and his nonsense. We wouldn't have let the senile old fool come otherwise.'

The rain was falling steadily as we slipped and slithered our way back up the muddy track to the main road. That morning's traffic hadn't improved it, and the thick soupy mud was splashing up on either side of the car as we lurched from pothole to pothole.

'Where d'you keep the lifebelts, Rick?' Patrick asked. 'Stored under the seats?'

'What?'

'Well, I only ask 'cos we appear to have sprung a leak.'

I glanced down at the brown muddy water sloshing around Patrick's feet. 'Yes, sorry about that,' I said, 'that foot-well does tend to leak a little.'

'A little! I don't want to be here when the tide comes in.'

Our progress back across the forest was erratic. One of the problems with the Ford Prefect was that its windscreen wipers ran off the exhaust or something like that – I never really understood it. Whatever it was that powered them, they only performed as fast or as slowly as the revolutions of the engine. This meant that if I was bowling along at a good speed, in good conditions, with not a cloud in the sky, the wipers would have worked quite well. However, if I was crawling along in zero visibility in thick fog or torrential rain, then they'd barely manage to squeak and judder their way across the windscreen at all. Even more inconvenient, they always stopped completely when the car was going uphill.

The only antidote to all those shortcomings was to put your foot down and drive like a maniac. So our trip back to Kington began with a series of snail-like hill climbs, each followed by a suicidal dash down the other side to clear the windscreen before the next ascent.

'I begin to wish I'd walked,' Patrick said as he repositioned his feet on the dashboard, clear of the murky waters splashing about on the floor below.

We had gone three or four miles when a rhythmic thudding started to come from the nearside back of the car.

'Wonderful,' Patrick said, 'a puncture!'

'Is it?'

'Yeah, pull over before you wreck the tyre.'

Ignoring the mud, and the water trickling down the side of the road, Patrick squatted in the pouring rain trying to force the jack into the corroded jacking-point.

'I don't like the look of this very much mate, but get the hub cap off and loosen the nuts, then we'll see – and watch out for your knuckles.'

The warning was wasted. The last nut put up a spirited resistance and finally gave when I was least expecting it. The blood flowed freely from my right hand.

'Okay, let's see what happens,' Patrick said as he started, very gingerly, to turn the jack handle.

We both watched for any sign of the car being lifted, but nothing happened. Then there was a sort of soft crunching noise, like a dry biscuit being crumbled. Patrick stopped. 'Well, that's that,' he said, peering under the car. 'The jacking-point's rotten. The jack's going straight through the chassis.'

'Great. What do we do now?'

'I'll lift the car and you change the wheel.'

'You sure?'

'Yeah, no weight in this wreck. Just don't hang about once I've got hold of it.' He turned round and with his back to the car grabbed hold of the wing and lifted the wheel clear of the road. 'At least the bloody wing hasn't come off – yet,' he said through gritted teeth. 'Get on with it, Sunshine, don't bugger about!'

Considering I had to work between Patrick's legs as he stood there like some latter-day Colossus, it went quite smoothly. As soon as the last nut was on, Patrick dropped the car like a stone, and we leant against it getting our breath back. We were wet, greasy, muddy and bloody.

'Oh well, I s'pose it could have been worse,' he said, as he brushed himself down, smearing the grime even deeper into his clothes. 'At least neither of us were wearing our Saville Row gear.'

'No,' I said, 'there is that to it. Mind you, I reckon it'll take me all Saturday to clean the car.'

'No, boy – put it through the car-wash at Kington Motors.'

'What car-wash?'

'Just installed it. Opened this week,' he went on. 'Bloody great thing with big brushes and hoses and stuff, all automatic. You just sit in the car and watch it all happen.'

Surrounded by our customary fug of exhaust smoke, we rattled onto the forecourt at Kington Motors.

'You go and get the token for the machine,' Patrick said, 'and I'll drive it round the back. I'll see you round there.'

At the back of the garage building, there was a large metal gantry on wheels. It was hung with giant bottle brushes, hoses and sprayers. It was the first car-wash in the area and quite a novelty.

'I'll drive it through,' Patrick said. 'I know how it works. Give me the token.'

I settled into the passenger seat beside him as he drove forward and parked the car under the contraption. He turned off the engine and started to wind down the window. As usual it complained bitterly and stuck half-way.

'Does it always do this,' he asked, forcing the handle round another half-turn.

'Yes, there's nothing you can do about it.'

As I spoke, there was a metallic click from behind the door panel and the window wound down fully without any further problem.

'As you were saying,' Patrick said. He wound it up and

down two or three times to prove the trouble had been taken care of.

'Ain't science wonderful?' he said. Reaching through the window, he put the token in the slot and pressed the start button. I made myself comfortable as I got prepared to enjoy my first fully automatic car-wash.

'I don't believe it,' Patrick said.

I glanced round and saw him gazing at his window handle. It wasn't attached to the door anymore.

'It just come off in me bleedin' hand,' he said.

I looked at his window. It was still open.

We sat like rabbits paralysed by a stoat as the spitting hoses crept closer and closer to the gaping window. When they finally sent the first jets of icy water into the car we both tried to take evasive action, but there was nowhere to hide. Next came the rotating brushes, each long nylon fibre licking into the car like a probing, vicious little scourge. At that point Patrick threw himself on top of me – merely, it should be pointed out, in an attempt to get out of the way rather than to protect me. As the brushes drummed and thundered their way along the car, he started it up and put it into gear.

'You can't,' I said, pointing to the large sign forbidding us to leave the car-wash while it was in motion.

'You can stuff that. I'm not just sitting here waiting for that lot to come back and do us over again.' He revved up the engine and let out the clutch. As if she could sense the urgency and danger of our plight, the car leapt forward a couple of inches, stalled and refused to re-start.

'Aaaaaah!' Patrick said, echoing my sentiments exactly. We sat, helpless, as the brushes thundered their way back along the wildly rocking vehicle and the hoses doused us for the second time. It was like being on the receiving end of a not-very-funny practical joke twice in very quick succession.

'Good God! Quick, Margaret, come quick and have a look at these two.' Duncan was sprawled in a chair in Gallery One, with a mug of coffee in one hand and a cigarette in the other. Margaret appeared from Duncan's office, stood and stared at us for a moment in silent disbelief, then fell about laughing. 'Now don't tell me, boys, let me guess,' Duncan

59

went on, clearly warming to his task, 'You've been fighting over Mrs Porter – no? Well then, perhaps you were ambushed by Indians as you came back over The Forest – jolly dangerous country up there. Did anybody else on the wagon train make it or are you the only survivors?'

'Ho, ho, ho,' Patrick said, with all the sarcasm he could muster, as he squelched past Duncan on his way to what was euphemistically known as the Rest Room.

'Well, I don't know,' Duncan went on like a dog with a bone, 'here am I, fresh as a daisy after a dozen calls and a three-hundred-mile round trip, and there are you two, after a simple little house clearance, looking like something the cat dragged in. I just don't understand it. How do you boys manage it?' He really was thoroughly enjoying himself.

'Actually,' I said, 'we had a bit of trouble with the car.'

'A bit! A bit of car trouble! Why, Richard, the only way your car could be held responsible for the way you look now would be if it had just run you down – it hasn't has it? Only, if it has it's been very naughty and I shall have a serious word with it.'

'Oh, very funny,' I said, finally losing my temper. 'It's all right for you. You don't have to drive it. It's bloody dangerous. The thing's a disaster area! The windscreen wipers don't work, it burns more oil than it ever does petrol, the jacking points are rotten, it smells disgusting, the windows don't work, there're bloody great holes in the floor that turn it into a swamp every time it rains, and now it's got a puncture.'

'But apart from that it's all right, is it?'

'Oh, what's the point? You wouldn't be seen dead in it anyway.'

'Oh, wouldn't I? Well, I'll tell you what – the next day of calls I have, I'll take your car, and you can have the Jag for the day, if you need to go anywhere. What's more, I promise you that if I come back looking a quarter as bad as you do now, I'll get you a new car. Okay?'

'Okay!'

Chapter 6

I was standing with no shoes on, on a George III mahogany sideboard, trying to hang an oil painting, when Duncan wandered up. The picture was a Yorkshire landscape by Edmund John Nieman Junior, a sought-after nineteenth-century English artist, and we had high hopes for it. Its gilt framed canvas was well painted, large and very heavy.

'Oh, you're going to hang that there, are you?' Duncan asked.

'Yes,' I said, straining to shorten by another link one of its hanging chains.

'Oh . . .' Duncan paused, 'you think that's the best place for it, then?'

'Yes.'

'Oh . . .'

'Why do you ask?' I said, after a long pause.

'Oh . . . no reason . . . just . . .'

'Yes?'

'I would have thought the light was better in Gallery Two.'

'It's too big for Gallery Two, it would overpower every other picture in the room, and the light reflects off its glass there as well.'

'Oh, do you think so?'

'Yes,' I said, still struggling to raise the left-hand side of the picture by one link.

'Oh, well, I suppose you could be right.'

'Yes!' I said.

'You've not forgotten about Jason Kingsbury?' Duncan went on, lighting a cigarette.

'Who?'

'Jason Kingsbury. I told you about him – he's joining us, starting this morning, I told you.'

I finally secured the chain on the Nieman, turned round and looked at Duncan. 'DP, I've no idea what you're talking about. I have no idea who Jason Kingsbury is. You've never mentioned him to me.'

'No, no, now that's nonsense,' Duncan exhaled a billow of smoke and wagged his finger at me. 'I distinctly remember telling you about him last week and, anyway, you were here when he came in for his interview on Saturday morning.'

'Last Saturday morning was my first Saturday off in over a month.'

'Oh, was it?'

'Yes,' I said. 'Now, who is Jason Kingsbury, and what's he going to do here?'

'Mmm, well I'm blowed, I was certain I told you about him.'

'DP . . .!'

'Yes, yes, well, he's a nice young lad – Harold Kingsbury's youngest son. You know Harold – the property developer?'

'Yes.'

'Well, Jason's just finished his A-levels and left public school and he wants to learn the business, so I've offered him a job as a porter . . . you know, I was certain I'd told you about this.'

'Well, you didn't,' I said, 'but thank goodness we've got somebody starting.'

We had been short-staffed for six weeks. Our normal complement of one full-time porter and me, to handle about a thousand to twelve hundred lots every month, stretched us to breaking point each sale anyway. We could call on Jim and Patrick if we were in a fix, but they couldn't always drop everything for us. Even with Jason Kingsbury joining us, we'd still be hard pressed to be ready for the view day on the coming Friday.

'You need to go left hand down a bit on that picture, you know,' Duncan said as he stood back and looked at the Nieman.

'Are you sure?' I replied. 'I've only just raised the left side because it was too low.'

'Certain – the left side's higher than the right.'

I grabbed hold of the frame, managed to lift it enough to take the weight off the chain and let it out one link again. 'How's that?' I asked.

Duncan took a couple of steps back and put his head on one side. 'Well, I'm damned! You know you were right first time. Sorry about that.' He turned to go as I heaped curses upon him under my breath. 'So, don't forget,' he said, 'Jason should be here by ten – he's moving into digs at the moment – then there's the delivery from Southbourne.'

Duncan's sense of timing and presentation when it came to the breaking of bad news was legendary. He would lob the bombshell into a conversation when you were least expecting it and usually in no position to argue about it. On this occasion the words had drifted innocently over his shoulder as he left the gallery. On the receiving end, I was completely immobilised having just unchained the picture again. 'Duncan!' I shouted.

Rather to my surprise his head popped back round the door. 'You called, Sir?'

'DP – what delivery from Southbourne?' I asked, half turning to look at him as I groped blindly to shorten the chain again.

'Mrs Wade's.' he said. 'I told you all about it the other day. Your trouble is, and I don't like having to say this, Richard, you just don't listen!'

'You've never mentioned to me that Mrs Wade was even thinking of selling anything,' I said, eventually securing the Nieman again and jumping down from the sideboard. 'What's she sending in?'

'About a dozen pieces of furniture – you're right, that picture does look better – including those two nice card tables, you remember them, blind-fret carved, they'll go really well . . .'

'Yes, but which sale's it all for? It's not in this sale, is it?'

'No, no, she didn't make up her mind until after this catalogue had gone to press. No, we'll just pop it in the store for the next sale.'

It was the nonchalant way Duncan said these things which used to drive me to distraction: 'We'll just pop it in the store.' By that stage the store was completely inaccessible. The only way into it was through Gallery Four and that was groaning with furniture. I pointed out the problem to Duncan as I put my shoes back on.

'I expect you'll manage. You'll have Jason to help you and perhaps the boys on the truck will give you a hand.'

'Perhaps they will,' I said, with growing impatience, 'but what if Watson's don't have time to help us?'

'Watson's?' Duncan's tone set all sorts of alarm bells ringing inside me.

'Duncan – it is Watson's doing the job, isn't it?'

'Not exactly – no.'

'Who is it, Duncan?'

'You know what a fussy old bird Mrs Wade is. If Watson's boys had walked through her front door she would have had a seizure. I've just taken two months to winkle this lot out from under Christies' upturned noses, you don't really think I'd take the chance of losing it now by having Arthur marching into her drawing room and goosing her, do you?'

'Who's doing the job?'

'It had to be a smart-looking prestige firm . . .'

'Who is it, Duncan?'

'. . . a set-up with a bit of class.'

'It's Burton and Farmer, isn't it?' I said.

'Mmm?'

'Is it Burton and Farmer?'

'Yes.'

'I knew it.'

The relationship between auctioneer and removal firm is a special one. To start with, since the auctioneer usually arranges the collection of things for sale, if the client has problems with the carrier, the client blames the auctioneer. The converse is also true of course; a difficult client is always considered by the carrier to be entirely the fault of the auctioneer. Another important angle is that of honesty. The auctioneer has more opportunity than anybody else I can think of to steal and pilfer and get away with it. Not only is he often left alone in houses, he's frequently the only one who knows that a particular item is worth anything anyway. So, an auctioneer has to be scrupulously honest, and so do

64

his carriers. Watson's were beyond reproach, and when it came to honesty, so were Burton and Farmer's men. The problem with the latter was one of attitude. They were fine with the clients, oiling their way around them with great skill. The trouble began when they arrived at The Galleries. Then they worked by the book, or at least, how they interpreted the book. They did no more nor less than they believed they had to, and the biggest bone of contention was the unloading of goods. As far as Burton and Farmer were concerned, their responsibility stopped at the threshold; as far as we were concerned, we expected them to put the furniture in whichever gallery we chose. We said that was no more than they'd do if they were moving a customer to a new house – they'd put the beds in the bedrooms, the dining table in the dining room and the cooker in the kitchen. Their reply to this well-reasoned argument was the oral equivalent of two fingers. The only way they could be persuaded to co-operate was by the application of substantial bribes, although for the sake of propriety these were always referred to as tips. Duncan tossed pound notes around like confetti and had no trouble with the men at all. I, on the other hand, had appalling problems because I wasn't permitted to dip into the petty cash tin in the way he did. Even more irritating, Duncan would always pretend that he didn't buy off the crews at all, but that instead he simply controlled them by firmness. It used to drive me mad.

'For goodness sake, Richard,' he went on, 'I do hope you're not going to make your usual song and dance about the Burton and Farmer boys. I must have demonstrated to you a dozen times that you simply have to be firm with them.'

'Duncan, immediately they walk through the door and see you're not here, they'll know there's no chance of a tip and they'll get bolshie.'

'Richard, I've told you before: you can't buy the respect of people like that, you must earn it – be firm, don't let them push you around, show them who's boss. Now, I must go or I'll be late.'

It was pointless arguing with him.

'And, by the way,' he went on, 'after all that fuss you

made the other week about your car, and just to demonstrate how you over-react to things, I'll use it today for my calls while the Jag's being serviced. See you later.'

From the moment of his arrival it was obvious that Jason Kingsbury was going to be an asset. He was bright, strong and keen. More than that, he was energetic. Being naturally cautious, I have always held a sneaking admiration for people who attack problems head-on, grappling with them and solving them as they go along. I've also always marvelled at those superhumans among us who can exist on two or three hours sleep a night – people like Bill Grigson. Jason fitted into that category and could power along all day and most of the night without showing any obvious signs of wear and tear. I, on the other hand, was quite capable of going to sleep standing up in the middle of a crowded room.

Whatever our differences were, we worked well together from the outset, and between us had managed to clear a way to the store by the time Burton and Farmer's pantechnicon pulled up outside the main doors.

Burton and Farmer had several teams of men, most of them middle-aged and not entirely unreasonable. However, they had one team of four youths and, to a man, they were offensive, surly, and thoroughly uncooperative. As the street doors opened, and the familiar pock-marked face of their loutish foreman appeared, I abandoned any hope of a reasonable dialogue.

'Where's the old geezer?' he asked Margaret Graham, who had come out of her office to see who it was.

'If you're referring to Mr Parkes, he's out. Richard will tell you where we want the furniture.'

'He can tell us what 'e likes. If Parkes ain't 'ere there's no chance of a tip, so all this gear goes right 'ere, darlin'.' He pointed down at the floor where he stood, just inside the door.

'If you're not prepared to unload it properly,' I said, taking over from Margaret, 'just leave it on your truck and take it to your depot, and I'll sort it out with your managing director. I've had enough of this nonsense every time you deliver a few sticks of furniture.'

'Get knotted, mush – this junk comes off this truck wever you like it or not.'

'I don't mind tipping you if that's all this fuss is about,' Jason suddenly volunteered. Margaret and I turned and stared at him.

'I'm not talking pennies,' the foreman said, looking at Jason with obvious suspicion, 'the rate's a quid an 'ead, little boy.'

'Four pounds – okay,' Jason said enthusiastically.

'Jason, you mustn't,' Margaret intervened, 'DP won't refund you.'

'I don't mind, let's get going.'

Quickly, and with very little grace, the Wade furniture was rushed upstairs, through Gallery Four and dumped in the store.

'That's four quid then,' the foreman said, holding out his hand to Jason less than fifteen minutes after the price had been agreed.

'Er, no money I'm afraid' Jason said with a disarming smile.

'What?'

'No money! I don't have any money on me. Well strictly speaking I do, but only about ten bob and you're certainly not having that – sorry! But thanks very much anyway, you and your chaps really were a great help, I don't know how we would have managed.'

The foreman looked incredulously at Jason, then at his colleagues, then back at Jason. 'You must want to bloody well die, Sonny!' he said, taking a step towards his smaller and still smiling adversary. 'You are just about to get filled in!'

The first punch was a short jab to the solar plexus; the second was a vicious left hook which, it must be said, was beautifully timed, arcing up and meeting the recipient's jaw as he was doubling over from the previous blow. He snapped upright as it hit him and went over backwards like a felled tree. Fortunately his fall was broken by an armchair and a pile of rugs, otherwise his head would undoubtedly have split open on the concrete floor.

'Jason!' Margaret screamed. 'Oh, my God, I think he's dead!' We both stood looking down on the prostrate figure.

'No, look, he's twitching,' Jason observed, sounding only mildly interested, 'I expect he'll be all right.'

As he lay on his back just inside the door, a trickle of blood dribbled from the side of the foreman's mouth and then down his scarred cheek. His left leg kicked and twitched involuntarily as his three crewmen stood in the doorway looking at their fallen champion. None of them showed any keenness to continue the argument with Jason on their colleague's behalf.

The foreman's eyelids flickered, opened, closed and then opened again. 'Wha-appened?' he slurred, as he tried to sit up, but instead rolled sideways off the pile of rugs. 'Where-is-e-I'll-kill-im!' He managed to get onto all-fours, began to stand up, but slumped back to the floor again. He looked like a big beached fish.

At last two of his crew stepped forward and, standing on either side of him, hauled him to his feet and guided him to the door. As they manoeuvred him through the doorway he looked back at Jason, and appeared to be about to leave him with a threat or at least with an insult. He opened his bloody mouth, but no sound came out. He turned away and was helped to the cab of the lorry by his friends.

'Well, that's that,' Jason said brightly as he closed the door behind them.

'Lord knows what DP will say when he hears about this,' Margaret said, sitting down in the armchair the foreman had so recently bounced off. Her hands were trembling.

'Does he have to know?' I asked. 'After all I can't imagine that lot will rush into their managing director's office when they get back to complain they were beaten up for trying to extort money from the staff of Wilson's Auction Galleries.'

'You've got a point,' she said. 'Okay, let's not mention it unless we have to. And now I'm going to get my lunch, I can't stop shaking.'

'You realise,' I said, as Jason and I wandered along the street to the local pub, 'as your immediate superior, I have to reprimand you very severely for what you did this morning.'

'Absolutely,' he replied.

'Right, consider it done.'

'Absolutely,' he said again.

It's said that Kington used to have a pub for every week of

the year, and if your spiritual requirements were otherwise inclined there were very nearly as many churches. The Brickmakers' Arms, always known to the locals as The Brickies, was a survivor of those halcyon days. By virtue of their long-standing tenancy, the landlord and landlady, Harry and Elsie Porter, had been able to resist all the brewer's entreaties for the pub to be modernised. The odd bit of formica had managed to creep in but it was so out of place it just added to the pub's surreal quality. It still had its original layout with Saloon, Public, Tap Room and Off-Sales, splitting the place into a series of small cubicles huddled around a central bar. The furniture was chiefly 1930s and 1940s Front Room Rejects: easy chairs with twanging springs, so low that nobody ever sat in them, stained oak draw-leaf tables, old dining chairs and the occasional stool. The saloon bar was carpeted with a worn, patterned Wilton, but all the other bars made do with lino and the odd rug. Only the outermost edge of the lino retained its pattern, elsewhere – with the exception of bits that got a lot of through-traffic, where it was worn through to the boards below – it was a uniform grey-brown. All the paintwork was nicotine brown or yellow, and the Victorian etched glass windows, which boasted 'Fine Ales & Stouts', protected the incumbents from the prying eyes of potential customers. For, if The Brickies didn't actually discourage passing trade, it did nothing to attract it either. Mind you, any stranger who did brave the glares of the regulars and the squalor of the surroundings was likely to get as warm a welcome from Harry and Elsie as they would from any landlord and landlady.

Harry and Elsie Porter were a perfect fit. Harry, short and round, habitually dressed in check shirt, silk cravat, cardigan, cavalry twills and carpet slippers, would sit on his stool behind the bar beaming and sucking away on one of his big black briar pipes. Elsie matched Harry almost exactly in construction, and would move through the bar like a great Tudor galleon. She created the best sandwiches in Kington and would commute between the bar and her kitchen on the first floor with a grace remarkable for one so large. When the production line ceased she'd settle behind the bar with

Harry and drink sparkling wine and brandy in quantities which would have stopped strong men in their tracks.

On special occasions a local police sergeant would pound out singalong numbers on an ill-tuned piano with three sticking keys, but at all other times music came from Harry's 1950s reel-to-reel tape recorder. The choice was limited to crackling slavonic violin concertos or Michael Holliday ballads. Harry never tired of either, and would sit smiling at the ceiling, keeping time with his fingers on the bar.

'There's nobody here,' Jason said as we entered the deserted public bar.

'Probably not,' I said. 'If we're the first ones in, Harry and Elsie won't have bothered to come down yet.' Their time-keeping was as personal as everything else about them. One of them usually drew the bolts on the doors at the proper time, but apart from that they both stayed upstairs until half past twelve at the earliest. Bottling-up was done by an experienced regular and each person served himself until Harry took up his rightful place in the bar.

'Two rounds of chicken please, Elsie,' I shouted up the stairs.

'All right, my dear, be down in two ticks,' Elsie's voice percolated down from the kitchen.

I walked behind the bar, pulled two pints of bitter and threw the money in the till.

'Is it always like this?' Jason asked as we sat at the bar.

'Yes, but there'll probably be quite a few locals in soon.' As I spoke, the saloon bar door opened and two men in quiet grey suits and loud ties walked in. Anybody coming into the saloon was a rare thing in itself but when, having looked around, they appeared to decide to stay and have a drink, they became very nearly unique. I went back behind the bar and walked round to the saloon serving hatch.

'Can I help you?' I asked.

'Two gin and tonics,' the smaller of the two said without a flicker of a smile. He was perspiring slightly and had blonde eye lashes which made his eyes look piggy. I got the drinks and put them in front of him on the bar.

'We'd like ice and lemon,' he said, looking at the drinks with obvious disapproval.

'I'm sorry, there isn't any at the moment,' I replied. 'I think the landlord or landlady will be down with both shortly.'

'How much do I owe you?'

'I don't know, the prices aren't marked. Settle up with the landlord or landlady . . .'

'Yes, don't tell me – when they come down,' he interrupted. There really was something very unfriendly about his manner. I went back to my seat and was talking to Jason when, after a while, the piglet appeared at the hatch again. He rattled the glasses on the bar. I ignored him. He rattled the glasses again and I ignored him again.

'Can I have some service here?'

He was perspiring quite freely now. I got off my stool and wandered round to the hatch. 'Same again?'

'Unless you have ice and lemon this time.'

'No.' I put the fresh drinks down in front of him.

'I suppose you still don't know how much these are,' he said.

'No.'

Something seemed to snap inside him. 'What sort of barman are you?' he snarled. 'You don't know the price of drinks, you have no idea about service . . .'

He seemed momentarily undecided about which short-coming to register next, so I took my chance. 'I'm the sort of barman who's trying to have a quiet drink with a colleague. I'm the sort of barman who has to be back at work by two o'clock. I'm the sort of barman who's a customer!'

'What?'

'I'm a fine art cataloguer, what are you?' I said, drawing myself down to his full height.

'I'm the district manager of the brewery that owns this pub,' he said, very slowly and quietly, his piggy little eyes staring into mine, 'and that,' he continued, hissing at me as he drew closer, 'is my managing director from London.'

I glanced across at his companion. He was seated uncomfortably on an old woodseat chair next to an unlit paraffin heater. He fidgeted as he gazed round the walls at the old calendar pictures of fluffy kittens, and the odd outdated brewery promotion poster.

71

'I'll go and se if Mr or Mrs Porter is down yet,' I said, backing from the bar.

I sprinted upstairs and dashed into the kitchen where Elsie was putting the finishing touches to the sandwiches. 'Elsie, Elsie, the district manager's downstairs and he's not happy.'

'Really, dear?' she said, arranging the garnish. 'Why, what's upset him?'

'I think I have,' I said.

'Well done, dear, he's a miserable little sod at the best of times. I hate those nasty beady pink eyes of his – reminds me of a ferret.' She swung her superstructure around the kitchen, weaving in and out of the furniture with ease. 'Harry's in the bathroom having a shave, tell him to get his skates on, darling, and your sandwiches are on the table, take them down for me, there's a love.'

Travelling at her top speed by the time she reached the landing, she seemed to float down the steep stairs. I marvelled again at how such a big woman could be so light on her feet.

'Harry, Harry,' I shouted as I knocked on the bathroom door, 'the district manager's downstairs.'

'Ooh crikey!' The bathroom door opened and Harry spilled out, clad in vest, a pair of underpants which began two inches below his armpits and ended two inches below his knees, socks and his faithful carpet slippers. He careered past me, wiping off the remaining shaving soap with a towel. 'District manager you say?'

'Yes, and his managing director from London.'

'Coo, like having royalty to tea,' he gurgled. 'Bit of a lark, eh!'

I had no real need to worry about Harry and Elsie of course. With their security of tenure nothing short of bankruptcy or death could remove them from the pub against their will. Unfortunately, they were very nearly the last generation of publicans to have such favourable arrangements, and both the British pub and the British public are the poorer for their passing.

That afternoon, Duncan slipped back into The Galleries very quietly and went straight to ground in his office. This was unusual. He normally checked to see if anything interesting had come in for sale while he'd been out. After about half an hour he went out again and eventually reappeared just a little before half past five.

'Richard,' he said, returning my car keys, 'as I thought, that little car is basically jolly sound – for it's age – but I'd already given it a lot of thought and I feel the time has come to look to the future.' He had started to pace up and down the gallery with his hands behind his back – always a sure sign of an important announcement. 'You're going to be doing an increasing amount of mileage,' he continued, 'and so I decided last night it would be wise to trade in the Ford before its mileage gets any higher. To this end, I've just done a deal with Barns Cross Garage on a second-hand Morris 1100. It'll be ready for collection the day after tomorrow.'

'That's fantastic!' I said.

I couldn't have been more surprised.

'Well, Mr Anthony and I expect you to look after it of course.'

'Of course.'

'Oh, there's one other thing,' he said, as though it was almost too trivial to mention, 'somebody must have backed into the Ford while it was parked in Langton this morning. The front offside wing's had a bit of a knock, must have been a lorry, I think. It doesn't matter though, the garage knows about it. It won't affect the part-exchange.'

'Gosh,' Jason said, when we got to the car park, 'must have been quite a lorry. It's really bent that wing, hasn't it?'

It had. Both head light and side light were gone and the bumper was a write-off.

'Is Mr Parkes usually so generous?' Jason went on. 'About the new car I mean.'

'No,' I said, 'no, he's not.'

'Well, it's a good thing he'd decided to get you a new car anyway, wasn't it?'

'Yes, wasn't it?'

I smelt a rat.

It was nearly two months before I eventually weedled the real story out of Margaret, and then she swore me to secrecy. Apparently, Duncan had had a terrible time with the Ford, but things had actually reached crisis point on the coast road out of Langton. He was bowling along at a reasonable speed for the first time that morning, when he allowed an attack of over-confidence to get the better of his judgement. He pulled out to overtake an articulated lorry – something I wouldn't have attempted for all the money in the world. The road had been quite clear except for an oncoming truck in the far, far distance. He pushed the accelerator to the floor, only to find it had very little effect on the speed of the car; if anything, it seemed to go a little more slowly. So he changed into what he absent-mindedly thought was third; it was of course second, and the car almost stood on its nose. By now, the distant oncoming truck wasn't so distant anymore. Duncan slammed his foot to the floor and, with the engine screaming and its customary plume of black smoke now pure papal white, he crept two thirds of the way past the articulated lorry. Unfortunately, two thirds of the way was not enough. The distant truck was on him, towering over the Ford, lights flashing and horn blaring. The only place for Duncan to go was a bus lay-by on the far side of the road, and that was where he went. He missed the bus shelter comfortably but destroyed an inconveniently placed metal litter bin on arrival.

In all the years I knew him, Duncan never told me the true story of the damage to that car, and if ever the vehicle came up in idle conversation, he would always refer to it as 'a jolly good little motor'.

Chapter 7

Viewing days always stirred mixed emotions in me. Two days set aside before each sale for the general public to saturate The Galleries in search of unidentified rarities and undervalued trinkets. Most of the regular trade – the dealers – viewed before the official viewing days. It didn't matter to them that pictures weren't hung or some of the furniture was still stacked and not easy to get at. They knew what they were looking for, and had often already spotted it in the catalogue, even though it might only have been represented by an ambiguous single line of print. The trade wanted to view quickly and in peace, without queueing and jostling. Their time was money and they would almost certainly be covering several sales in a day, each one probably miles from the next.

There were certain exceptions, however, and some of the older dealers used to be happy to sit down and have a cup of tea and a natter. Many of them had known Duncan for twenty years or more, and trusted and liked him. They were the ones who took time to regale us with the latest trade gossip and scandal: who'd just worked one over on whom; how some particularly unpleasant type was enticed into paying twice as much as he should for something; and, of course, the ridiculously high prices being paid at auction. It should be added that, in the late sixties, a price variation of ten per cent was considered the financial equivalent of an earth tremor.

Some of the dealers would travel round in pairs just for the company and economy of transport. The two I remember best were Joe Levene and Fred Hart. Both in their late fifties, they'd perfected a double act of one-liners and insults. Joe, who was always smart and charming, dealt in good English and Continental furniture and works of art. Fred was grizzled, sported designer stubble when Bob Geldof was barely more than a twinkle in his parents' eyes, and smoked a disgusting old pipe that had a mouthpiece green with age and decay. He claimed he was the only card-carrying Communist Party member to deal in antiques west of the German Democratic Republic, and maintained his stock was formed in his own likeness – he'd buy anything old and ugly.

'What about that, you old fool?' Joe would say. 'You like that do you?'

'That? Nah – it's 'ideous!'

'So you don't want me to bid on it for you then?'

'Course I do, you damned idiot, I must 'ave it – can't live without it!'

Harold Middleditch and his wife were another pair of regulars. Harold had once been one of the most important dealers in the south east, and even in semi-retirement, he still had a coterie of wealthy private customers for whom he bought and sold. Mrs Middleditch was a great character with a sparkling sense of humour untarnished by her long years of crippling ill-health. On arrival at The Galleries she would plump herself down in the most regal chair she could find and start reeling off anecdotes. I never heard her repeat herself once. If their visit coincided with the erratic opening hours of The Brickies, as many Wilson's staff as would fit would pile into the Middleditch Bentley and be ferried to the pub, where Mrs Middleditch would be greeted like a long lost sister by Elsie. She'd then down a pint of Guinness like a pro.

One of Harold's small pleasures was a game of torment he played with Agnes Bromley. Agnes helped us out at sale time and was in charge of displaying porcelain. She had her own little trade mark, which was to put a vase of freshly cut blooms from her own garden on the piece of furniture we expected to make the highest price. If any important dealer came to view the sale, she'd hover by the piece with a duster in her hand to underline how highly we rated it. Harold Middleditch, who viewed very thoroughly, would invariably completely ignore the star turn. He'd examine every other lot around it and eventually turn to go to another gallery.

This always proved too much for Agnes. She was a roly-poly character of advancing years, and a fervent, no-nonsense chapel-goer. 'Ahem!' she'd cough theatrically, as she stood, arms folded across her ample bosom, fingers drumming on either bicep. 'I think you've overlooked something, Mr Middleditch.'

Harold Middleditch would turn in puzzlement, then his eyes would apparently light for the first time on the prize lot. He'd return to it, break off a buttonhole, compliment Agnes on the flowers and walk off, still without having looked at the piece of furniture. It was a simple little pantomime which never seemed to lose its charm for the two players.

The official viewing days were chiefly the domain of the private buyer, collector or browser. Patrick and I used to take an overview of things in the main gallery from a vantage point on the staircase. I believed then, and I still believe now, that every form of human life milled about below us there: mouthwateringly beautiful women; ugly, sharp-featured old crones; gentlemen farmers; overblown little barons of local industry; academics; scrap merchants; spoilt children; abandoned parents. The rich, the poor, the happy, the sad – they all came and went. Some in too much of a hurry to be polite. Some wanting to linger and talk, too lonely to go. We had our favourites, those we looked forward to seeing, and there were those we'd go to any lengths to avoid. Any new member of staff would have to endure a dreadful initiation period as they found themselves saddled with every problematic client we had. Those of us who knew the ropes could melt into the furniture and *objects d'art* like chamelons. The unfortunate novice would find himself monopolised by one obnoxious, objectionable or just plain boring character after another.

'Where's lot 153? . . . where's lot 89? . . . show me the James II tankard . . . what will the Shayer farmyard scene make? . . . what number's the table in Gallery Three . . . you know the one, you must do, it's . . . it's . . . it's dark brown . . .'

By five o'clock on Saturday afternoon, at the end of the

second day, as we checked the silver back into the strong-room, we had aching feet and little conversation left. All we wanted to do was get home as quickly as the news that nothing had been stolen from the silver would allow.

The Friday view of the sale containing Alan Porter's aunt's pieces went off without any problems, other than those suffered by Jason as part of his apprenticeship. He had been collared for an unprecedented one hour, forty-seven minutes by one Mrs Weinberg. As far as Patrick and I knew, no man had spent that long with her and kept his sanity. Jason seemed unlikely to be certified, although by the end of this extra-ordinary feat of endurance, he did seem to find it difficult to put together a coherent sentence and his eyes kept rolling round in a strange way.

By a quarter to nine the next morning he'd recovered almost completely and was helping the rest of us display the silver again, when Anthony Wilson arrived on the scene.

'Good morning, Mr Anthony,' we all chorused, like primary school children.

'Morning, morning – thought I'd have a quick look around.'

'You should think about buying Alan Porter's aunt's diamond solitaire, Anthony,' Duncan said, as he came through from the strongroom with a tray piled high with bundles of spoons and forks. 'I'm sure Daphne would be appreciative.'

'Solitaire? . . . Solitaire? . . . Good one is it, old boy? . . . Eh? . . . Eh?'

'Very nice indeed – it'll be a good buy at anything under seven hundred.'

'Really? . . . Really? . . . Seven hundred? . . . Not out of the way is it? . . . Not out of the way at all. After all, bound to be a good investment . . . Eh? . . . Eh?'

'I would think so; and isn't your anniversary soon?' Duncan gave me a sly look as he laid out the lots on the table.

'Yes . . . Yes . . . Absolutely right, old chap . . . And Daphne has hinted that a little bauble wouldn't go amiss as it happens . . . Better have a look at it.'

'Pat!' Duncan called out. 'Open up the jewellery case and show Mr Anthony the diamond solitaire.'

Patrick hurried into the gallery and hauled a bunch of keys from his pocket. He unlocked the display case and put the ring into Anthony Wilson's pudgy, pink little hand. The stone winked and flashed as he held it up to the light.

'Jolly good! . . . Jolly good! . . . Er . . . No doubt about it being genuine, of course?'

'Genuine what?' Duncan asked, checking off a few more lots and sounding vaguely mystified by the question.

'Genuine diamond, old boy . . . You can get some damned clever fakes these days you know . . . I was reading about it in the *Telegraph* the other day.'

Duncan smiled. 'No, Anthony, I can personally guarantee you have in your hand a genuine diamond.'

'Good . . . Good . . . I'll certainly give it some consideration then, Duncan . . . Anything less than seven hundred you say?'

'That's it.'

Anthony Wilson bumbled around The Galleries, generally getting in everybody's way, for another quarter of an hour. Then he left for the estate office. Shortly after nine o'clock, one of our popular, regular private buyers, John Bingham, arrived. John was an ebullient local businessman who thoroughly enjoyed the atmosphere of auctions. He had little knowledge of antiques but, with Duncan's assistance, he'd bought quite well over the years.

'What's good on the menu today, Duncan?' he asked.

'Nice diamond solitaire, John.'

'No thanks, I saw it in the catalogue, it'll be too rich for me – might give me serious indigestion!' he grinned. 'I'll have a look at lot twelve thirty-three though – the watch fobs.'

'Pat, open up for Mr Bingham, please – the watch fobs.'

The next visitor was less welcome. It was Jacob Raseby, a Langton silver dealer of few words and less charm. The sheen on his bespoke suits usually put our silver to shame, but on this occasion we were spared such a comparison since he was huddled inside a camel overcoat. 'Wanna see da watch fobs,' he demanded.

Patrick wrinkled his nose to leave no doubt as to his feelings about Mr Raseby, then he unlocked the cabinet and

79

handed him the fobs. At just that moment, Agnes Bromley inadvertantly altered the course of the day for us all. She failed to notice the upturned corner of a rug on the floor just outside the strongroom. She was carrying the final tray of silver and went down with a crash that must have been audible in the High Street.

'Mrs Bromley! Are you all right?' Duncan said, rushing to help her.

'Yes, yes, I'm all right. Oh, what a stupid thing to do . . . Is any of it broken? . . . Is any of the silver broken? I'll pay for it if it is.'

'Never mind the silver,' Duncan said, 'is any of you broken?'

'No, I'm all right, I've just bumped my knee – oh, do stop fussing, you're like a lot of old mother hens!'

Amid her protests, Jason and I crawled about under tables and chairs retrieving the errant pieces of silver, while Duncan and Margaret winched Agnes back to her feet. Under a barrage of further protests, Margaret led her away to check on her knee. As Duncan, Jason and I carried the silver through to Gallery One, Raseby was just leaving. 'What was that row?' he grunted.

'Mrs Bromley had a fall,' I said.

'She all right?'

'Yes, I think she's just a bit shaken, thank you, Mr Raseby,' Duncan replied.

'Good, she's getting on a bit for that sorta thing,' he said, and let himself out.

'There you are boys, even Jacon Raseby has a good side,' Duncan said, 'perhaps there's hope for the human race after all.'

It was shortly after ten o'clock that Agnes gave in to Duncan's insistance that if she wasn't going to go home, she must take the day easy sitting by the jewellery cabinet. Handing her the keys, Patrick glanced at the display inside once more. His face suddenly fell and paled – something was obviously terribly wrong.

'It's gone,' he groaned, 'it's bloody gone!'

'None of those "Bs" when I'm around if you don't mind young Patrick,' Agnes ticked him off.

'Sod the "Bs", the bloody solitaire's gone!'

We all rushed over to the cabinet.

'Where was it?' Duncan asked.

'Just there,' Patrick said, miserably, 'next to the watch fobs. They've been moved over so I didn't notice the gap in the display.' For a moment he stood looking completely dejected, then his eyes took fire. 'Jacob-effing-Raseby!' he said.

'Don't you dare "F" in my presence,' Agnes said, by now fully recovered and steeped in Sunday-best chapel zeal.

'It was that bastard who had it,' Patrick went on undeterred. 'I bet the sod lifted it when Agnes went arse over ti . . . Ahhh!' The three-foot rule which, along with her duster, Agnes Bromley always carried like a staff of office, crashed down across Patrick's knuckles before he could finish.

'I've told you, my boy, I don't care how big you are or what you say at home, I won't have all this effing and blinding when I'm around, I just won't put up with it . . .'

'Yes, thank you, Mrs Bromley,' Duncan interrupted, 'I think he's got the message. Are you certain it was Raseby, Patrick?'

'Yeah – he's the only person who could have had it. Anyway, the only other people who looked at the jewellery this morning were Mr Anthony and Mr Bingham – neither of them would have half-inched it, would they?'

'Pretty unlikely, I give you,' Duncan said, 'and it would explain why Raseby left in such a hurry. He usually views all the silver. He wouldn't have come all the way over here to look at one lot of watch fobs – no it's him all right. Margaret, call the police!'

The local CID were with us within half an hour. We were all questioned, except for Patrick who was grilled.

'So you take each piece out individually and hand it to the customer,' the sergeant recapped, looking at his notes, 'then you close the cabinet. Then, when the customer has finished looking at that bit, you take it from him, open the cabinet, put the thing back in the cabinet, then give him the next thing, and so on.'

'Yes.'

'So there's never more than one thing out at a time, and the customer never puts his hand inside the cabinet?'

'Never.'

'So how did Raseby nick it if he never even asked to see it?'

'I'd just handed him the watch fobs . . .'

'Hold on, what *are* watch fobs?' the sergeant interrupted.

'They're gold mounted seals that hung from a gentleman's watch chain,' Duncan explained.

'Not very big then?'

'No. Only about an inch to an inch and a half, but there are four in the one lot, tied together with string. Do you want to see them?'

'Yeah, in a minute,' the sergeant said, turning back to Patrick. 'So you'd just handed Raseby these fob things, then there was the big crash in the other gallery. Exactly what did you do then, Mr Watson?'

'I looked up, and I think I took a few steps away from the cabinet – to try to see what had happened.'

'Had you closed the cabinet door, or pushed it to?'

'I don't think so.'

'When you returned to the cabinet, did Raseby hand the fobs back to you?'

'That's what I've been trying to remember. I'm almost certain he didn't. He just stood there talking to me until the others came through with the silver, then he asked them what had happened. I should have known he was up to something, usually the most he'll do is grunt at you.'

'Okay,' the sergeant said, 'so what we're saying is that you give Raseby the watch fobs – Mrs Bromley falls over – you're distracted – you step away from the cabinet and take your eyes off Raseby – he sticks his hand in – grabs the ring and drops the fobs – you return to the cabinet – he engages you in conversation until the others arrive – then it's "Good Morning, Mr Raseby." You wouldn't be looking for the ring to be missing anyway because he only looked at the fobs and there they are, back in the cabinet.'

'Yes.'

'Sounds plausible enough to me,' Duncan said.

'Oh, it's plausible enough,' the sergeant replied, 'but as

evidence goes, it stinks. In the middle of Mr Watson's vital testimony we've got two "thinks" and one "almost certain" Not a lot of good really, Mr Parkes.'

'Well, you're not suggesting the lad should perjure himself are you?'

'No, no, don't get me wrong, sir. All I'm saying is that Raseby's a slippery sod. I nicked him myself four years ago and his Brief ran rings round me in court – I'm not up for that again, thank you very much.'

The sergeant looked pensively at his notes. 'No, the only way we'll have him is by nailing him with the ring on him, and the chances of that are slim – he's been gone for an hour and a half already.' He turned to the plain clothes constable with him. 'Let's get after him, anyway. Put out a call to bring him in. Do his shop and his flat. Take his car apart. Give him a real going over. Even if we can't get this one to stick, we'll let him know that we know it was him.'

The constable nodded and left without saying a word.

'We'll need the addresses of the other two, please, Mr Parkes,' the sergeant continued.

'Other two? What other two?'

'The other two people who had access to the cabinet this morning – Wilson and . . . er . . . Bingham,' he said, leafing back through his notes to find the names.

'But you can't possibly suspect them, surely . . . I mean . . . good God . . . Anthony Wilson's my senior partner – he owns the place.'

'And he was also the last person you all saw actually handling the ring. With the exception of Mr Watson, nobody here could really testify, hand on heart, that the ring was back in that cabinet when your partner left this building. After all, neither Bingham nor Raseby even asked to see it.' Duncan looked utterly miserable but didn't argue. 'I'm sorry, sir,' the sergeant went on, 'but if we don't make a show of going after the other two as hard as we go after Raseby, he's just as likely to accuse me of harassment.'

'Okay,' Duncan said, 'but it'll be all right for me to ring them and warn them what it's all about, won't it?'

'No it will not, sir!' the sergeant looked horrified. 'And if you do any such thing you'll be seriously impeding the course of this investigation, and I'll come down on you like a ton of bricks!'

Duncan squirmed with discomfort. Whatever happened, whatever he did, whichever way he jumped, disaster was inevitable. The fuse was lit and there was nothing he could do to extinguish it. 'Give the sergeant the addresses, Margaret,' he said, abandoning himself to fate.

'Wilson's Galleries,' I said, answering the telephone.

'Who's that?' The voice at the other end was Mr Anthony's. Distorted by rage though it was, it was still recognisable as that of the firm's senior partner.

'Er . . . it's Richard here, Mr Anthony,' I said.

'I want to speak to Mr Parkes. Put him on, *immediately!*'

I looked across the desk at Duncan and gestured that the call was for him. He shook his head vigorously and raised his hands as if to push the phone away. I clamped my hand over the mouthpiece.

'You must speak to him,' I whispered, 'I think he's going to burst a blood vessel.'

'No, no, get rid of him. I'm not strong enough yet,' he hissed back at me.

'But what shall I tell him!'

'Tell him I'm with a client! Tell him I'm out! Tell him I'm dead! Tell him anything you like, but get rid of him.'

'Er . . . Hello . . . Mr Anthony?'

The barked response suggested the blood vessel was due to go at any moment.

'. . . I'm afraid Mr Parkes is with a client at the moment,' I struggled on, 'but I'll get him to call you immediately he's free.'

'Make sure you do, young man!'

The line went dead. Duncan and I sat staring glumly at each other.

'I'd better get back into the galleries,' I said, 'we've got a lot of people out there, it's almost three o'clock.'

'You stay where you are, Richard. Every time that phone rings, you answer it. You're my last line of defence – Margaret's already disappeared somewhere.'

As he spoke, the telephone jarred into strident life again.

84

We sat looking at it, then Duncan reached over, picked it up and handed it to me.

'Wilson's Galleries,' I said, with some difficulty – my mouth was like sandpaper.

'This is John Bingham – who's that?'

'Richard Harton, Mr Bingham,' I said, still trying in vain to produce some saliva.

'I don't expect Duncan's available, is he, Richard?'

'Er . . . no, I'm afraid he's not.'

'What a surprise . . . and what a pity, because I have a very funny story to tell him.' John Bingham didn't sound as though he was particularly amused. John Bingham sounded rather unstable, like a fully extended rubber band, or an unexploded bomb that was ticking. 'Never mind,' he went on, quietly and too deliberately for comfort, 'I'll tell you instead, and then you can tell Duncan, and then you can all have a good laugh about it.'

'Er . . .' I said, looking at Duncan, whose tortured facial expressions must have been mirroring my own.

'The story begins,' John Bingham continued, 'with me, my wife and children about to have lunch at home with some guests. The chap just happens to be my most important American client. He's over here with his wife and children, they're staying the weekend with us – a nice quiet weekend in the English countryside, away from all the crime and violence of New York. Well, we'd had a couple of gins on the terrace – it's such a beautiful day for late autumn, don't you think, Richard?'

'Yes . . .' I wriggled, nervously. The bomb was ticking away. It was just a matter of time until it went off, and I was sitting on top of it.

'We had just begun our first course – an avocado mousse,' he went on. 'It was just a light lunch, you understand – fresh salmon as a main course, that sort of thing – when there was a knock at the door. Not expecting anyone . . . Wonder who it can be . . . Get up . . . Go to the door and open it. Who do you think I find there, Richard?'

'Ah . . . er . . .'

'Oh, come on, have a guess.'

'I . . . er . . .'

85

'No? Can't guess? Never mind, I'll tell you – four bloody great policemen, Richard, four policemen, that's what I found outside my front door. FOUR!'

'Er . . . er . . . ah . . .'

Duncan was now sitting with his head in his hands, staring at his littered desk top, unable even to look at me.

'"Mr Bingham?" they said, "we'd like to have a chat," they said. "Best if we come in, sir," they said. So in they came, and then, Richard – and this is the funny bit – in front of my wife, my children, my best client and his family, they accused me of stealing a diamond ring I've never even seen! Then, as if that wasn't enough, they searched my house, Richard – they searched my bloody house!' His voice was rising with every word and trembling with rage. I could have sworn that the phone itself was radiating heat.

'I'm very sorry, Mr Bingham,' I began, 'I know how you must feel . . .'

'No you bloody don't! You have no idea how I feel! If you knew how I felt, you and every other member of staff and partner at Wilsons would have left the country or taken to the hills by now. You can tell Duncan that I'm not done with this. I've been slandered, humiliated and insulted – *I want blood*!'

'I'll certainly tell him you called, Mr Bingham, and I can assure you . . . Mr Bingham? . . . Mr Bingham? . . .'

It was a waste of time, he'd already hung up.

I slumped back in my chair and looked at Duncan who was taking out his frustration of a piece of twisted metal that had once been a paperclip.

'Another satisfied customer?' he said. 'You know, I could just about bear all of this if I really thought we were going to get Raseby, but that so-and-so's going to get away scot-free. I can feel it in my water.'

The telephone rang again. I reached to answer it, but Duncan brushed my hand aside and lifted the receiver himself.

'Wilson's Auction Galleries – good afternoon . . . Oh, hello sergeant . . . Yes, okay, I'll be here all afternoon, just bring it along . . . Thanks for letting me know.'

'What's happened?' I asked as he put the phone down.

'They stopped Raseby in his car going back to Langton. It would seem he went on somewhere from here, rather than straight back to his shop. More importantly, they searched him and found a diamond solitaire ring in a hidden pocket in his overcoat, and he's reluctant to tell them where he bought it.'

'We might get him after all then,' I said.

'Mmmm, we might,' Duncan replied, 'we'll see. You may as well get back to the galleries, Richard. Nothing more we can do until the police arrive.'

'Okay, but don't forget you're supposed to call Mr Anthony.'

'No, I can't seem to forget that however hard I try,' he said, starting to sort through the papers on his desk.

Some time later, a young, spotty faced uniformed constable appeared in The Galleries. Margaret saw him into Duncan's office. The rest of us went on half-heartedly dealing with the crush of viewers, waiting with fingers crossed for confirmation that Jacob Raseby was going to go down. The lanky figure of the young policeman reappeared after a few minutes. He stood just inside the door, putting his helmet on and adjusting the chin-strap. Then he stepped outside and closed the door behind him. We all waited. At last, Duncan came out of his office and made for the door as well. Just as he was about to leave, he turned, looked at us across the packed room and gave us the thumbs-down signal. It was the wrong ring. Raseby had got away with it.

It was late by the time we'd checked away all the silver and jewellery that evening. Fortunately, nothing else had gone adrift, but we were all dispirited by the day's events.

'Come on you lot, it's not the end of the world,' Duncan said, 'I think we could all do with a drink before we knock off.' He was carrying a tray with an assortment of bottles from the drinks cupboard in his office.

'Get some glasses from the mixed lots in Gallery Four, and some water, please, Jason. What would you like, Mrs Bromley – a little nip of your favourite, perhaps?'

'Well, Mr Parkes, as you know I don't hold with strong

liquor, but I must say, a little cherry brandy would be warming.'

'Quite right, Mrs B. What about you boys – scotch or beer?' We all slumped on whichever piece of furniture came to hand. I lay back in a deep, comfortable armchair and gazed up at the ink-black rooflight above me. I could just make out the first stars of the night. Suddenly, Duncan started to giggle. We all turned and looked at him.

'Oh dear, I was just thinking of Anthony when I went up to see him this afternoon – he was apoplectic. Apparently, the police went mob-handed to the estate office, gave him the third degree and scared him half to death. He would probably have been all right if he hadn't said he played golf with the Chief Constable.' Duncan shook his head and giggled again.

'What's going to happen about Mr Bingham?' I asked.

'Don't worry,' Duncan said, wiping his eyes, 'I've just spoken to him on the phone, and he's calming down. I've also told him there's a case of champagne on its way to him by way of compensation. I think he's realised he'll be able to dine out on today's fiasco for months.'

'What about Mrs Porter? Does she know that Aunty's solitaire's been stolen?'

'Ah, now there's an altogether more delicate matter,' Duncan said, laying back in his chair and looking up at the ceiling, 'of course, it's covered by our insurance, but the news itself could be most distressing if not broken in the right way. No, I fear I may have to sacrifice several hours of my day of rest tomorrow, just to break the news to Antoinette and console her in her grief at losing a much loved family heirloom.'

'Mr Porter's still away then?' Patrick said, with a long and meaningful sniff.

'Mmm, now you come to mention it I do believe . . .'

'Phone's ringing!' Margaret said, 'who on earth's calling at this time of night?'

'I'll get it, Margaret,' Duncan said, jumping up, 'we've already had John Bingham and Anthony screaming for blood and vengeance. Now we have nothing to fear but fear itself.'

He wandered into his office and we listened as he picked up the telephone.

'Wilson's Auction Galleries – how can I help you? . . . ah . . . hello, Mr Raseby . . . I'm sorry, I didn't quite catch that . . . I'm sorry, it's a very bad line – you've just been what? . . . released? . . . released from where, Mr Raseby? . . .'

Chapter 8

According to his letter, Christopher Evans had noticed a snippet in the national press about a particularly good price we'd got for a Japanese ivory figure. He'd written to us immediately enclosing some photographs of his 'own modest collection' asking if we would be interested in selling it.

'Interested!' Duncan said, as he leafed through the pictures. 'I should say so. There are nearly three hundred pieces and, if they're all up to the quality of these, they are superb.' He passed the photographs over to me. All the carvings appeared to be late nineteenth-century and were certainly the best of their type I'd seen in my four years at Wilson's. It was unusual for such a large collection to be offered to us, and particularly unusual that the owners should live so far away, for Mr and Mrs Christopher Evans lived in Ramsey on the Isle of Man.

Provincial auctioneering is normally a very localised activity. At Wilson's, a good eighty per cent of the things we sold came from within a twenty-mile radius of Kington, so tens of thousands of pounds worth of ivories from a couple we'd never heard of, who lived three hundred miles away, was a very pleasant surprise.

'You'll have to go up and take care of it all, Richard,' Duncan said. 'Best thing will be for you to motor up with Jim and Patrick. You can list everything, sort out reserves on the spot if necessary, and Jim and Patrick can pack as you record everything. I'll get Margaret to book you all into a hotel overnight. I must say, I wish I could go myself, there's nothing to beat a good bracing sea crossing.'

It was a bracing five thirty in the morning when I saw the

90

lights of Watson's van coming along the track to my home. I picked up my briefcase and overnight bag and went out into the wet, cold February darkness to meet them. I'd been up for over an hour and had checked the contents of my bag three or four times. I don't think I ever go away anywhere without forgetting to pack something. Although this does lend a certain added excitement to travel – wondering all the way there what it is I'm not going to have when I arrive – it also tends to make life unnecessarily difficult. I once mentioned my recurring problem to a much travelled friend of mine. He said that he'd devised and adopted a system of packing which was guaranteed to make my trouble a thing of the past. The secret was simply to pack from the feet up – you started with shoes, then socks . . . then trousers . . . shirts . . . sweaters . . . jackets and so on. I tried it and arrived for a long weekend in Washington DC without any underpants or cufflinks. I abandoned his system and returned to my own random method. At least I've never found myself without underwear again.

I climbed into the van and Patrick tossed my luggage unceremoniously over his shoulder into the back.

'Got your passport, mate?' he asked. 'They're a funny lot north of Watford.'

'Yeah,' Jim said, steering the van round the potholes as we made our way slowly along the track, 'you can't understand what they're saying and they've all got hairs on the palms of their hands.'

The conversation quickly dwindled away and we sat in silence as we headed north in the darkness. When I say we sat in silence, I actually mean we didn't talk. Watson's Transit van was anything but silent. The engine throbbed and thundered away so loudly that conversation could only be carried on by bellowing at one another. On top of that, the dozen or so empty tea chests on board rumbled and bumped about behind us every time we hit a piece of uneven road.

The Thames slid, thick and oily, beneath Chelsea Bridge when we motored over it. I gazed out at Sloane Square, Park Lane and Marble Arch as we rattled on. I never really felt comfortable in London. Although I enjoyed my occasional visits, I always experienced a feeling of relief when I found myself south of the river again.

By the time we got on the M1 we'd grown accustomed to the blanket of noise in the cab, and conversation was going on again in short staccato bursts. One of the exchanges had resulted in the decision to breakfast at the first motorway service station we came to. It turned out to be a fine example of the genre, specialising as it did in the traditional British Motorway Breakfast: two rashers of bacon afloat on a sea of grease, an egg fried until it could have doubled as an ice hockey puck, and a sausage, apparently filled with liquidised egg boxes.

Back on the road, Patrick and I settled down with our newspapers. I stoked up my pipe, and Patrick worked his way steadily through a pack of Players Number Six. Before very long, the acrid blue fog we created became too much for Jim.

'Stone me! Open your sodding window, Richard – the visibility's worse inside than it is out.'

'It don't open,' Patrick said, without looking up from his paper. 'Dad did something to it last week and I haven't had a chance to fix it. You'll have to open yours.'

With a few carefully selected adjectives and nouns, Jim cranked down his own window. Both his voice and the thundering engine of the van were drowned at once by the roaring wind that filled the cab. The mud-coloured spray, thrown up by the lorries surrounding us, lashed in through the open window and spattered his face.

'Close the bloody thing for Chrissake, Jim!' Patrick bawled, as he tried to regain control of his wildly flapping tabloid.

'Only if you two stop smoking for half an hour, otherwise I'll need oxygen before we get anywhere near Liverpool.'

'All right, all right,' Patrick muttered, as he stubbed out half a cigarette, 'it's Richard's fault, anyway. That portable bonfire he carries around with him's enough to make anybody chuck up.'

I think the landscape of the north always appears harsh to a southerner, especially one brought up among the soft green pillows of the South Downs. Certainly, nothing I'd

92

ever seen compared with my first sight of the city of Liverpool. Perhaps my early visits to London, when I was a child in the mid-fifties were the nearest thing to it. Bomb damage was still evident then, with surviving buildings teetering alongside gaping holes in the earth where their neighbours once stood. I remember being fascinated by the fireplaces stuck to the walls, two or three floors up, just hanging there in full view, each one surrounded by its own individual square of wallpaper as though it were part of some surreal patchwork quilt. Below, in the labyrinth of basement passages, buddleia and willow herb grew out of the rubble as if they'd been there forever.

Liverpool brought back those memories, but it was worse, far worse than anything I'd seen in London. Driving towards the docks, vast areas of what must have been streets of terraced houses were laid waste. Then there'd be an entire terrace left standing with every window and door boarded up, as though the residents had been caught in some lightning welfare state pogrom. The only sign of life was the odd feral cat stalking whatever prey it could find amongst the devastation and abandoned cars.

'What have they done with the people?' I asked.

'Up there,' Jim replied, pointing through the driving rain at a group of barely visible, grey concrete towers. 'Multi-storey flats, dozens of them, people stacked one on top of the other, twenty, thirty floors up. That's no good, we ain't made to live like that – nobody can tell me we are. They should never have done it. Not here, not London, not nowhere.'

Jim sat and brooded as we drove on in silence, through the urban wasteland that I'd known only as the legendary home of The Beatles and the other Mersey groups. Now that I'd seen Liverpool, the thing that surprised me most about it, was that it was just a musical revolution it produced, not a political one.

'I reckon we should get the tickets and everything then go and have some lunch,' Patrick said, breaking the silence.

'Yeah,' Jim said, 'steak and chips. I fancy steak and chips. We've got to get something solid inside us, it looks like being a bumpy ride.'

He was right, it did look like being a rough crossing. The wind had begun to buffet the van and the rain was drilling horizontally against metal and glass. Lunch seemed a good idea. A steamy little cafe near the docks was chosen, where I worked my way through a huge plate of chips, something that appeared to have once been the sole of a boot, several slices of flaccid white bread and butter, and a mug of hot, strong tea. Jim and Patrick pronounced it passable, so I went along with the majority verdict while making a mental note to avoid the steak and bread in future.

We boarded the ferry, abandoned the Transit and made ourselves comfortable in a sort of lounge area.

'Time for a little shut-eye,' Jim said. 'Wake me up when we get to Douglas.'

We didn't have to wake Jim when we got to Douglas. Jim was awake long before then. He was wide awake when we headed out into Liverpool Bay and the open sea beyond. The ferry rolled violently as she started to smash her way through the heaving seas that raged between us and the Isle of Man. The rain and spray dashed against the big observation windows making it almost impossible to see out. It wasn't long before the general clamour of conversation which had filled the lounge became little more than a soft, low murmer. Knuckles whitened as hands gripped seats and tables, and faces greyed as eyes stared hopelessly at any fixed object. It was about fifteen minutes before the first person clawed his way to his feet and lurched unsteadily in the direction of the toilets. He was followed by another, then another, each grey grim face set in an expression of deepest, darkest concentration. I'd always thought of myself as a reasonably good sailor, but I began to suspect that my constitution was going to be severely tested on this little voyage.

'Fancy going on deck?' I asked.

'What, in this lot?' Patrick scowled at the filthy conditions outside. 'You've got to be joking.'

I looked at Jim, but he just looked straight ahead. His face was pallid and minute beads of perspiration gave his skin a glossy sheen.

'Fancy going outside, Jim?' I asked, again.

'Nah,' he said, through tightly clenched teeth. Then he rose shakily to his feet and, looking neither left nor right, he joined the procession of tormented souls on their way to the lavatories.

'And then there were two,' Patrick observed, laconically, as his brother left us. 'He's never been too good when it gets choppy.'

A few minutes later, and just two seats from Patrick and me, the first passenger seriously to underestimate his resistance to *mal de mer* suddenly had a second look at his lunch. His companions jumped from their seats in panic, skidded about on the wet floor, then one of them fell over.

'Perhaps we should go outside after all,' Patrick said, looking away and pulling up the collar of his donkey jacket.

To our surprise, the rain had stopped, although the screaming gale still lashed spray up and down the deck. We made our way aft and stood looking back through the spume at the faint outline of the coast.

'Oh dear,' Patrick said, glancing over my shoulder, 'stand back. Here he comes again.'

I turned round and saw the stooped figure of Jim making its unsteady way towards us, clinging grimly to the rail. His complexion was so horrible he seemed to possess a strangely luminous tinge. His mouth was clamped tightly shut, his lips were white and his eyes stared wildly, like those of a cornered animal desperately seeking somewhere to hide.

'Feeling better?' I asked.

'Yeah . . . Nah . . .'

'What did he say,' I asked Patrick.

'Not sure,' he replied, backing away as his brother drew closer.

'. . . Nah . . . Argh . . . Ergh . . .' Jim went on as he stumbled across the wind-swept deck towards us, '. . . Argh . . . Yergh . . . Woorf!'

'Cor blimey,' Patrick said, as the remainder of Jim's lunch passed between us at head height and quickly vanished into the spray, 'I wouldn't want to be standing on the docks when those chips arrive. It'll be like getting hit by shrapnel.'

'Ergh . . .' Jim said, rather lamely as he turned to go. We watched him, shaky and hunched as he zig-zagged away from us, round the corner and out of sight.

'Will he be all right?' I asked.

'Yeah, best to leave him alone. I don't know about you, but I don't half fancy sitting down.'

The only available seat appeared to be a huge pile of coiled rope next to the stern rail. We waddled over to it and threw ourselves down. It was surprisingly comfortable, so there we stayed until Douglas came into view.

Getting up to go and find Jim and the van, Patrick caught my arm.

'Oh dear, Sunshine, you'd better have a look at the back of your raincoat.'

I took it off and examined it. It was fawn in colour and impressed across it was the perfect tarry imprint of the thick coils of rope I'd been reclining on. From a distance, I must have looked like a giant fossil on legs.

'Oh, sod it!' I said. 'Let's hope it's not tipping it down when we get to the Evans's.'

Patrick was all right. His black donkey jacket appeared as pristine as it was when we started the crossing. We found Jim seated in the lounge. He was uncommunicative, but plainly over the worst. We made our way through the crowd of ghastly, exhausted faces to the car deck and waited to disembark.

For some reason it took an age. By the time we'd spilled onto the quayside with the other vehicles, the light was going fast.

'Which way for Ramsey?' Jim asked.

'Over there,' Patrick replied, looking at the atlas and pointing to the right.

We hadn't gone far when Patrick looked up. 'I'm going to have a fag, boy – all right?'

'If you must,' Jim replied, 'but definitely no pipes.'

As we motored along the narrow road which snaked towards and up Snaefell, the weather closed in again. Before long it was pouring so hard I could barely make out the dry stone walls on either side of us. Patrick and I chain-smoked his cigarettes until the ashtray was full.

'Window!' Patrick shouted.

'What?' Jim asked.

'Open the window, I want to chuck this fag-end out.'

'Bloody fags,' Jim grumbled, winding down his window as the cigarette was propelled under his nose into the darkness.

'Did that actually go out?' Patrick asked.

'Must have done,' Jim said, 'I can't see it on the floor.'

We rumbled on for another mile or so before I became aware of a strange smell. 'There's something burning,' I said.

'Yeah, I thought I could smell something,' Patrick said. 'It's that bloody fag-end, that's what it is.'

'Well, find it!' Jim barked. 'Don't just sit there like a couple of prize prats.'

That was easier said than done. The size of the cab didn't permit much movement, but Patrick and I did our best to search the floor area.

'It's no good,' I said, 'we'd better pull over, I can't see the thing but that smell's getting stronger and stronger.'

Almost immediately, as if on cue, the van began to fill with smoke. Jim needed no further entreaties. He braked hard and threw open his door. Straight away, tongues of flame began to leap and flicker in the darkness of the cab.

'Fire! Fire!' he shouted, as he jumped into the darkness. Patrick and I bailed out of the passenger door into about nine inches of mud, and looked back into the van. The smoke had cleared and there was no sign at all of fire. However, on the other side of the Transit, Jim was leaping about in the middle of the road like a dervish. He was spinning wildly, thrashing away at a fire which seemed to have its seat in the right hand pocket of his jacket.

'It's me bloody hanky! Me bloody hanky's on fire!'

It was; as was his jacket which, encouraged no end by the force eight gale that was ripping across Snaefell at that moment, promised to turn into a major blaze.

'Get it off! Get it off!' Patrick shouted, as he leapt forward and tore the donkey jacket from his brother's back. He threw it down on the wet grass verge and stamped it into the mud.

'Look what you've done,' Jim complained, as he picked up the smouldering ruins of his wardrobe. 'Absolutely buggered! It's covered in mud now!'

'So what?' Patrick snorted. 'Unless there's a new fashion for one armed, one pocketed donkey jackets, that one's buggered anyway.'

'Might have been able to repair it,' Jim muttered, looking at the shapeless mess of charred cloth, 'and clean it,' he added. There was something so ludicrous about the idea of repairing and cleaning Jim's jacket that I began to laugh and set off my companions. Fortunately, there wasn't another vehicle for miles. Had there been, anybody in it would have been quite justified in concluding we'd escaped from a lunatic asylum. Why else would a group of grown men be falling around hysterically in lashing rain, in the teeth of a gale, two thousand feet above sea level?

'How on earth am I going to explain the state we're in to the Evans's?' I asked, once we'd got underway again.

'You could say we'd driven off the road into a swamp,' Jim suggested.

'Which then caught fire,' Patrick added.

'Thank you both very much – you're a great help.'

'No good getting nasty with us,' Jim responded, 'you're the ideas man; the brains behind this trip. We're just labourers. We don't get paid enough to be intelligent, do we, Pat?'

'No, Jim, we only get paid enough to be really stoopid.'

'It's serious,' I said. 'God knows what they're going to think.'

'You'll just have to brazen it out, mate,' Jim said, 'pretend you know what you're talking about, that'll take their minds off what we look like – it always works for DP.'

'DP seldom looks as though he's been mud-wrestling in a bonfire.'

'He does have a point there, Jim,' Patrick said.

The Evans's home was a handsome whitewashed house on three floors, standing in a walled garden, with a wide expanse of gravel outside the front door. As we drove through the open gates, two lanterns, one on either side of the front door, shed a blaze of light over the whole area.

'So much for Plan A,' I said.

'What was that?' Patrick asked.

'Slipping in unnoticed, under cover of darkness.'

'Yeah, not much chance of that,' Jim said, as he turned off the engine, 'the place is lit up like a Christmas tree.'

We left the worst soiled and burnt coats in the van, and lined up on the doorstep. Then I rang the bell. The sound of footsteps on bare boards approached the door which was opened by a distinguished looking, grey haired man in his late fifties or early sixties. He was smiling as the door swung back, and to his great credit, his expression changed only momentarily when he saw us.

'Mr Evans?' I said, as quickly as I could, 'I'm Richard Harton of Charles Wilson and Company. I'm sorry we're late, we were delayed by the weather.'

'Oh, don't mention it, Mr Harton. My wife and I felt for you – it must have been bloody. Come in, come in.'

We all squelched into the entrance hall where we left puddles of muddy water on the polished oak boards. The lighting in the hall revealed the true horror of our collective appearance. Individually, Jim won the rosette. Patrick and I were just wet and muddy, but Jim was wet, muddy and smeared with black, sooty streaks.

'I must say,' Christopher Evans went on, 'you poor chaps really do look as though you've been through it. Get those shoes off and we'll dry them out – looks as though you've been wading about in a swamp.'

'Which then caught fire,' Patrick muttered.

'Sorry?'

'I just said it'll be nice to see a fire, sir.'

'Of course, come on through. I'll show you where you can wash and tidy up, and then I'll get some drinks – whisky all right?'

Mrs Evans provided us with soup and toast to go with our scotch, and before long we were feeling almost civilised again. Once we'd finished the meal and had our glasses recharged, Mr Evans led us into the dining room where he'd assembled his collection. It was everywhere, and was just as impressive as the photographs had led us to believe.

'We'll be sorry to part with them,' he said, looking around at the hundreds of fine carvings that filled the room, 'they're just like old friends, but we're spending more and more time abroad, and security's becoming a problem, even on this little island now.'

While Jim and Patrick went out to get the tea-chests from the van I had a closer look at some of the more impressive pieces. One thing I'd learned from Duncan was that, when dealing with a new client, it was as well to demonstrate quite early in the proceedings that you had a good knowledge of the subject in hand – especially if you hadn't. When it came to Japanese ivories, my knowledge, like Duncan's, was adequate rather than scholarly. So, I'd done a little swotting-up for appearances sake.

'Mainly *okimono* from the Meiji period,' I observed, as I cast an eye over the pieces.

'Yes,' Mr Evans replied, 'there're a couple of *inro* and three or four *netsuke* but, as you say, most of the pieces are *okimono* and they all date from the Meiji period.'

Jim and Patrick, who'd arrived back with the tea-chests, witnessed the learned exchange with a great deal of smirking and nudging which suggested they were not altogether convinced about the depth of my knowledge of oriental art. Fortunately it all went unseen by Mr Evans who was plainly impressed by my opening remarks.

'Isn't this *bijin* beautiful,' I said, looking for a few more Brownie points, as I picked up a graceful carving of a young woman.

'Isn't she? By Shingyoku, as you'll see from the signature.'

I turned the piece over and studied the neat Japanese characters on the base. 'Oh, yes,' I said. 'Shingyoku.'

As it happened, I wouldn't have known Shingyoku's signature from a hole in the head. Come to that, I couldn't have identified the signature of any Japanese carver. I knew that, Jim and Patrick knew that but the important thing was, Christopher Evans didn't.

'Yes,' he said, 'I can always remember that one, but the one of *benkei* there, despite being one of my favourites, always eludes me. Have a look, is it by Toshichika or Rishu?'

Jim and Patrick stopped rustling around in the tea-chests and stared at me. Their faces were expressionless.

'Ah, the *benkei*,' I said, clearing my throat, 'yes, well, let's see.'

100

The sea of figures swarmed before me. I'd done enough preparatory work to know that an *okimono* was a standing ornament or figure, a *bijin* was a beautiful girl, and the Meiji period ran from 1868 to 1912, but I hadn't come across *benkei*. I knew that an *oni* was a demon, a *ho-o* was a pheonix, *shi-shis* were lion dogs, and *minogame* was a hairy-tailed turtle, but I had no idea what or who *benkei* was. There were probably two dozen figures in the rough area gestured to by Christopher Evans and I had to pick one of them – the right one! I briefly considered dropping to the floor in a dead faint, but rejected the ploy as impractical. Taking my fragile professional future in my own hands, I reached out and picked up the most impressive carving of the bunch. It was a figure of a fiercesome looking warrior.

Christopher Evans didn't react. I'd got it right! I'd actually got it right! Now all I had to do was bluff my way out of the problem with the signature.

'Ah, ha,' I said, in one of my most inspired pieces of subterfuge, 'as I thought!' I held the piece up so the owner could see the signature.

'Oh, yes,' he said, 'I don't know why I can't remember that one's by Toshichika.'

I wiped away the beads of perspiration that had collected above my upper lip, and Jim and Patrick resumed their activities with the tea-chest, exchanging wry smiles as they did so. It had been too close for comfort.

It was a great relief when Christopher Evans agreed it would be best to fix reserves – the lowest prices at which we'd be permitted to sell the carvings – after we'd got the collection back to Kington, researched and catalogued it. I hadn't relished the idea of sitting up until the early hours, fixing prices on three hundred individual ivories. Even without that job we didn't finish listing, marking and packing until almost a quarter to eleven. We arranged to call back early the next morning to collect the cargo, then we set out for our hotel a few minutes drive away.

The Watsons were hardly able to contain themselves until we got in the van.

'A particularly 'squisite *oki-noki-poki*, Mr Evans,' Jim said, in mincing tones.

'Oh, yes,' Patrick replied, in similar vein, 'it's by Mishi-Titty, as a man of your experience in the field of Jap'nese carved stuff would instantaneously recognise.'

'Actually, I didn't know that, Mr Evans,' Jim went on, 'I don't fink I've got to that chapter in "Noddy's Guide to Ivories" yet.'

There are times in one's life when there's nothing to be gained by offering resistance. That mercifully short journey to the hotel was one of them.

The hotel was a comfortable, family-run place, perched right beside the sea, and the three of us fell gratefully into our beds within minutes of our arrival there. I think it's generally acknowledged that the noise of the sea is one of the most soporific sounds on earth, but for some reason, on that particular occasion, it had quite the opposite effect on me. I was absolutely exhausted when my head hit the pillow, and wide awake five minutes later. I tossed and turned for an hour, then gave up trying to sleep and began to read instead. I eventually dropped-off to sleep at about four thirty – twenty-four hours after I'd last slept.

'Mr Harton – your alarm call – it's six thirty.'

The bright sounding receptionist on the other end of the telephone was obviously smiling as she spoke – smiling at half past six in the morning! She was plainly a sado-masochist. I stumbled around and unpacked my shaving kit, or at least, part of it, since I soon discovered I'd forgotten to pack my razor. So that was what I'd overlooked this trip. I knew it was pointless seeing if Jim or Patrick could lend me one, they never took razors with them on one night stops. I was simply destined to bid a corporate farewell to the Evans's looking like an escaped convict. It was just one of those trips. Fortunately, once again, our clients did nothing to suggest they doubted the wisdom of their choice of auctioneers. They were a very charitable and trusting couple.

The journey back to Kington was uneventful but tedious and we were all relieved eventually to draw-up outside The Galleries. Duncan, who'd stayed late to let us in, appeared at the door, bubbling with excitement.

102

'How was the trip, boys? . . . You all look ghastly . . .
How did you get so muddy? . . . Are the ivories as good as
they looked in the photographs, Richard? . . . Why haven't
you shaved? . . . Did you have to fix reserves on the spot?
. . . What are the owners like? . . . I wish I'd gone on this
little jaunt – it must have been fun . . . Why are you all
looking at me like that?'

Chapter 9

'. . . at one hundred and fifty pounds then . . . all done at one hundred and fifty pounds? . . . Against you at the back at one hundred and fifty . . .' Duncan paused, hammer raised, for two perhaps three seconds, staring directly into the eyes of the dealer at the back of the room. Reluctantly, the man raised his hand once more.

'. . . One hundred and sixty . . . at one hundred and sixty pounds . . . The gentleman's bid, away at the back, at one hundred and sixty . . . All done?'

Duncan's ivory gavel cracked down sharply on the rostrum as he scribbled the name of the buyer and the selling price in his book.

'John Wilmot – one hundred and sixty pounds,' he confirmed in an aside to Margaret and me.

We both sat at a table below and to one side of the rostrum. As well as keeping her own record of buyers' names and sale prices, Margaret, as auctioneer's clerk, used to handle all the commission bids – the bids left by people who couldn't attend the sale. It was a good system. For one thing, the auctioneer had no note in his book of the bids that had been left, so nobody could reasonably accuse him of 'running-up' the commission bids when there was no bidding in the room. Furthermore, Margaret guarded her clients' interests like the she-tiger guards her cubs. She would fight every inch of the way to buy the lots as cheaply as she could for her bidders, and, generally, her clients appreciated her efforts.

My job was one which earned very little appreciation on the part of the buyers – I wrote out their bills. As each lot was sold, I entered it in triplicate in a thick, heavy ledger. I spent every sale day flicking backwards and forwards through the alphabetical sections, trying to remember who'd already got a bill running and who'd just bought for the first time that day. When Duncan was selling flat out at a hundred and twenty lots an hour I'd have to work like a maniac.

'That concludes today's sale of furniture, ladies and gentlemen,' Duncan continued, raising his voice above the general hubbub as the specialist furniture dealers got up to go, 'which brings us to lot 573 – the first of the carpets and rugs.'

Tom Jeffreys was busy at the cashier's desk – a sort of glorified cupboard under the stairs – dealing with people who wanted to pay. His assistant arrived in front of me with a fresh list of buyers who had asked for their bills, and I was flicking through the ledger, tearing out the ones she wanted, when I heard Duncan say something which turned my blood to ice and my backbone to jelly.

'. . . and now I'm going to hand over to Mr Richard Harton who will take this section of the sale. Please be kind to him, it's his first time on the rostrum – come on Richard, up you get.'

If I'd had the courage I would have hurdled the first two or three rows of chairs, sprinted through the gallery, out of the door and never been seen again. Instead, trembling from head to toe, nausea gripping at the pit of my stomach, I took Duncan's gavel and clambered onto the rostrum.

At Wilson's, we had an improvised rostrum made up of furniture included in the sale. The base was usually a substantial old dining table covered with a rug; on top of that we would stand some sort of small side table covered with a velour table-cloth which hung down to the floor; finally, a dining chair, preferably one with arms, would complete the set-up. It was perfectly adequate and, of course, much cheaper than having a proper rostrum made.

'Good afternoon, ladies and gentlemen,' I said, my voice rising and falling at will, completely out of control. 'We'll continue with the carpets and rugs, beginning with lot 573.'

I was running out of breath and the more I tried to breathe in, the less air I seemed to get.

'A Shirvan rug, woven with latch-hook medallions on a madder and blue ground, four feet ten inches by three feet five inches,' I read from the auctioneer's book as I gasped in yet more air. I began to feel light headed. The prospect of crashing, unconscious, to the floor went through my mind. I forced myself to take a long, deep breath. I held it, then breathed out. Another, I held it, then breathed out again. Suddenly I felt much better. At least I'd regained control of my breathing, even if my heart was still pounding away like some manic tom-tom.

'Now, what will you bid me? . . . Sixty pounds? . . . Forty then? . . .' Panic swept over me again. What happens if nobody bids? What do I do then?

'Thirty pounds,' said a kindly looking man three rows back.

'Thirty pounds I'm bid,' I squeaked, 'may I say thirty-five?'

A group of rug dealers stood by the showing table, where Jim Watson was displaying the lot in question. Not usually known for being the most charitable members of the trade, even they took pity on me. 'Thirty-five,' one of them said, waving his catalogue.

'Thirty-five,' I echoed, 'may I say . . .'

'Forty,' interrupted the kindly man.

'At fort . . .'

'Forty-five,' the dealer cut in.

'Fifty,' the man said.

'One hundred,' said the dealer.

'And ten,' the man replied.

I couldn't get a word in edgeways. I just kept swivelling about in the rostrum, pointing vaguely to where the bids were coming from.

'One hundred and twenty,' said the dealer amidst a chorus of protest and disapproval from his colleagues.

'And thirty,' returned the man.

'He can have it,' the dealer snorted, making a note in his catalogue and turning away.

Now was my chance. 'At one hundred and thirty pounds then . . . Are you all finished at one hundred and . . .'

'One hundred and forty,' Margaret said.

106

I looked down at her and saw that both she and Duncan were pulling faces and looking theatrically at the clerk's book. I glanced down at my book. Next to the lot number, in bright red ink, it said, 'R £150'. A reserve, that's what they were trying to tell me, I'd almost sold my first lot twenty pounds under reserve!

'At one hundred and forty pounds . . . at one hundred and forty . . .' I persisted, lamely, '. . . at one hundred and . . .'

'Fifty,' said the dealer at the showing table, to another vigorous chorus of disapproval from his companions.

'One hundred and fifty,' I said, looking down at my book to check the reserve figure once more. 'All done at one hundred and fifty pounds? . . .'

I brought the hammer down.

'Hampstead Carpets,' the buyer called out while his colleagues stood around shaking their heads.

'Hampstead Carpets – one hundred and fifty pounds,' I repeated as I went to record the details in my book.

That was an exercise which proved more difficult than it should, since in my excitement I'd been holding the hammer in my right hand and the pen in my left. I went to swap them over, and in doing so, dropped the hammer against the microphone stand. My ineptitude was picked up, amplified and blasted out through the loudspeakers at the back of the room. Anyway, I'd sold my first lot!

'Lot 574 – a Yomud saddle bag and one other . . .'

It took me about an hour to sell fifty lots, whereas Duncan would have sold twice that number in the same time.

'Never mind,' he said, when I clambered down at the end of my ordeal and apologised for how slow I'd been, 'you didn't cost us any money, and once you'd stopped shaking, you actually looked as though you were enjoying it. I think we'll make an auctioneer of you, Richard, perhaps even a good one.' He gave me a congratulatory slap on the back as he climbed back into his seat.

I don't think I was ever again as frightened as on that first occasion. I always suffered from butterflies before every auction, but nothing like the cold, almost paralysing fear that swept over me that day. I shudder at the thought of the sort of state I would have been in had Duncan given me any warning of my debut. I suspect I would have been absent without leave.

Over the next year or so Duncan taught me most of the tricks of the trade: how to take bids 'off the wall' to get the bidding started quickly; how always to stare directly at somebody when you're taking those non-existent bids – the person you stare at is usually too petrified with fear to move, let alone speak, so everybody else is convinced it's a genuine bid; how to hang on those extra few seconds when the bidding has apparently stopped – in at least three cases out of ten you get a late bid from somewhere; and, finally, how to get out of trouble when you've just sold a lot for less than the reserve price. It happened only rarely, but when it did, there was always a special quality to the momentary attack of blind panic that seized one. To bring your hammer down at five thousand pounds whilst noting, almost simultane-ously, that the reserve price in the book is seven thousand five hundred, is one of life's great sobering experiences. The initial chill wave of nausea rapidly gives way to a hot flush that feels as though it's lighting up your ears like red traffic lights, then come the cold, clammy drops of perspiration. And a perfectly reasonable reaction it is too, since the auctioneers have to make up the difference between the sale price and reserve on such occasions.

Duncan's salvage technique worked like a dream, but only on two conditions. Firstly, you had to bring it into play *immediately* you brought the hammer down; secondly, you had to be prepared to crush anybody who argued with you. The trick was to pretend somebody else was bidding when you knocked down the lot, and that you had initially missed their bid.

'I'm sorry, sir. You were in time,' he'd say, staring straight into the eyes of some terrified non-combatant who'd just been sitting there minding his own business. 'At five thousand five hundred now . . . May I say six thou-sand? . . .' If the person, who thought he'd bought it for five thousand, complained, Duncan would glare at him over his gold rimmed spectacles and say: 'The gentleman was in time. The decision is mine. The bidding is his at five thousand five hundred. Will you bid me six thousand?'

Whatever the reply, it didn't matter. Wilson's were off the hook.

Chapter 10

I always enjoyed the drive out to Ditchley. The road from Kington clung tight to the line of the Downs, and was bordered on either side by fields and woodlands. It was crystal-clear early spring, with just a few small pockets of mist still hanging in low lying fields. The day was perfect, and I had enough calls in my diary to keep me out of The Galleries all morning and, with luck, part of the afternoon as well.

My first appointment was at ten o'clock with a Miss Beatty who said she had an oak coffer for sale. Her address, Rowan Cottage, turned out to be a little semi-detached red brick house, partly hung with flaking old clay tiles. To get to the simple, boarded front door you had to climb a steep flight of four narrow, worn brick steps. I took two steps up and gave the old iron knocker a couple of bangs. Immediately I touched it a great barking and howling began inside the cottage. I stepped back down onto the garden path and stood there listening while heavy canine bodies hurled themselves against the inside of the door. I've never been frightened of dogs but I was quite grateful the door was stout and secure. I didn't much fancy having what sounded like an entire pack of hounds leaping to greet me at head height.

'Git back, yer lot,' a deep bass voice boomed somewhere in the cottage, 'git away frum that thur door, I tell yer!' The voice had a lovely Sussex bur to it and was obviously that of a real countryman. The howling and whining grew even more frenzied as a pair of boots clumped through the cottage towards the door. 'Git back yer so an' sos, git back in thur an' do as yer told!'

There was more scrabbling and whining, then the sound of

a door being closed. The pack had obviously been confined. A bolt was drawn at the top of the door followed by a second at the bottom. Finally, a key turned in what sounded like an old, substantial lock, the door opened and a great wave of doggy odour broke over me. I found myself looking at a pair of heavy brown brogues surmounted by a pair of khaki ankle socks which, in turn, surrendered to a pair of the most muscular calves I've ever seen. They were covered in thick black hair and wouldn't have looked out of place in the back row of a rugby fifteen. My gaze faltered for a moment but then continued it's ascent: tartan skirt, beige sweater and, finally, grey shirt. I couldn't really see much beyond that since the face was partially obscured by the largest bosom I've ever encountered. It loomed over me, like some sort of geological phenomenon, defying accurate definition. In fact, it seemed to defy lots of things – gravity, credibility, several of the basic rules of structural engineering and certainly adequate description. I took another step back down the path and the face, round and moonlike, came into view. It had quite a passable moustache and was topped by an unruly mop of grey hair.

'Yass,' it said.

'Miss Beatty?' I suggested, rather tentatively.

'Yass,' it said, again.

'Good morning, Miss Beatty. I'm Richard Harton of Wilson's Auction Galleries.'

'Oh, yass – yer've come to 'ave a look at moy chest, an't yer?'

I very nearly took another step back down the path but I stopped myself. I could only hope it was her coffer she was referring to.

Miss Beatty invited me to come in, and led the way into the semi-gloom of her parlour. I noticed that one renegade dog had avoided incarceration. It was a black and white, rough haired Jack Russell and it had wicked, beady eyes.

'Dun't yer wurry 'bout 'im. If 'e gives yer any trouble, yer jus' belt 'im.'

'Right,' I said.

'That's moy chest – wha'd'yer think?'

It was a nice oak coffer with original carving. That made a

change since most of the carved oak we saw had been messed about by our Victorian forebears. Carved on the top frieze was the date '1690'.

'My ol' dad used ter say it were 'Enery the Eighth's, but Oy spec 'e jus' made tha' up – silly ol' sod.'

'I should think the date on it's about right, which makes it William and Mary rather than Henry VIII,' I said, bending down to have a closer look at the piece. In doing so, I nearly came nose to nose with the Jack Russell. It had plainly sneaked around the other furniture just to get at me. It showed its teeth in a sneering snarl as a growl gargled away deep in its throat.

''Ere, git outta it yer little begger!' Miss Beatty boomed, bringing the coal shovel – the nearest thing to hand at the time – thumping down across the offender's back. It let out a sharp yelp, glanced up at its mistress, sneered at me again, and stiff-leggedly strutted off towards the kitchen range.

'Can yer sell it?' Miss Beatty asked.

'Yes,' I said, 'but it won't make a huge amount, probably a hundred to a hundred and fifty pounds.'

'Tha'll do foine. The money'll be more use than the chest. Wha' about tha' ol' kettle an' them candlesticks an' all?' she asked, pointing to the brass and copperware on the mantelpiece over the range.

'Yes, we can sell them.'

'Roight – yer gonna take all on it now?'

'No, I'll arrange for our carriers – Watson's Removals – to give you a ring to sort out a time when they can come and collect the things.'

'All roight than, Oy'll wait ter 'ear from 'em.'

'Shall we fix reserves on the things now?' I asked.

'Oy dunno – wha're them whan the're at 'ome?'

'The lowest price at which we'll sell 'em . . . them . . . I mean.'

'Nah, Oy'll leave all tha' ter yer – I rackon yer 'onest 'nough.' She gave me a great horse-toothed smile. I was quite warming to Miss Beatty, even if her gender was open to question. She showed me to the door amid a fresh chorus of baying from the inmates of the other room. Then, just as I was about to step outside, the Jack Russell made his last bid for my ankles. He'd been stalking me all the way down the narrow passage from the parlour, but hadn't been able to get past the bulk of Miss Beatty's undercarriage. At last, he saw an opening and hurled himself to his mistress's right. Without even glancing down at him, Miss Beatty lifted a brogued foot and stamped down on his neck, pinioning him to the floor. The terrier let out another yelp and lay quite still. Miss Beatty, who'd carried on talking while executing her perfectly timed interception, lifted her foot. The dog got up, shook itself, flashed me a withering glance of undiluted hatred, and strode back to the parlour.

'Li'le ol' sod 'e is,' Miss Beatty said.

I had one other call to make in Ditchley village. It was on the widow of an old local gardener. She had suggested to one of the village worthies – a lady who happened to be a client of ours – that she had a 'Chinese china gravy boat' that might be worth something, but she didn't know what to do about it. So it was that I was due to visit Mrs Pierce, despite being absolutely certain it was going to be a waste of time. The likelihood of the Chinese gravy boat being anything other than late nineteenth-century willow pattern worth a few shillings was very remote. Nevertheless, along I went to Mrs Pierce's council house.

She was a nice, sparrow-like little woman, who insisted that I have coffee and biscuits before I saw the piece. It stood, wrapped in yellowing newspaper, in a cardboard box on the dining table.

'It was given to my mother-in-law when she married Ted's father – Ted was my husband,' Mrs Pierce told me. 'She was a house maid and it was the lady of the house that gave her it.' If I'd had any doubts about the gravy boat being worthless, that story dispelled them. From Land's End to John O'Groats, hundreds, perhaps thousands of families still treasure completely unsaleable tat donated to their ancestors by upper crust employers. Handed over in a blaze of charity and *noblesse oblige*, the very worst examples will almost certainly have a pedigree going back to a member of a European royal family.

'It's got a few chips round the rim,' Mrs Pierce continued, 'so we never used it for gravy. It's a bit big anyway. Ted's mum used to put flowers in it.'

'I think we'd better have a look at it,' I said. It was time to get the disappointment over and done with.

Mrs Pierce pushed the box over to me and I started to remove the aged wrapping paper. It was the *Daily Sketch* from the 1950s – in mint condition it would probably have been worth more than the heirloom. Then I saw it, and I couldn't believe my eyes.

'Good Lord!'

'Is it worth anything, Mr Harton?' Mrs Pierce asked.

'Well, it's a good job you never used it for gravy.'

'Why, what is it?'

'It's a bourdaloue – a lady's portable chamber pot.'

Mrs Pierce raised her hands to her mouth in horror. 'But it can't be, pots are round and that looks like . . . like . . . well, like a big gravy boat.'

'I know,' I said, 'it's specially designed to be easily portable, easily concealed and easily used in public.'

'In public!'

'Yes, specifically in church, in fact.'

'In church!' Poor Mrs Pierce was absolutely scandalised.

'Yes,' I said, 'it's actually named after a Jesuit preacher called Louis Bourdaloue who used to preach at the court of Louis XIV. His sermons were so popular that people had to take their places hours before he was due to start. This could prove a bit of a strain so the ladies needed some means of relieving themselves without leaving their seats. The bourdaloue was the answer. It could be carried, hidden in a lady's muff and pressed into service as and when necessary.'

Mrs Pierce sat staring at the piece. 'So, how old is it, then, Mr Harton?' she asked.

'Well, I'm afraid it's not Louis XIV. It's later than that. I think it's probably about 1740 and, despite the Chinese-style decoration, it's not Chinese or even French, it's English. Lastly, it's not porcelain, it's pottery – what we call Delftware. Apart from that you were absolutely right about it.'

'Oh, my goodness,' Mrs Pierce said, obviously thoroughly confused, 'does that mean it's not worth anything?'

'On the contrary, I'm certain it would make at least a

thousand and possibly more.'

Mrs Pierce gripped hold of the edge of the table. 'A thousand pounds?' she whispered.

'Almost certainly more.'

'Can you sell it for me then?'

'Yes, I'd be delighted to take it with me now and put it in our next sale.'

'You take it, Mr Harton, please,' she said, looking across the table at the thing as I held it, 'I don't want to touch it again in case I break it – my blood runs cold when I think of how it's been treated over the years. You just take it away, now. *Please*!'

I gave Mrs Pierce a receipt and went back to my car with what, I suspected, would be my best find of the month.

Next stop was Woodcombe, near the coast. A Mr Briggs was about to move house and had some furniture surplus to his requirements. His house, which stood just outside the village, was a large, mock Tudor creation dating from the 1920s. Mr Briggs, a solid businesslike man, answered the door and invited me into an unusually large, square entrance hall. Six doors led off the hall, but it was what stood on either side of them that caught my eye. Over each door there was a small mahogany canopy, a little more than the width of the doorway itself. Each canopy was supported by a pair of carved mahogany pillars – one pillar on each side of the doorway. I stood and gaped at them.

'Rather unusual feature isn't it?' Mr Briggs said.

'Do you know what they are?' I asked.

'Er . . . not quite sure what you mean, Mr Harton, they're just carved pillars as far as I'm concerned. Why, have they some special significance?'

'They're bed posts,' I said, 'all George III period, mainly Hepplewhite designs.'

'You mean they're from four-poster beds?'

'Yes.'

'How extraordinary, I'd always assumed they were no older than the house.'

'No,' I said, 'they're eighteenth-century and of some value.'

'Really?'

115

'Yes, certainly five hundred pounds a pair and probably more.'

Mr Briggs did not look happy. 'I wish you hadn't told me that, Mr Harton,' he said, 'I've just sold the bloody things with the house!'

'Isn't there anything you can do?' I asked.

'Absolutely nothing. We exchanged contracts two weeks ago and we're due to complete at the end of next month.'

'Oh, no!'

'Oh, yes,' he said, staring at one of the pairs of posts, 'and since I've sold the entire property for forty-five thousand, I'm less than delighted to learn that these damn things are worth three thousand-plus on their own!'

Mr Briggs did have half a dozen bits of furniture worth selling, but that was an anti-climax, and I suspected when we parted that he wished I'd never set foot in his house – he'd been far happier not knowing about his bed posts.

My next appointment was in Southbourne, where I was due to meet Mrs Edwina Williams at two o'clock. I stopped for a pub lunch on the way. I knew I'd need all the strength I could muster to deal with Mrs Williams. She was an occasional visitor to Wilson's and when there, always saw something she swore was identical to one she had at home. Naturally, there was never any similarity between the two objects, so my visits were nearly always a waste of time. The problem was that she did have some nice things and we needed to stay in contact if we ever wanted to sell those for her. To that end, Duncan, in the sort of act of selfless generosity for which he was known, presented Mrs Williams to me as my very own client. Now it was always 'nice Mr Harton' she asked for. On this particular occasion, Mrs Williams was adamant she was the proud possessor of an *art nouveau* silver photograph frame which was the absolute twin of one we'd sold a month earlier. I had no choice but to go through the motions.

Unlike the full-blooded, baying pack that greeted me at Miss Beatty's, the doorbell at Mrs William's home set off a high-pitched stereophonic yapping on the other side of the front door. It was her brace of pekinese. I had nothing against Ching and Chang personally, I'm just not

116

particularly fond of the breed, so they were another good reason for getting the job over and done with as quickly as possible. The snuffling and yapping reached its own version of a crescendo as my client opened the door.

'Mr Harton,' Mrs Williams gushed, 'so prompt, as always. Do come in. Now out of the way Ching, Chang, don't pester poor Mr Harton, I'm sure he's terribly busy. Do come through Mr Harton. Have you had lunch? Is there anything I can get you? A sandwich? A drink? Coffee? Would you like to wash your hands? Do sit down. Get out of Mr Harton's chair, Ching! At once, or I'll shut you in the kitchen! Do sit down, Mr Harton – just relax!'

It was the same every time I went to see her. Mrs Williams was like a diminutive, blue-rinsed typhoon for the first few minutes, then she'd settle down. You just had to sit it out and, every now and then, insert 'yes' and 'no' into an otherwise one-way conversation.

'I'll go and get the photograph frame,' she said, 'it's absolutely identical to the one you had in the sale.'

While Mrs Williams went to get her treasure, Chang sauntered across the bright and comfortably furnished drawing room. He stopped at my feet and sniffed my shoes, socks and eventually my right trouser leg. Then, without warning, he stood on his hind legs, wrapped his front paws around my shin and started pumping away at my ankle with exaggerated pelvic thrusts. His bug-eyed little face was a picture of concentrated lust.

'Chang! Stop it!' I whispered.

Chang took no notice, but Ching, who was sitting on the settee, began to show some real interest in the floorshow. I shook my leg to discourage his brother's passionate advances but Chang seemed to misinterpret my action, and his eyes bulged even more as he stepped up the rate of his pumping. I could hear Edwina Williams crossing the hallway just outside the door, so I jumped up and gave a violent kick. Chang was instantly disengaged. He sailed across the room, bounced on the edge of the huge Chinese carpet, and slid along the parquet flooring until he was brought to an abrupt halt by a Regency rosewood bookcase. None the worse for wear, he gathered himself up and started to come at me

117

again. He obviously liked his women to treat him rough. Fortunately, just at that moment, Mrs Williams reappeared.

'Chang!' her shrill voice of command stopped the amorous pooch in his tracks. 'Will you please go and sit down with your brother!'

Chang gave her a resentful look and waddled over to the settee. He didn't climb onto it though, but just sat on the ground next to it, shooting lecherous glances at my leg.

'There we are, Mr Harton,' Mrs Williams went on, handing me a rather nasty, plated picture frame, 'just like the one in your last sale.'

'I'm afraid not,' I said, 'it's not silver.'

'Are you sure?' she said, looking crestfallen. 'I know I couldn't find any hallmarks, but it has got a maker's mark – I thought it might be American.'

'Where's the maker's mark?' I asked.

'On the side, just there, look – E.P.Copper – sounds an American sort of name, don't you think?'

'I'm afraid that's not the maker's name, Mrs Williams,' I said, 'that stands for Electro-Plated Copper.'

'Electro-Plated Copper? . . . Oh, how stupid . . . I hadn't thought of that . . .'

She was momentarily covered in confusion, but help was at hand. Chang was about to take her mind off her embarrassment over the photograph frame. Unseen by either of us, he sneaked across the room, and like some fanatic on a suicide mission, suddenly hurled himself at my right leg, pumping away for all he was worth.

'Oh, my goodness! . . . Oh dear! . . . Oh no! . . . Chang! . . . Stop it! . . . Stop it! . . . *stop it!*'

I grabbed hold of him by the scruff of the neck and disengaged him from the object of his affection. 'It's not his fault,' I said. 'I was in a house with a lot of dogs earlier today. I think one of them must have been on heat.'

'Nevertheless, Mr Harton,' Mrs Williams went on, taking the panting lothario from me, 'I'm so ashamed, I've never permitted such . . . such . . . such naughty-man-things in my house before, and I'm certainly not putting up with it now. You're going straight to your basket in the kitchen, Chang. Naughty dog! Would you mind terribly if I let you out of the back door, Mr Harton?'

'Not at all,' I said, secretly delighted at having the opportunity of making such a quick get away.

We proceeded through to the kitchen, with the unfortunate Chang being held out at arm's length in front of Mrs Williams like a piece of fish that had gone off. Once in the kitchen he was promptly deposited in his basket.

'What's that?' I asked, looking at Chang's bedding.

'That, oh, it's a bit of old rug,' Mrs Williams replied, 'I cut it into four pieces so that Ching and Chang had two pieces each to dry themselves on after splashy walks. With two each, they always had one each that was dry, you see? Unfortunately, I've only got two left now. I burnt the other two – they'd got so dirty.'

'Oh, I see.'

'Why do you ask, Mr Harton? I know that old thing wasn't worth anything. I bought it at a jumble sale.'

'Oh, no reason,' I said, 'I just wondered what it was.'

Driving away from Mrs Williams, I decided I'd done the right thing. I'd already upset one person by telling him he'd given away three thousand pounds worth of Hepplewhite bed posts. There seemed no point in letting Mrs Williams know she'd dismembered and burned a Nain prayer rug worth somewhere in the region of two thousand pounds. It would only have upset her, and she already had Chang's unpleasant social habits to worry about.

The last call of the day was at a house on the southern outskirts of Kington. It was a place I'd always admired, an old flint-built rectory with rows of large sash windows looking out over the Downs towards the sea. I drove through the white gates, past a sort of small lodge and up the gravel drive. The owner's name, according to the notes Margaret had given me, was Hugh Cartwright, and he'd got a desk he wanted to sell. He turned out to be a good looking man in his forties. Tanned and obviously fit, he looked as though he'd just come back from a holiday in the sun.

'Sorry about the route march,' he said, as he led me through the house, 'but the desk's in here.'

I followed him into a small sitting room with a window providing a distant view of Kington.

119

'Used to be my late wife's study. She loved it. It was handy being right next to the kitchen – warm too – but it doesn't get used now, so I thought I'd have it knocked through into the kitchen and make it a sort of breakfast area. That's the desk. I don't know if it's any good or not.'

It was a small, elegant, lady's writing desk which looked very French in style. 'Oh, yes,' I said, 'it's quite nice. It's actually called a *bonheur du jour*.'

'I always wondered if it was French.'

'Well, despite it's name it is, in fact, English – dates from about 1860.'

'What's it made of, Mr Harton?'

'The wood's walnut and these metal mounts are ormolu.'

'Fine, I was wrong about everything, then,' Hugh Cartwright laughed. 'What do you think it would make?'

'Somewhere in the region of three to four hundred pounds.'

'That's not bad.' He leant against the wall, hands in pockets, looking thoughtfully at the piece. 'The only reason I'm hesitating at all about selling it,' he went on, 'is because it was my wife's, so there's a sentimental attachment, but . . .' He was obviously finding the decision a difficult one to make. '. . . but my daughter's adamant she doesn't want it . . .' There was the thud of a door closing somewhere. 'I think that's her now. Let's just check that she's sure she doesn't want it – Antonia?'

'Yes.'

'Come here a minute, darling.'

A few moments later, the half open door opened fully to reveal the most beautiful girl I'd ever seen. She was tall and slim with raven hair tied in a pony tail. She wore a sweater which had seen better days, tight fitting riding breeches and riding boots. Her face, suntanned like her father's, was spattered with dried mud.

'This is Mr Harton from Wilson's, the auctioneers in Kington.'

'Hello,' she said.

'He thinks Mummy's desk would probably make three to four hundred pounds, so if you're certain you don't want it . . .'

120

'No, I keep telling you I don't like it, Daddy. I know you want me to have it, but I really don't like it. I never have. It's too fussy . . .'

'All right, all right,' Antonia Cartwright's father put up his hands to ward off any further criticism of the piece. 'Okay, it's all yours, Mr Harton – take it away.'

I watched his daughter as she turned in the doorway to go. I wanted to say something to make her stay.

'Any chance of a cup of tea once you've got your boots off, darling?' Hugh Cartwright asked. 'You'd like a cup of tea, wouldn't you, Mr Harton.'

'Yes, I would, very much indeed,' I said.

Hugh Cartwright took me back through the house to the drawing room. It was long and light with French windows leading onto a terrace for the warmer days and evenings. I glanced round. There were some nice pieces of furniture and some good pictures, but it wasn't a showcase, it was a home.

'We inherited bits and pieces,' he said, as I looked at one of the oil paintings, 'and my wife bought the rest. She used to like poking around salerooms and antique shops. I'm afraid I don't have the faintest idea about anything in that line.'

While he was speaking, Antonia brought in a tray with tea things. I leapt over to make room on a table for it. 'Thank you,' she said, with the faint suggestion of a smile.

'What about this table over here, Mr Harton?' Hugh Cartwright asked, oblivious to the fact that in a matter of minutes I'd become wholly besotted with his daughter. 'Is this one any good?'

'For goodness sake, Daddy, let the poor man have his tea.'

'That's all right,' I said, 'I don't mind.' I decided that if I couldn't make any other lasting impression on Miss Cartwright, I could, at least, lead her to believe I was the absolute last word in fine art auctioneers. The table was a perfectly straightforward George III side table with a single drawer. It was plainly 'right' and hadn't been messed around. I could see that from the other side of the room, but I thought I should probably seize the opportunity to display not only the depth of my knowledge, but my thoroughness

121

as well. I went over the piece with a fine-toothed comb. I checked every inch of it, finishing with a second examination of the drawer lining. I bent over the open drawer, peered at the dovetails, then shut it firmly as I stood up to give my considered opinion.

'Well, it's George III, about 1780, mahog . . .' It was as far as I got. Something caught me by the throat as I was standing up and jerked me back down again. My chin hit the top of the table as I found myself on my knees, trying to work out what had happened.

It didn't take long: when I'd closed the drawer, I'd slammed my tie in it.

Antonia let out a shriek of laughter and threw herself backwards onto the settee where she rolled about hysterically. As I struggled to unjam the drawer and retrieve my tie, her father clutched hold of the mantelpiece to steady himself, as he too howled with laughter. I'd made a lasting impression on the Cartwrights after all.

Chapter 11

The worst thing about Perry Gascoigne was that he kept crying. He certainly seemed incapable of setting foot in Marshlands without exploding into tears. Even allowing for the fact that his companion had died suddenly, we all felt Mr Gascoigne's grief was on an epic scale. He'd lived with Bernard Smartley for the better part of ten years and, at forty-five, was over twenty years Smartley's junior. When Mr Smartley succumbed to a massive heart attack over dinner one Saturday night, poor old Perry lost not only his companion, but also his meal ticket. If Gascoigne knew why his lover had chosen to leave everything to his goddaughter rather than to him, he never shared the confidence with us. Mind you, there was no reason why he should. After all, we'd been retained by the goddaughter to sell the contents of his home, so it wasn't really surprising if he looked on us as mercenaries.

'You take him round this time,' Duncan said, 'and do try to get him to make up his mind. Everytime I suggested a piece this morning he just burst into tears.' We were trying to get Mr Gascoigne to choose two or three pieces from the house to keep as mementos. It had been Mary Bryant's, the goddaughter's, idea. She hadn't even specified any upper limit on value, and had actually refused to do so when we suggested it.

'No, let poor old Perry have whatever he wants,' she'd said, 'he's such a sad little man these days.'

Regardless of her instructions, Duncan had made it clear that he wanted 'poor old Perry' kept as far away as possible from the Queen Anne silver monteith bowl – a special type of punch bowl – which was expected to make the highest price in the silver section; and the John Frederick Herring farmyard scenes which were certain to do the same in the collection of pictures.

'The last thing we need is Weepy Willy wandering off with the best lots in the catalogue,' Duncan said. 'Try to get him to concentrate on things of sentimental value, like crocheted tea-cosies or *petit point* hot water bottle covers.'

'And what if he looks like choosing the Worcester dessert service?'

'Oh, just take his mind off it. Ask him why he thinks the late lamented left him up the financial creek without so much as an index-linked annuity. That should do the trick!'

'You're all heart Duncan. Has anybody ever told you that?'

'Frequently . . . watch it, here he comes!'

As the front door started to open, Duncan was gone – up the old creaking oak staircase in four bounds, away along the landing and out of sight.

Miserable though he was, Perry Gascoigne still cut a sartorial dash. With black soft kid boots, a black cloak that trailed on the ground, dark glasses and a leather cap, he looked like a cross between Zorro and a Russian revolutionary.

'Oh, hello, Mr Harton,' he said, sounding very tired, as he looked up from closing the door, 'so you've drawn the short straw this afternoon then.'

'Not at all, Mr Gascoigne,' I replied, almost certainly overdoing the sincerity, 'it's just that Mr Parkes is expecting Mrs Bryant in about half an hour to discuss the sale.'

'Oh, Mary's going to be here, is she?'

'Yes.'

'Well then, I'd better choose what I want and go. I wouldn't want my presence to embarrass her – after all it's her house now.'

'I'm sure there's no question of your presence embarrassing . . .' The words were lost on the air. Perry Gascoigne had already flounced off towards the dining room. I crossed my fingers in the hope that we weren't heading for the Worcester.

'I've decided what I want, you know,' the caped figure

said over its shoulder as it flapped and billowed its way through the low, oak panelled drawing room.

'Really?' I said, crossing my fingers harder.

'Yes, and you needn't worry, I'm not going to take all the most valuable things – I know that's what Mr Parkes is frightened of.'

'Oh, I don't think so . . .'

'I've decided,' he went on, ignoring my spiritless defence of Duncan, 'that all I want is the pair of Sheraton card tables.' I uncrossed my fingers. We could certainly live with the loss of the 'Sheraton' card tables, but it crossed my mind that I should probably tell Mr Gascoigne that the tables weren't actually eighteenth-century. Fortunately, he saved me further soul-searching.

'I know they're not really Sheraton, but we bought them together one day in a little antique shop in Kensington. It was run by a friend of Bernard's – I used to be quite jealous of him – and we'd had a wonderful lunch in a French restaurant in Church Street, and we were both a bit tiddly . . . and . . . these tables . . . these tables will always remind me of that day . . .' He clutched hold of the dining room door, and once again the tears streamed down his face as he sobbed uncontrollably. I reached into my pocket and got out a freshly laundered white handkerchief which I offered him.

'. . . No . . . no thank you . . . I've got one here somewhere . . . I've already used one of Mr Parkes's.' He groped about under his cloak, produced a red and white spotted handkerchief the size of a head scarf and blew his nose noisily. 'Anyway, it's the tables I want,' he concluded.

'Fine, I'll see they're withdrawn from the catalogue. Would you like us to arrange delivery of them?'

'Not yet. I'm coming to the sale and I'll probably buy some other things.' I obviously looked very doubtful about the suggestion. 'Don't worry, Mr Harton,' he went on, blowing his nose again, 'I can afford it. I know everybody thinks I'm destitute, and that Bernard left me flat broke, but he'd provided for me in other ways, and I'd always kept my flat in Southbourne. I shall just move back in there – nobody need worry about my finances . . .'

'That wasn't my concern, Mr Gascoigne,' I said, aware

125

that I'd accidentally ruffled his feathers. 'I was just thinking that you'd probably find the sale itself rather distressing. Believe it or not, even we can find the break-up of a home very sad.'

'Oh, I don't doubt you're human as well. It's just that you disguise it so expertly! Anyway, I'm coming and that's that!'

'Okay, I'll see we reserve you a seat in the front row.'

'The good news is,' I told Duncan, 'that Perry Gascoigne only wants the pair of card tables in the dining room.'

'Well done. What's the bad news? Does he want us to go round and play snap with him?'

'The bad news is,' I continued, 'that he's adamant he's going to attend the sale.'

'Oh, hell! We'll need a second marquee to store the Kleenex tissues.'

'It's Margaret for you,' Jason shouted, waving the telephone out of the open window at me.

'I'll ring her back in ten minutes,' I said, 'if we don't press on we'll never have the place ready for viewing.'

'No – she said it's urgent.'

I cursed liberally as I disentangled myself from the piles of strawberry netting outside the old barn. I'd catalogued the stuff in six lots the day Perry Gascoigne had come and selected the pair of card tables, but I could only seem to find five bundles now it came to putting lot tickets on them. I blew on my hands as I crossed the lawn. For spring it was exceptionally cold, we'd had a frost the previous night and Marshlands was in quite an exposed position. Jason handed the telephone to me through the window as I stood straddling the flower border.

'Yes, Margaret.'

'Richard – we've got a bit of a problem. An Inspector Davies from Southbourne police is coming to see you later this morning.'

'Why – what have I done?'

'Nothing, he'll explain everything. I'm just calling to let you know that Duncan's agreed to his plan. I can't really say anything else over the telephone.'

'Can't you give me a clue?'

'No. Bye.'

Inspector Davies of Southbourne CID turned out to be a big, cheery sort of man, who was evidently enjoying his current piece of investigation.

'As I explained to Mr Parkes,' he said, 'I can't give you any details, but one of our sources has passed us information which leads us to believe that a burglary attempt will take place on Saturday night, after the second viewing day. On the strength of this information, I have requested that we be allowed to have two men in attendance at the house from this evening through until the day after the sale. Mr Parkes has agreed.'

It was fine by me. The last thing we needed was to lose all the best pieces two days before the sale, and since our security was pretty well non-existent a helping hand from the boys in blue seemed a good idea.

'My chaps will move in about five o'clock this evening, Mr Harton,' Inspector Davies went on, 'and I'd quite like to have another one here during the day, working as a porter. He can keep an eye on who's coming and going. Mr Parkes has also agreed to that.'

'Now there's a surprise,' I said, as I thought of the expression on Duncan's face when he heard that he was going to get a porter for four days without paying him.

'Sorry, Sir?'

'Oh, nothing, Inspector, nothing.'

From a security standpoint, Marshlands was a shambles. It was, basically, a sixteenth-century timber-framed house which had been so extensively added to that the original structure was now buried deep in the centre of the present building. In form it was roughly M-shaped and, externally, it presented a different architectural style to each point of the compass. Internally, it was warm and friendly. Its main shortcoming was that it had miles of passageways, especially on the first floor, and dozens of unprotected windows. It also had three separate staircases.

It was the combination of the passages and windows that posed the problems when the two policemen allotted to the case sat down that afternoon to agree routes for their periodic, nocturnal patrols. It took some time, but they

127

eventually decided that, despite the complicated floor plan, it would probably be best if one of them took charge of the first floor and attics, while the other based himself downstairs. So, at the end of a busy but uneventful first viewing day, Detective Constable David Chapel withdrew to the master bedroom while Detective Constable Christopher Beardmore bolted the front door behind us as we left.

'Hope they have a quiet night,' Duncan said as we walked over to our cars.

'Oh, I think they're spoiling for a scrap,' Jason replied.

'Yes, I got that impression too,' Margaret said.

'Well, I think it's disgusting,' Mrs Bromley added, 'all this greed, and crime and violence; and the language those two policemen use too, it's disgusting, absolutely disgusting.'

'If you hadn't had your ear jammed up against the keyhole of their door, you wouldn't have heard anything,' Patrick said, immediately breaking into a sprint to stay out of reach of Agnes's right hook.

'You cheeky young monkey, you wait until tomorrow morning,' Agnes Bromley shouted after him, 'somebody's going to get a good hiding round here before long.'

Her words were to prove more prophetic than she could ever have imagined.

Shortly after eight o'clock the following morning I parked my car behind Duncan's in front of the house. He and Margaret were already standing on the doorstep waiting for one or other of the resident watchdogs to answer their knock at the door. As I walked up I heard bolts being drawn and then a key turning in the lock. As the door opened, Detective Constable Beardmore came into full view.

'Ouch!' Duncan said as he looked at him.

'Oh, Lord! Are you all right?' Margaret added.

'Yeah, jesh fine, it looksh wursh than it ish,' the policeman said through tightly clenched teeth.

'You sure you haven't broken anything?' I asked, looking at his blackened eye and badly bruised and swollen jaw.

'Well, shertainly no bonsh, but we did shmash a little table on the shtairs – I hope it washn't valuable.'

'Oh no, not you as well,' Duncan said, ignoring Christopher Beardmore as David Chapel wandered into view. He was in much better shape than his colleague, although he'd obviously taken a blow above his left eye and there was dried blood on his shirt.

'I take it you had intruders,' I said.

'Not exactly,' DC Chapel replied, 'we may as well tell you what did happen. We're never going to live it down anyway, and it'll be all round the station as soon as Jones hears about it.'

Whatever it was he was talking about, I was quite sure he was right. Cliff Jones, his undercover colleague, had been an instant success as a porter the previous day, but I don't think he'd stopped talking once from the moment he put on his apron to the moment he took it off again.

We gathered round to listen to the two policemen's account of the previous night's excitement. Due to the discomfort experienced by Constable Beardmore every time he opened his mouth, he left most of the talking to David Chapel.

'It had been quiet as the grave,' he said, 'but we'd been checking the place, room by room, every hour on the hour. At midnight we'd agreed to begin half hourly checks. We'd finished the two o'clock one, and I'd gone back to the main bedroom again and was reading the paper, when I heard a noise on the back staircase. I knew it couldn't be Chris because he'd finished his rounds when I finished mine, so I edged my way along the landing, in the pitch black trying to avoid all those creaking boards. Then I could just make out this figure on the stairs. I jumped out in front of him, he rushed me, I swung him round, got him off balance and we both fell down the stairs – top to bottom.'

'Hell!' Duncan said. 'You're lucky you weren't killed. Where were you when all this was going on?' he asked, looking at Christopher Beardmore.

'I wash falling down the shtairsh too,' Constable Beardmore replied.

Duncan looked uncomprehendingly blank.

'He was the bloke coming up the stairs,' David Chapel said, just to clarify things, 'he wanted a pee and you've stacked about a thousand catalogues in the downstairs loo.'

'But why didn't you shout out and let him know it was you?' Margaret asked DC Beardmore.

'I didn't hear him coming – firsht I shaw of him wash when he jumped me and then I thought he wash a villain.'

Duncan looked from one to the other policeman and shook his head.

The View that day was so packed we had to regulate the number of people coming through the house in the afternoon. House Sales always attract more attention than ordinary sales. The trade like them because they can usually be certain that the things on offer haven't been on the market for many years, and locals love them because it gives them a chance to give way to their worst voyeuristic fantasies – like peeping through a keyhole, but without the risk of getting caught. Marshlands had the added advantage of offering the more puritanical neighbours the bonus of being 'absolutely disgusted'. This is, of course, one of the great British pastimes.

'Where did the young one sleep then? . . . You don't mean? . . . Not together . . . Ooh! . . . How disgusting!'

It went on all day in hushed tones, accompanied by nudges, winks and rolled eyes. We had no trouble living with it. These were the same people who'd come back on the day of the sale and pay twenty pounds for a bread bin, two plastic washing up bowls and three bald brooms just so they could say they'd come from Marshlands.

'Okay, Pat,' I said, 'five o'clock on the dot – close the door. Let's get them out.'

Patrick and I had been standing on the landing looking down on the still crowded entrance hall as we counted off the last seconds of viewing. He eased his way through the crowd on the staircase and made for the front door.

'I'm sorry ladies and gentleman,' I boomed from my raised position above the throng, 'but it's five o'clock and we must close the viewing now.'

I received the customary black looks from those who'd arrived late, and I overheard the usual protests being made to Wilson's staff.

'This is absurd . . . Come all the way from London . . . Come all the way from Langton . . . Haven't seen the silver . . . This is disgusting . . . Where's Mr Parkes?'

I was about to wander off through the house to let the

other staff know it was time to shut up shop when I glanced down and saw Patrick in the process of turning a late arrival away from the front door. She was slim and dark, dressed in a heavy sweater and faded blue jeans, and she was as stunningly beautiful as the day I'd first seen her. I barged my way down the stairs, through the crowd and across the hall, reaching the door just as she was going.

'Miss Cartwright,' I called, 'hold on!'

She turned, saw me and smiled. 'Hello,' she said, 'I'm too late, I'm so stupid. I hadn't noticed the time, and it's the last day, isn't it?'

'Yes, but if you'd like to hold on for a moment, just to let the crowd clear, you can have a look round while we're clearing up.'

'Are you sure?'

'Yes, absolutely – we'll be here for an hour or so yet.'

She followed me through the front door, against the flow of viewers, and I parked her on an oak settle just inside the door.

'Miss Cartwright's going to have a look round while we're tidying up,' I told Patrick, who was still standing at the door and had watched my pursuit of the young lady with quiet interest.

'Of course she is,' he replied, with a bright smile.

'You must stop calling me Miss Cartwright, it makes me feel like a maiden aunt. Please call me Antonia.'

'Fine,' I said, 'I'm Richard.'

'And I'm Patrick,' Patrick said, stepping forward and pushing me to one side.

She shook hands with him and laughed, 'Hello, Patrick,' she said.

As I turned to go through the house to check that the viewers were clearing, Patrick caught my arm. 'Very nice mate,' he said, 'she'll take some holding on to, but go for it – if you feel rich enough.'

'What do you mean?'

'Well, she's not the sort of bird who'll settle for a night at the boozer followed by a fish supper, is she?'

'No – I realise that.'

'Well then, you're going to have to dig into your piggy

131

bank – but my advice is have a crack at it. I reckon she's a goer.'

'Thank you, Patrick. I think I can manage, but should I need you to take round the collection boxes, I'll let you know!'

The truth was that I had grave doubts as to whether I could even begin to manage. Antonia Cartwright may well have been the girl of my dreams but this was reality. She was sitting there in the flesh in the hall of Marshlands, thumbing through a sale catalogue, and before she left I had to devise a way of seeing her again, but alone, just the two of us. All right, I could simply ask her out to dinner, but neither my salary nor my experience of local eating places was likely to be up to the standards she was accustomed to.

'Who's that pretty girl in the entrance hall?' Duncan asked, 'Patrick said she was something to do with you, Richard.'

'Well . . . not really . . . That is, her father sold a desk through us last sale, and she was late for the view, and . . .'

'Come on, Richard,' Duncan said, slyly and confidentially as he placed a hand on my shoulder, 'plunge in, you can't afford to hesitate with a girl like that – they're in short supply. You're lucky that Patrick and I are both married, otherwise . . .'

Everybody was so keen on giving me advice, when the one thing I really needed was a few moments alone with her. Our first meeting must have left her with the impression that I was a complete idiot, and now I had to disprove it, quickly.

I managed 'accidently' to find myself in the same room as Antonia on four occasions as she wandered around Marshlands. Each time we were interrupted by other members of Wilson's team. On the final occasion it was Agnes Bromley who'd bustled in looking for something that had never been in that particular room anyway. I was sharp with her and in return received a caustic, 'Very sorry to have disturbed you, Sir, 'cept that some of us have to keep on working while others give guided tours.'

'Oh dear, I think she disapproves of me being here,' Antonia said, 'I really should go.'

'No, no, don't worry, she's always like that.'

'Well, I really should go anyway, it's getting late and Daddy was expecting me back for tea.'

'Oh, I see. I'll see you out, anyway.'

As we walked through the house to the front door, I asked her, as nonchalantly as possible, whether she'd be coming to the sale the following Tuesday. 'I shouldn't think so,' she said, 'I think I'm going to be in London. Anyway I'm only looking for cheap bits of furniture – I'm moving into our little lodge cottage – and I should think this lot's going to be very expensive.'

'You're probably right,' I said, as I opened the front door for her. She stepped outside. 'Bye, bye, Richard.'

She was going. She was getting away. When would I ever see her again? I might never get another chance.

'Would you like to come out to dinner later next week?' I blurted.

'Oh, I'm sorry, I can't, I think I'm going to be in London all week.'

'The following week, perhaps?' I persisted, having abandoned any pretence at cool disinterest.

'Still no good,' she said, I'm going abroad for two or three weeks next weekend. Sorry.'

'Never mind,' I said, completely crushed, hopeless and humiliated, 'it doesn't matter. Goodbye.'

'Bye,' she said, and walked off in the gathering twilight towards the makeshift car park in a nearby field.

Although Wilson's were selling the contents of Marshlands, the sale of the house itself was being handled by a Southbourne estate agent called Thomas Collyer. This created two problems. The first being that since he had introduced Mary Bryant to us, he was entitled to a share of our commission by way of an introductory fee. This was an arrangement that always caused Duncan and Mr Anthony great discomfort in the area of the wallet pocket. The second problem was potentially less costly but certainly a great diplomatic conundrum. It was that Thomas Collyer imagined himself to be a brilliant auctioneer – astute, witty, urbane, just what every auction needed.

'The trouble is he's a complete bloody disaster area,'

Duncan said, the evening before the sale, 'he misses reserves, doesn't get buyers' names, forgets prices, and sells about thirty lots an hour. He introduced a house sale to us before your time, Richard, and I let him sell the carpets and rugs. I still wake up screaming about it sometimes. He fell out with the trade, insulted the vendor and completely cocked-up the book. It took us a day to sort out the bills and we ended up having to buy most of the lots ourselves.'

'Why don't you just tell him he can't get on the rostrum this time?'

'Oh, God, he'd scream and shout and hold his breath until he was sick. What's more we'd never get another piece of work from him. No, we've got to let him sell something and it's going to have to be outside effects. He'll still cock it up, but better he screws up lawn mowers and garden rollers than anything else.'

'But what about . . .?'

'I know, I know the garden statuary. That's what I wanted to talk to you about. There's only half a dozen lots, but they're quite nice, and he's just as likely to knock them out for a few pounds if we don't keep an eye on him, so I want you to clerk while he's selling.'

'Oh, thanks very much!'

'I know it's a pain, Richard, but I'll still be selling the silver when he's doing the garden stuff, so Margaret will still be clerking for me. Just try to keep him under control.'

'All right,' I said, 'I'll try, but we're bound to have some sort of disaster tomorrow, it's all gone too smoothly so far. Even the burglary tip-off turned out to be a dud.'

'Oh, I don't know about that,' he said, 'I suspect the tip-off was genuine enough. I think they were just scared off by the noise of our brave boys beating one another's brains out.'

'And Cliff Jones going up to any vaguely suspicious looking viewer and saying, "'Ello, 'ello, 'ello, what's goin' on 'ere," ' I added.

'Yes, he's the least covered undercover policeman I've ever seen,' Duncan mused as we headed for our cars and the nearest pub, 'he might just as well wear his helmet under his cloth cap.'

*

134

When Duncan took the rostrum a few minutes before ten
o'clock the following morning, the marquee on the lawn at
Marshlands was packed to capacity. All the larger pieces of
furniture stood around the sides of the tent. Everything else
was lined up in the house, ready to be carried along a
covered way to the marquee, shown beside the rostrum, and
then transported back to the relative safety of the house
again. Many of the regular dealers were perched on the
chests of drawers that lined the sides of the marquee nearest
the rostrum. Everybody, including Duncan, was wearing an
overcoat – the spring temperatures had not improved and
there'd been frost on the ground again when we'd arrived
that morning.

'. . . finally,' Duncan said, as he concluded his opening
remarks, 'no lots to be cleared without payment; no lots to
be cleared during the sale unless by special arrangement; all
lots to be cleared by midday on Saturday. We begin with the
furniture in bedroom number one – Lot number one – a
George III-style mahogany chest fitted . . .'

'I have a serious complaint.'

Duncan was stopped in his tracks. The person with the
complaint was a tweedy middle-aged woman with half-moon
glasses and a voice like a regimental sergeant major. She had
been seated three rows from the front but had sprung to her
feet to express her grievance.

'That man is ruining that piece of furniture,' she
continued, pointing an accusatory finger at the dealer
perched on the first lot, 'he's scratching the drawer fronts
with the heels of his shoes!'

'Ooooh!' came the chorus of mock horror from the rest of
the dealers, as they decided to enjoy this early comic
diversion. Duncan always maintained that he could cope
with any interruption or disaster during a sale, providing it
didn't happen in the first twenty lots. He was absolutely
right. It takes that many lots to get into your stride, and on
this occasion Duncan was not in his stride.

'I . . . I . . .' he said.

As luck would have it, the dealer so happily reclining on
the chest in question was none other than Fred Hart. His
eyes lit up at the unexpected opportunity of having a

slanging match with a fully paid up member of the local gentry.

'I shall take some savage woman, she shall rear my dusky race,' Fred said, flashing his yellow teeth and jutting out his stubble-covered jaw.

'I beg your pardon!' the good lady replied.

'Tennyson, Madam. Are you doing anything tonight? Only I think I'm in love.'

'Well, really!'

The dealers rocked with laughter while everyone else looked on, amazed.

'Madam – sit down please,' Duncan said, grasping the reins again, and not a moment too soon.

'But I insist . . .' the lady protested.

'Madam – *sit down!*' Duncan thundered.

Mouth open, she dropped back into her seat, obviously shocked by the force of Duncan's command.

'That's right, Sir, don't you take no nonsense from . . .' Fred tailed off, sensing that discretion was the better part of valour, as Duncan glared at him. However, he couldn't quite suppress a snort of laughter as he buried his face in his catalogue.

'Lot number one – the mahogany chest,' Duncan said, slowly and firmly, 'what will you bid me. Start me at fifteen pounds, someone.'

'Five,' the protesting lady cried out, shaking her catalogue violently above her head.

'Twenty,' Fred said, smiling maliciously at her.

'Twenty I'm bid,' Duncan went on. 'Twenty-two?' he queried, looking back to the lady bidder.

'Twenty-two,' she shouted, still shaking her catalogue furiously.

'Fifty,' said Fred, still smiling and not taking his eyes off his opponent. Since the chest was worth no more than twenty-five pounds on a good day, and Fred Hart knew it, I concluded he was teaching the complainant a lesson.

'At fifty pounds then – all done at fifty?'

The lady's catalogue lay still in her lap.

'Hart – fifty pounds,' Duncan said as he brought his hammer down. Immediately, Fred drummed his heels furiously on the front of the chest. His adversary shot him a glance that should have turned him to dust on the spot.

'I can do what I like to it now,' he shouted at her, 'it's mine, all mine.'

'Fred! Really!' Duncan complained. 'Behave yourself!'

'Sorry, Sir, I got carried away.'

As Duncan moved on to the second lot of the sale, the indignant underbidder on lot number one collected her belongings together and stalked from the marquee.

Following the initial hiccup, the sale proceeded according to plan with Duncan in good form and prices going through the roof. The greatest success turned out to be our somewhat doubtful decision to sit Perry Gascoigne next to Thomas Collyer. As it was, Perry was so busy telling Collyer the intimate history of each lot as it came up for sale, he only remembered to dab at his eyes once, while Collyer only had time to pass one note to Duncan. It was a respectful suggestion that Duncan should slow down a little since the writer felt he was going too fast for the dealers. Duncan read it, screwed it into a very small ball, dropped it on the floor and increased his selling rate by another ten lots an hour.

It was nearly half past three when Duncan came to the silver section of the catalogue.

'So that we're not still here at midnight,' he said, 'Mr Thomas Collyer will sell the outside effects whilst I'm selling the silver.'

'We'll still be selling at midnight anyway, with Flash Collyer on the rostrum,' Patrick muttered as we made our way outside, 'he thinks he's so bloody funny, I swear he drags it out as long as he can.'

I had to admit that Thomas Collyer did come over as being an awful bore. He was a big man, in his early fifties, with a loud voice – most of his whispered asides to Perry Gascoigne during the morning could have been heard in the car park. During the luncheon interval he'd punished the Booths Gin severely, and consequently had been rather more subdued during the afternoon session. I'd noticed his head nodding on more than one occasion as his several chins slowly came down to rest on his barrel chest. He'd remain still for a few moments then jerk upright with a snort, glancing round and smiling amiably as though he'd just entered the marquee. I couldn't make up my mind whether it was a good or bad thing that the cold afternoon air seemed to have revived him.

'Right,' he bellowed to the gathering of thirty or forty pinched faces in front of us, 'I'm going to sell the outside effects as we walk around the out-buildings so you'll have to keep up because I don't intend to waste any time.' He paused and delved about in the sleeve of his overcoat, eventually producing a handkerchief. He blew his nose loudly, stuck the handkerchief back up his sleeve and continued, 'Our first lot is number eight hundred and one – one bundle of strawberry net . . .'

'No, Sir,' I interrupted to a chorus of echoes from the assembled company, 'you've turned over too many pages. The first lot is number seven hundred and seventy-five – the quantity of terracotta flower pots.'

'What? What?' Thomas Collyer spluttered as he thumbed back through the book, dropping his pen in the process. 'Oh yes, I see. It's the book,' he explained to the restive crowd, 'it's not put together properly.' I retrieved his pen and handed it back to him. 'You'll have to do something about these books,' he said to me, 'they're terribly badly laid out.'

'Yes, Sir,' I said.

'Now, where are we? Ah, yes lot seven hundred and seventy-five – a quantity of terracotta flower pots. There they are,' he said gesturing to a group of about fifty pots, 'what will you bid me. Ten pounds?'

Nobody moved a muscle.

'Five then?'

Still nobody moved.

'Two?'

'One pound,' said a wizened little man in the front row of the otherwise immobile crowd.

'A pound? One pound?' the auctioneer said, sounding personally insulted. 'Oh, I don't think that's good enough!'

'Then you can stuff 'em,' the former bidder said, to a loud guffaw of laughter and some applause from the crowd.

'No, no,' Thomas Collyer said, 'I'll accept your bid.'

'No yer wun't,' the man said. ''cos I dun't want 'em no more.'

'But you bid, you bid, you can't just withdraw it . . .'

'Five pounds,' I said.

'What?' Collyer snapped, turning to me, rather flustered.

'Five pounds, Sir. I'm bidding five pounds.'

'Oh, yes, quite, five pounds I'm bid.'

He eventually sold the lot for seven pounds fifty and even then encountered a problem.

'At seven pounds fifty pence . . . For the last time at seven pounds fifty pence . . . Sold then at seven pounds fifty . . . Oh dear, where's my gavel?'

He'd forgotten it. I took mine from my pocket and handed it to him. He banged it down on his clipboard and then looked blank. 'How much?' he hissed at me.'

'What?'

'How much did I sell it for?'

'Seven pounds fifty. What was the buyer's name?'

'What?'

'What was the buyer's name?' I repeated.

'I don't know.'

'Well, find out.'

'It was the man in the front,' he muttered out of the side of his mouth.

'Ask him his name!'

While this exchange was going on, the prospective purchasers began to become a little impatient. 'Get on wiv it!' the wizened man said to a general ripple of support from his fellow sufferers.

'Your name, Sir?' Thomas Collyer demanded of him.

'Why, yer goin' ter report me?' the man replied, to an accompanying cackle of fresh laughter.

'I want your name because you bought the last lot,' Mr Collyer went on.

'No, Oi didn't.'

'Oh, yes you did,' our hero blustered.

'Oh, no he didn't,' chorused a handful of humourists in the crowd.

'I knocked it down to you at seven pounds fifty,' Thomas Collyer insisted.

'That dun't surprise me neither,' the man drawled, 'it's plain yer 'aint got no idea what yer doin'.'

'You bought the last lot for seven pounds fifty,' the almost scarlet Collyer shouted at the man.

'I thought you'd taken *my* bid,' intervened a lady standing just behind the wizened man.

'No, no, you were the underbidder.'

'No, I bid seven pounds fifty.'

'No, you only bid seven pounds,' Thomas Collyer said, wiping his brow despite the biting cold.

'Excuse me, but I do know what I bid,' the woman replied sharply.

'You bid seven pounds,' shrieked Collyer.

'Oh no she didn't,' chorused the crowd again.

It is not the done thing for an auctioneer's clerk to suggest that the auctioneer hangs up his gavel, but the situation at Marshlands was plainly out of control. I was desperately trying to think of a nice way of telling Thomas Collyer to go home, when fate took a hand in the proceedings.

Collyer had been getting increasingly animated as he conducted his oral brawl with the crowd, hopping up and down, and waltzing backwards and forwards as he spoke. Suddenly, he caught his heel in one of the bundles of strawberry netting, twisted and fell sideways into a pile of bean poles and seed trays. The merciless crowd loved it and a great roar went up as they collapsed with laughter. Patrick and I both stepped forward to help Thomas Collyer to his feet but it soon became evident that more than his pride was bruised.

'My ankle – I've twisted my ankle,' he said, wincing, as we sat him up.

'Oh dear, what a shame,' I said.

'Yes,' Patrick agreed, 'what a shame you won't be able to auction with a twisted ankle, Sir – and just as you were getting into your stride too!'

'Yes, I know, but I'm afraid that's it, I'm out of action,' Collyer said, massaging the injury. 'Would you mind terribly taking over, Mr Harton?'

'Of course not, Mr Collyer, it'll be no trouble,' I said, retrieving the hammer from where it had fallen among the seed boxes.

'Thank God for that,' Patrick muttered as Cliff Jones helped the ex-auctioneer to the house, 'perhaps we'll get

140

home in time for breakfast after all.'

'All right, ladies and gentlemen,' I said to the restless mob, 'since there seems to be a dispute about who bought the first lot, I'm going to offer it again, and five pounds is my opening bid . . . Do I hear five fifty? . . . Five fifty I'm bid . . . six . . . six fifty. . . seven . . . seven fifty . . . The lady's bid at seven pounds fifty . . . All done? . . . Sold at seven pounds fifty. Your name please, Madam?'

Chapter 12

Mrs Dorothy Foster demanded nothing less then immediate and undivided attention. Furthermore, since I'd been the one unfortunate enough to answer the telephone when she called, it was me she demanded it of. She was quite explicit, she wanted an experienced and competent valuer to come and value, for possible sale, the contents of Keeper's Cottage, Harcombe. She didn't want the valuer to come tomorrow, or even later today, she wanted him to come *now*.

'I'm rather committed at the moment,' I said.

'Please yourself,' she replied. 'Christie's have already seen it. If you can't be bothered to make an effort, it'll all go to London for sale.'

'But I can be there by midday,' I continued.

'Eleven o'clock at the latest,' she said.

I counted very slowly to ten. 'Eleven o'clock it shall be,' I said.

'And what is your name?'

'Harton – Richard Harton.'

'Barton?'

'Harton – "H" for Harry.'

'Harold Barton, right, I'll expect you at eleven sharp, Mr Barton.

Harcombe was a pretty little village only a few miles away, but that didn't make it any less inconvenient having to trail there at the drop of a hat. I was still in charge of accounts at The Galleries, although somebody else now did the donkey work, and having just had three sales in quick succession – two at The Galleries, and the house sale at Marshlands – there was a lot of tidying up to do. On top of that, I was due

142

to interview a candidate for the newly-created post of personal assistant to none other than me. Duncan had resisted the idea for a long time, but had eventually given way when he found Margaret was no longer available to type his letters because she was too busy typing mine. As a result, Miss Kate Bentley was due at The Galleries at a quarter to one. I had hoped to present a facade of order and efficiency, but I already sensed she was going to be exposed to Wilson's Auction Galleries as they really were.

Keeper's Cottage was right in the middle of Harcombe, next to the small village green and opposite the little old shingle spired church. The cottage itself appeared to be minute, and as I approached the front door it crossed my mind that Mrs Foster might be nothing more than a time-waster. All my doubts on that score were dispelled immediately she opened the door – time was one thing Dorothy Foster did not waste.

'Come in. I'd be grateful if you would wipe your feet thoroughly, Mr Barton. There are valuable rugs throughout as I hope you will recognise.' As she spoke she eyed me up and down and I felt that, at any moment, she'd tell me to wipe my nose and not slouch. 'Before you say anything,' she continued without pause, 'I want you to value a pair of pictures in the sitting room. I shall then decide, on the strength of your opinion on those, whether there is any point in your examining the rest of the contents. Follow me, please.'

I followed the square, dumpy figure through to the next room. There was certainly nothing frivolous about her. She was like an old-fashioned school mistress. Her steel grey hair was drawn back tightly in a bun, while her dress was plain and strictly untilitarian. I noticed that a faint odour of mothballs accompanied us into the sitting room. As we entered the room, she very deliberately – and obviously entirely for my benefit – picked up a Christie's valuation from the table just inside the door.

'Those are they,' she said, pointing to a small pair of Venetian scenes hung on either side of the window, 'and don't put a ridiculously high value on them either, or I'll just send the whole lot straight to Christie's.'

143

I decided the time had come to stand on my professional dignity. 'Mrs Foster,' I said, turning suddenly to face her, in the hope that a surprise attack would catch the old trout off-guard, 'I shall give you the same opinion on these pictures as I would give anybody else on any other item – my honest view of what I think they are, and what I think they will make under the hammer, wherever they are sold.'

'No more than I would expect,' she said, plainly unruffled by my bluntness. She was going to be even tougher than I'd first imagined.

I took down one of the oils and had a close look at it. It was a view of the Doge's Palace, painted on canvas, and it was in what appeared to be it's original eighteenth-century carved wood frame. Its partner was a study of the Santa Maria Della Salute. Both were well executed and there was no sign of a signature on either.

'I like them,' I said, quite expecting some caustic reply about my personal likes and dislikes, but none came. 'I don't know who they're by, so at this stage I'd go no further on attribution than to describe them as eighteenth-century Venetian School, although with a bit of research we might well come up with an artist. Christie's may already have done that, of course,' I added, fishing furiously to see how I was doing.

'And value?' Mrs Foster said, treating my baited hook with disdain.

'Well, they're in their original frames which is always good . . . Offering them just as eighteenth-century Venetian School . . . I would say . . . somewhere in the region of . . . three hundred and fifty pounds, perhaps more.'

My fate was sealed. I stared into Dorothy Foster's cold grey eyes and waited. Slowly, she opened the Christie's valuation and held it so I could read the first page. Item number one read: '18th-century Venetian School, a pair, carved wood frames – £300/400'

'Shall we go on,' she said, as just for the merest moment, the faintest suggestion of a smile flickered on her lips.

I shall always remember the Keeper's Cottage contents for one piece of furniture in particular. It was a magnificent yew wood gateleg table dating from about 1700. When the

D-shaped leaves were up it measured over six feet in length. There wasn't a join in the top. Each leaf and the centre section were made from single yew planks from a tree that must have been massive.

'You know, Mrs Foster,' I said, running my hand over the silk-smooth golden table top, ' the timber used to make this table must have come from a tree planted while Henry VIII was still a child, perhaps even before he was born. Puts things into perspective doesn't it?'

'What's it worth?' she said.

I don't recall my reply, but I do remember that, when the table was sold, it made what was then considered to be the staggering price of fifteen hundred pounds. I've never seen one to compare with it though, and I've no doubt it would make fifteen thousand if it were offered today.

I drove back to Kington feeling justifiably smug. I'd got hold of a very nice contents that had been bound for London; I'd seen one of the nicest pieces of country furniture I was ever likely to see; I'd even eventually explained to Mrs Foster that my name was Harton not Barton, and I was only going to be a few minutes late for my appointment with Kate Bentley. The sky was blue, the birds were singing and, with the exception of my total inability to convince Antonia Cartwright that I was anything other than a gauche country bumpkin, all was well with the world.

Still, my complete lack of progress with Antonia cast a dark, dark shadow over everything else. My performance so far had been pathetic. I could actually feel myself blushing when I recalled the ghastly incident with the tie. I had to think of some way, any way of seeing her again. But how?

Both Margaret and Jason were waiting for me when I walked through The Galleries' door.

'Kate Bentley's waiting in your office,' Margaret said. 'I've already had a chat with her and she seems competent enough technically.'

'But?' I said, sensing Margaret was less than convinced about the suitability of the applicant for this new and prestigious post.

'But, she's rather unusual.'

'In what way?'

145

'You'll see. Oh, and by the way, there was a call for you while you were out – an Antonia Cartwright. She asked if you could ring her as soon as you got back, the number's on your pad.' My stomach started to churn. She'd called me! But why! What could she want? I had to call her right away before I did anything else.

'Hold on, Richard,' Jason said, catching me by the arm as I turned to go to my office and the telephone, 'she'll have to wait. I've got a problem.'

'What?'

'I'll give you a clue – it's small, round, has a heavy accent, and bought a load of bronzes in the last sale.'

'Oh, no!'

'Afraid so. It's Mrs Weinberg.'

The very mention of Mrs Weinberg always brought on acute ambivalence in me. One part of me regarded her as a rather lovable old lady with a great gift for making beautiful music, while the other part of me just recognised her as an amazing nuisance who would go to any lengths to avoid paying bills. She was certainly adept at using a 'poor little old lady' routine as and when necessary, and she'd long since learned I was the best one at Wilson's to try it on.

Mrs Weinberg had, along with many others, fled Germany for England in the 1930s. All she had brought with her was a small suitcase and a prodigious talent as a cellist. Her career as a professional musician had taken off in a big way by the late 1930s, and during the 1950s she was in constant demand on both sides of the Atlantic. Unfortunately, her private life was not as happy as her professional life, and by the time I met her she was a rather lonely, fat little old lady living in a modest flat in Langton. Her only vice seemed to be that she bought things at auction which she couldn't afford to pay for. She was obviously wheeling and dealing to supplement her income, trying to sell the things for a profit before she paid for them. It was some time, however, before I learned of the scale of the operation. It was one of the old Langton dealers who had told me about it.

It would seem that Mrs Weinberg started by renting a couple of run-down flats in one of the less fashionable areas of Langton. She'd furnish each one in turn, right down to the last napkin ring, then put an advertisement in one or other of the local papers announcing: 'Elderly widow moving into Old People's Home for medical reasons – entire flat contents must be sold urgently – NO DEALERS.'

Of course, every sharp operator for miles around homed in on whichever flat it was. Before long, her advertisements became so well known she had to change her tack. She started to select individual dealers well outside the Langton area. They would be telephoned and given a heart-rending account of her present terminal illness, and how she had to move into a hospice. In a one-way conversation punctuated with sighs and sobs, she'd explain in her strong German accent how she couldn't go to the local dealers because she had no idea what any of her things were worth, and she'd been told that all Langton dealers were crooks. She could only do it to each dealer once, but that was generally enough. Once Mrs Weinberg had a dealer in one of her flats, she didn't let him go without a fight. Even if she didn't unload the whole contents on him, he'd generally buy something just to get out of the flat again.

Reluctantly, I wandered through to Gallery Three where I could see the dumpy figure of Mrs Weinberg standing by her most recent purchases. She looked up as I approached and beamed at me.

'Ah, Mr Harton,' she said, clasping her hands together, 'goot, goot, now ve find out vot is vot.'

'Hello, Mrs Weinbeg. How can I help you?'

'It's deez bronzes vot I bought in da last zale. Vot you know 'bout zem? I ask Jazon but he know nuzzing, zo I zay I vait for Mr Harton becoze he iz zo clever.'

'It's very kind of you to say so, Mrs Weinberg,' I replied, well aware that Jason had simply chickened-out of telling her the truth. 'What would you like to know?'

'Vell, in da cadalogue you juzt zay "a bronze vigure ov an adalete".'

'A bronze figure of an athlete – yes.'

'And "anuzer of a dizcuz drower".'

'Yes.'

'And "anuzer ov a javelin drower".'

'Yes, discus and javelin throwers.'

147

'Yah, now vot I vant to know eez, how old zey are?'

'They were cast in the '30s,' I said.

'1830s – I zee.'

'No, Mrs Weinberg, the 1930s.'

'1930s – mine Gott, zey are not zo old zen. Ver vur zey made?' That was the question I had not been looking forward to. There was only one thing I'd been looking forward to less, and that was Mrs Weinberg's inevitable reaction to my reply.

'On the Continent,' I said, trying one last sidestep.

'Yah, yah, but ver – Franze?'

'No . . . Germany.'

'Germany? Germany? Germany!' Mrs Weinberg said, her voice rising a little with each mention of the Fatherland. '1930s Germany – zat meenz zey are . . . zey are . . . zey are Narrzi!' Poor Mrs Weinberg pronounced the loathed word the same way Churchill had in his wartime speeches. 'Ach! *Mein Gott! Mein Gott!* Zey are Narrzi, Narrzi! Take zem avay! Take zem avay! Pleez, pleez, take zem avay!'

If anything, the reaction was slightly worse than I'd expected. I'd known it would be extreme, but the sight of Mrs Weinberg rotating slowly in the middle of the gallery, clutching her head in both hands, and shrieking alternately, *'Mein Gott!'* and 'Take zem avay!' was even more than I'd been prepared for.

'Mrs Weinberg.'

'Mein Gott! Mein Gott! Mein Gott!'

'Mrs Weinberg, please listen, Mrs Weinberg.'

'Take zem avay! Take zem avay!'

'Mrs Weinberg, I realise how upset you must be. If we'd been able to stop you from buying them we would have done so . . .'

'Narrzi! *Mein Gott!* Narrzi!'

'. . . We'll just put them straight back in the next sale for you . . .'

'Mein Gott! Mein Gott!'

'. . . You don't have to take them with you and, on just this one occasion, we won't charge you any commission for reselling them.'

'No commizzion?' Mrs Weinberg stopped spinning and

wailing, and checked she'd heard correctly.

'No commission,' I confirmed.

'Ah, zat eez very kind, zank you, Mr Harton. I just take my carriage clock and go now, zen.'

'Yes, I think that was the only other thing you bought last sale, wasn't it?' I was about to hand her the clock when a thought crossed my mind. 'Has Jason got your porter's slip?'

'Porter'z zlip?'

'Yes, Mrs Weinberg, you know – the slip you hand to the porter when you collect your purchases. It's attached to your receipt. You have got a receipt haven't you, Mrs Weinberg?'

'Rezeet?' Her round face expressed only uncomprehending innocence.

'Mrs Weinberg, you haven't paid, have you?'

'No, but zen you zaid I don't haff to, Mr Harton,' she said, giving me her most innocent look.

'I said no such thing, I said . . .'

'Yah, yah, you dit!'

'. . . I said, we would re-offer the bronzes on your behalf in the next sale, not that I'd take them off your bill this time.'

'Ach! *Mein Gott! Mein Gott!*'

'No, no, stop that straight away,' I shouted, coming to the end of my own tether, 'one more word and my offer of zero commission in the next sale is withdrawn – just one more word, I mean it!'

Mrs Weinberg was instantly silent. I escorted her to the cashier's desk where Margaret was temporarily stationed. 'Mrs Weinberg would like to pay for her lots, please, Margaret.'

'Right, and I think it may have slipped your mind that Kate Bentley is still waiting patiently for you in your office.'

'Oh! My God!'

'Yah, yah. *Mein Gott! Mein Gott!*'

Kate Bentley was indeed waiting patiently. She was sitting, one elbow on my desk, resting her head on her hand, reading the *Guardian*. She was a strikingly pretty girl, although it was her clothes which made the greatest initial impact. Her general concept of *haute couture* seemed to be centred around the local Oxfam shop. Her 1950s flower-printed dress and woolly cardigan were complemented by a pair of lace-up granny boots and a man's raincoat. Her handbag appeared to be an army surplus ammunition pouch suspended from a rainbow-coloured crocheted cord. Margaret was right, Kate Bentley was a little unusual.

'I'm sorry to have kept you waiting,' I said, 'I'm Richard Harton.'

'Kate Bentley,' she said. 'Don't worry, I don't have to rush anywhere.'

'Well, I think Margaret's explained the job to you. How do feel about it?'

'Fine.'

'It's boring, repetitive and routine,' I went on, lighting my pipe, 'the building's dirty, cold and damp, and the pay's awful.'

'Yes, that's more or less what Mrs Graham said. Do you mind if I smoke?'

'No, not at all, please go ahead.'

She poked around in her ammunition pouch and came up with a packet of cigarette papers, a rolling machine and a partly-used half ounce pack of Golden Virginia. I watched as she started to manufacture a cigarette, then I picked up the curriculum vitae Margaret had left on my desk. An expensive girls' school, followed by a London secretarial college, then quite a long list of firms and companies.

'You haven't stayed anywhere very long,' I commented.

'Nor would you in some of those places,' she replied. 'They were really boring.'

'What makes you think Wilson's will be any more interesting?'

'Oh, I just think it's unusual.'

'Well, it's certainly that. One thing, though – you're not taking this job because you like fine art, are you.'

'No, I don't know anything about it. Why?'

'Oh, it's just that we've had temps in the past who've taken jobs here because they've "just loved art and antiques" and they've always been unmitigated disasters.'

'Well, I might still be a disaster, but I couldn't care less whether Wilson's sell Rubens or raspberries.'

'Good. When can you start?'

'Tomorrow.'

'See you then.'

She swept her things back into the ammunition pouch, stood up and picked up the raincoat. 'I know I don't start officially until tomorrow,' she said, 'but I'm certain Mrs Graham told you you had to call somebody as soon as you got in – I think you may have forgotten.'

'Oh, my God!'

'What did Miss Cartwright want?' Jason asked, when I joined him Gallery Four where he was unpacking china.

'Precisely nothing.'

'How come?'

'Because, what with Mrs Weinberg and Kate Bentley – who's starting tomorrow, by the way – I forgot to call her, and when I eventually did there was no reply.'

'Oh, dear. Never mind. Have a look at this, it'll cheer you up.'

As a substitute for Antonia Cartwright, the item Jason had just unpacked was a non-starter, but otherwise it was really quite nice.

'What a pretty clock,' I said.

It was a perfectly standard French movement with a painted porcelain dial. What made it unusual was that it was set in a porcelain model of an artist's palette. The palette itself stood about a foot high and was beautifully painted with a rural landscape. It was such fine quality, it looked as though it had been executed by a miniaturist. As a final touch, the palette clock stood on a miniature carved ebony easel.

'How old is it?' Jason asked.

'1860 or 1870, I would have thought – no great age, but what fantastic quality. Set it up in the main gallery so that people can see it when they come through the door – it'll sell really well. Anything else come in with it?'

'A longcase clock just inside the front door, otherwise only this china and glass,' Jason gestured to a pretty ordinary looking collection.

I went back through to the main gallery and looked at the clock. It was a George III oak longcase (the correct term for a grandfather clock) with an eight-day movement and brass dial. Like oak furniture, oak cased clocks are normally the work of provincial makers for the simple reason that the country craftsman used readily available local timbers, whereas the top makers in big cities used more exotic and expensive imported woods like mahogany. The clock by the front door was a pretty typical example and was the work of a minor Kentish maker.

'What's it worth?' Jason asked.

'About sixty pounds, I suppose,' I said.

'Should I move it to another gallery?'

'No, leave it where it is until something better comes in.'

'Hello, it's Richard, Richard Harton. I'm sorry I didn't get back to you earlier but . . .'

'Oh, don't worry, I hope you haven't been trying all day, I've only just got in.'

'No, no, first time I've called.' It was a barefaced lie. I'd called Antonia Cartwright every hour on the hour and now it was 9 p.m.

'It was just that I wondered if you'd like to come to dinner on the tenth – it's Daddy's birthday and he needs cheering up, and you make him laugh.'

'Quite,' I said, as the still painful incident with the tie flashed before me once again.

'Oh dear, it wasn't meant to sound like that – I just mean we'd both love to see you. Can you come? I do hope so. I felt so rude at the house sale, turning down your invitation to dinner.'

'I'd love to come,' I said.

'Wonderful. It's seven thirty for eight, black tie. See you then. Bye.'

Black tie! Oh God! Why was nothing ever simple? Not only didn't I own a dinner jacket, the current state of my finances made the hire of one an economic impossibility. There was only one course of action open to me: I had to ask Duncan for a loan.

Chapter 13

It was always difficult to know just how Duncan would react to an approach for a loan. Whereas there was never any question about his reaction to a request for an increase in salary, a loan was different. The faintest suggestion that one's salary should, perhaps, be increased by the current rate of inflation would always bring on an analysis of the inherent instability of the art market, a summary of the bleak state of the British economy, and several tips on frugality and the need to tighten one's belt. In short, you stood no chance at all of getting a rise unless you were prepared to accompany your request with the threat of resignation, and then it could be a close run thing. Loans were different. Suggest a loan to Duncan on the right day and he'd open his wallet without a second thought. The problem was, if you caught him on the wrong day, you'd just get the frugality lecture and no cash.

All in all, I thought the timing looked quite auspicious. We'd had three good sales in a row; I was due Brownie points for having snatched Dorothy Foster's collection from Christie's, and, generally speaking, Duncan and I hadn't had an argument for ages. So, immediately after my telephone conversation with Antonia, I decided I'd tap Duncan for a loan first thing the next morning.

I made sure I was at The Galleries before Duncan. I noticed with some satisfaction the first thing to catch my eye was the French palette clock – just the sort of thing Duncan liked. That wouldn't do any harm to his frame of mine when he arrived. By a quarter past nine everybody, including Kate Bentley, was working away with quiet, beaver-like intensity. The place was a model of industry and efficiency.

Duncan's entrances were often dramatic. He'd frequently spill through the door piled high with boxes and files, unable to see where he was going and oblivious to the trail of papers, letters and other debris he was leaving behind him. But, even by his standards, his arrival that morning was really spectacular. I say 'arrival', but I suppose, technically, I should say 'arrivals' because, even if he didn't actually make two entrances, he certainly made two appearances. The first, admittedly, was extraordinarily brief, but none the less dramatic for that. Jason and I were working in Gallery One when I spotted Duncan's scrambled outline through the frosted glass of the front door. He was obviously piled high with boxes and was about to do one of his party tricks. He'd high kick the door handle and the door would swing open on its own, permitting him to enter without having to put down what he was carrying – not many men of his age could have managed it. We heard the impact of shoe on handle. The door lashed open, and whipped back against the oak longcase clock standing behind it and slammed shut again. We had a momentary glimpse of Duncan peering over a large cardboard box and then he was gone. It was like seeing something illuminated by a brilliant flash of lightning on a pitch black night. You end up being not quite sure whether you really saw it. Before Jason and I could compare notes on our visual impression of what was happening outside, what was happening inside captured our full attention. The Kentish oak longcase was on the move. The initial impact of the door had rocked it back on its heels, but now it was coming towards us. Like some resurrected mummy in a Hammer horror film, it was swaying violently from side to side, inching forward as it did so. It must have travelled about a foot across the gallery before it hesitated, looked me straight in the face and crashed full length onto the bare concrete floor. Its hood shattered in a storm of wood splinters and glass fragments which fanned out across the room. The furthest spread pieces of debris lapped around our feet as we stood, observing the scene of destruction, paralysed by the sheer suddenness of it all.

One phenomenon that always followed a major breakage was an eerie silence. On that occasion it was broken by Jason.

154

'S . . . H . . . One . . . T,' he said, articulating my own feelings surprisingly accurately. The door opened again and Duncan, now without his cardboard box, reappeared.

'What the hell was that?' he said.

'I think the wind caught the door,' Jason said, in his usual bright, helpful way.

'I know the wind caught the door,' Duncan replied, 'but what did the door? . . .' He stopped in the middle of his question as his eyes fell on the fallen clock.

'Who the hell put that there?' he snarled, his eyes darting from me to Jason and back to me again.

'It fell there,' Jason said, with a sort of keenness which suggested his strictly literal interpretation of Duncan's questions was innocent rather than malicious, 'when you kicked the door open, it fell there.'

'I meant, who put it behind the door in the first place?' Duncan said slowly, beginning to look really mean.

'I did,' I said.

'Well, what a bloody stupid place to put it,' he remarked as both Margaret and Kate, who'd been standing in their respective office doorways, slipped out of sight again like figures on a confused weather-house.

'We've had clocks there before,' I pointed out.

'And I've always said it was stupid. I knew this would happen one day, but you will not take any notice, that's always been your problem, Richard.'

It was pointless arguing with Duncan once he was in one of those moods, so I just kept quiet.

'Whose is it anyway?' he went on, bending down and picking at the wreckage.

'It's a probate lot,' Jason said, 'came in yesterday from a Southbourne solicitor. I thought you'd probably seen it.'

'No,' he said, still poking about in the debris, 'never seen it. Anyway, if it's a probate lot, with a bit of luck we can get it repaired and nobody will be any the wiser. Did anything else come in with it?'

'Yes, that,' I said, pointing to the palette clock.

'Oh, I say,' he said, brightening up at last, 'isn't that pretty.' He went over to the table where the clock was standing and, carefully gripping hold of the easel, picked it up.

'*No!*' I shouted, but it was already too late. Once again, Jason and I were limited to being helpless observers, as the delicately decorated porcelain clock parted company with its stand and soared off in ungainly free flight. It made a brief false landing on the edge of the table, then bounced onto the floor. Unlike the pieces of the longcase clock which had distributed themselves in a fan-shape, the fragments of the palette clock formed a rough circle around the brass-cased cylinder movement which was left spinning, slowly and incongruously on the concrete. Duncan seemed momentarily mesmerised by the vacant ebony easel, then he looked down at the abstract mosaic of broken porcelain on the floor.

'Oh, **** it!' he said, as Margaret and Kate repeated their earlier weather-house routine.

Chapter 14

'No commission! No commission! What do you mean, no commission?' Duncan was in the vilest of moods and, by then, so was I. We'd had two days of it, ever since the great clock disaster, and we were all feeling punch drunk. It didn't matter what any of us did, it was wrong; and now Duncan had found I wasn't charging Mrs Weinberg anything for selling her bronzes.

'Exactly what I said: I've agreed not to charge the old girl for reselling those bronzes. You know she would never have bought them if she'd known what they were.'

'*Caveat emptor*,' Duncan said.

'And she paid much too much for them,' I added.

'Oh, that's all right then,' he said, 'only I hadn't realised we'd become a registered charity. Now I know, I understand perfectly. I assume you also gave her a few pounds out of the petty cash.'

'Oh, for God's sake, DP!'

'Well, why not? Why cramp your style? You might just as well give away cash as commission – what's the difference?'

'That's it!' I shouted, as I grabbed my jacket from the chair. 'I've had enough!'

'Where do you think you're going?' Duncan demanded.

'Out!'

Although the spring had been dreadful, the worst I could remember, the days had at last become warm and dry, so I decided to drive the few miles to the coast and walk along the cliffs towards Southbourne. It was the right decision. For one thing, once Duncan and I had got that heated, a cooling off period was the only answer. The balmy breeze coming off the sea blew way the cobwebs, and a couple of hours walking put things back into perspective. I could only hope Duncan was also in a more reasonable frame of mind. The chief problem with walking out in the middle of a blazing row is that you've got to walk back in again at some stage, and that usually demands greater nerve than was needed to walk out. Whereas you can always find a good reason for slamming your way out of a room, it's pretty well impossible to find one for slamming your way back into it. That makes it almost inevitable that every dramatic departure is eventually followed by an embarrassingly undramatic return.

Fortunately, a diversion was under way when I arrived back at The Galleries: Watson's pantechnicon was parked outside, disgorging the contents of Keeper's Cottage. I had completely forgotten it was coming in that day. I'd fully intended to enter it all, and personally look after its distribution through the various galleries, but when I got inside I found Duncan had taken control.

'Hello, Dick,' he said, his face wreathed in smiles, 'super lot, this. Well done. Beautiful yew wood gateleaf – best I've ever seen.'

Obviously peace had broken out. Duncan only called me 'Dick' after one of our rows. It was a sort of coded message which meant, at least as far as he was concerned, hostilities had ceased. I knew neither of us would ever again mention – to each other, anyway – that morning's row or my three-hour absence from The Galleries. It would be as if the last two days had never happened. That was Duncan's way of doing things.

'Yes, it's quite a nice lot,' I said.

'Oh, super! Well done, Dick. Really well done!'

'He was like a bear with a sore head for about half an hour, then he decided to repair the longcase,' Jason said, recounting the morning's events following my sudden departure.

'Oh, no!' I said.

'Afraid so, Richard, but it's a small price to pay. Look at him now – happy, relaxed, positive. It obviously had a tremendously therapeutic effect on him.'

'I suppose so.'

Jason was right of course. The longcase clock was a small

price to pay for a fully rehabilitated DP, but it was still a pity
– it had been coming on so well.

I had been quite surprised to find that the damage done to
the hood of the clock, though extensive, was certainly
repairable. Most of the splinters had come from the inside of
the case, and I was reasonably confident that the repairs, as
long as they were done carefully, would be difficult to detect
on the outside of the clock. We'd also been fortunate that
neither the movement nor the dial had suffered any damage
at all. I'd laid out all the broken pieces of the case in the
store and had begun, over the previous two days, to
reassemble the thing. I thought it would probably take about
two weeks to do it properly. According to Jason, Duncan
had put it all back together in a little under twenty-five
minutes. The more I heard, the less I wanted to see the
finished product. Duncan Parkes possessed numerous
natural talents, but furniture restoration was not one of
them.

'Good God,' I said, 'I didn't know we had that much
glue.'

'Mmm,' Jason replied, 'at one stage I thought I was going
to have to cut him free. Every time he touched something it
stuck to him.'

I looked at the lop-sided hood. It was covered with lumps
of hardened glue where the over-enthusiastically applied
adhesive had oozed from the shattered joints. Stalactites of
the stuff hung all round the edge of the thing.

'Oh, well,' I said, 'I suppose we can scrape most of it off.'

'Yes, but you haven't seen the best of it yet.'

'You mean there's more?'

'Well, let's put it this way – I bet you can't open the door
or remove the hood.'

'Oh, no.'

'Oh, yes,' Jason said.

The hood of a longcase clock is constructed separately
from the rest of the case, so it can be removed to allow one
to get at the movement. Normally it just slides forward and
can then be lifted off. The door in it permits you to wind the
clock, adjust the hands and so on, without lifting the whole

hood off. Duncan's handiwork had put an end to all that on this particular clock. The movement was sealed away like a corpse in a tomb.

'It wouldn't have been so bad if he hadn't put the replacement glass in the door,' I said. 'At least we could have got at the dial then.'

'You know DP – nothing if not thorough. Would you like to see the palette clock now?'

'You don't mean . . .?'

'Yes! He repaired that as well.'

'No, Jason, I don't want to see it, really, I just don't want to see it.'

'Spoilsport. It's a completely new shape – looks like a shallow fruit bowl now.'

'Duncan, I wonder if I could ask you a favour?'

'Of course, Richard. What did you think of the clocks by the way? Pretty good job on the longcase I thought.'

'Yes, very solid repair.'

'Yes, that's what I thought. That clock won't fall apart in a hurry.'

'No, it certainly won't. The point is,' I persevered, 'I've got to go to a black tie dinner party and . . .'

'Ah, sorry to interrupt, Richard, but while I think of it, old Mrs Weinberg called while you were out.'

'Really, what did she want?'

'I think she's probably just getting a bit forgetful. She only wanted to confirm that we're not charging her commission on her items in the next sale. I said that was quite correct.' Duncan smiled benignly as he recounted the telephone conversation. I had to remind myself he was the same person who, just a few hours earlier, had wanted to know when we'd become a registered charity.

'Oh, good. The problem is,' I tried again, 'I've got to hire a DJ and all the kit and, quite honestly, I'm flat broke, and I wondered if you could lend me the hire fee until the end of the month?'

'My dear chap, why ever didn't you say? You don't need to hire one. I'll lend you one of mine.'

'One of yours?'

'Yes. I've got three or four different DJs. I'm sure one of them will fit the bill.'

'Er, well, it's very kind, Duncan,' I said. 'Are you sure they'll be the right size?'

'Absolutely. I'm a wee bit broader than you, I know, but there's nothing in it at all when it comes to height. No, I'm certain I can fix you up.'

I can't pretend I was as confident as Duncan about the similarity between our vital statistics, but I wasn't in any position to argue. It was agreed that he would bring in the full bib and tucker the following Monday for a fitting. As we wandered back into Gallery One, Jim Watson turned up.

'Hello,' Duncan greeted him, 'got something for us?'

'Only a complete van full.'

'Who's it from?'

'Your old friend, Mrs Weinberg,' Jim said. 'She phoned up in a great panic this morning saying how we'd got to get our biggest truck down to Langton right away. As it happened everything was booked out except the Luton Transit, and she nearly went spare about it not being big enough. I think she would have sent every stick of furniture she had if there'd been room.'

'What on earth's got into the old girl now?' I asked, turning to Duncan. 'She's never sent in a big load before.'

'Beats me,' he said, 'perhaps she's gone doolally.'

'Well, somebody has,' Jim went on, 'because she said the reason she was selling all this kit was because nice Mr Harton had said he wouldn't charge her any commission this sale.'

'What!'

'So I said, I think you'd better check that before I put all this gear on the van,' Jim went on, grinning. 'I got her to telephone, and would you believe it, nice Mr Parkes said that was quite right. So you tell me who's going doolally!'

161

Chapter 15

It was most unusual. We generally saw nothing of Anthony
Wilson from one sale to the next, yet here was his car parked
outside The Galleries at a quarter to nine on a Monday
morning. Even more curious, parked just behind it was an
incredibly battered old van. Like Mr Anthony's car, it was
empty, and there was only one place the former occupants
could be: inside The Auction Galleries. I drew into our
private car park behind the building and found Duncan's car
was already there as well. It seemed we had a full house, but
why?

The mystery was only enhanced by the scene awaiting me
inside The Galleries. Duncan, Anthony Wilson and two
other men were standing in Gallery Two, staring at a blank
wall and obviously discussing it at some length.

'I think this is the best place,' Duncan was saying.

'You may be right, you may be right,' Anthony Wilson
replied, 'but what do the experts think?'

The experts were a wonderfully unlikely pair. One of
them was stocky, but only a little over five feet in height,
with greying curly hair. His companion was tall and lanky
with unkempt blonde locks. Both were unshaven and wore
clothes that had seen better days.

'Oh, Oi don't t'ink dere's any problem at all, Mr Wilson.
Oi t'ink if dat's where you want it, den dat's where we'll put
it,' the smaller of the two experts said, confidently, in a
heavy Irish brogue. Then, turning to his partner, 'What do
you t'ink, Ray?'

'Oh, no trouble, Bernie, no trouble,' he replied without a
moment's hesitation.

The whole party turned as I walked up to join them.

162

'Ah, good morning, Richard,' Duncan said, 'just in time to give us the benefit of your opinion – where do you think the door should go?'

It was almost too good to be true. After two years of dithering it looked as though it was going to happen at last. We'd been desperately pressed for both office and storage space at The Galleries for years, but despite the fact that Anthony Wilson owned the empty building next door, he and Duncan had never been able to agree on what should be done to link the two properties. It wasn't a structural problem; the cottage leant itself to conversion and annexation. The obstruction was, as usual, financial. Anthony Wilson, as owner of the cottage, wanted, not unreasonably, The Auction Galleries to pay him rent for it. Duncan thought the suggested rent too high, and on top of that he wanted specific alterations made to the cottage before he'd even consider The Galleries renting it. Over the years, Anthony Wilson had got estimates from half a dozen different builders. Each time he decided it was far too expensive, and so the deadlock had continued. I couldn't be sure what it was that had so suddenly broken the log jam, but I had a fair suspicion it was something to do with Bernie and Ray. There was something about them which suggested their construction techniques would be less costly than normal builders.'

'I would have thought that was about the right place,' I said, in answer to Duncan's question.

'There it shall be then,' Anthony Wilson confirmed.

'Roight,' Bernie said, chalking a large 'X' on the wall, 'and we'll sort out de eventual layout as we go along den.'

'Fine, fine,' Anthony Wilson agreed.

'Er, haven't you got any plans for the conversion?' I asked, rather alarmed by the *laissez-faire* principles being employed.

Bernie and Ray smiled at one another, then at Anthony Wilson, then they all smiled condescendingly at me. 'Oi, don't t'ink we'll be needin' plans an' de loike for a liddle job loike dis one here, young man.' I'm sure he would have patted me on the head if he could have reached.

'No, no, my boy,' Anthony Wilson confirmed, 'it's the very fact that we're cutting out such unnecessary expenses that enables us to forge ahead with the project. That and the competitiveness of Mr Ryan's and Mr Rankin's quote.'

That confirmed my worst suspicions. Bernie Ryan and Ray Rankin were obviously a couple of cowboys, and the whole job was being done on the cheap. I should have guessed at first it was the only way it would get done.

'So we'll be startin' dis T'ursday afternoon, den,' Bernie confirmed to Mr Anthony and Duncan.

'And then there's the stage payments,' Ray Rankin reminded his partner.

'Dat's roight, Ray. I very nearly forgot – der's de matter of de first stage payment for de materials, Mr Wilson.'

'Yes, yes. What I've agreed is,' Anthony Wilson said, turning to Duncan. 'that I'll pay a third of the total now so they can get the materials; a third at the halfway stage; and the final third on completion of the work. You pay it out of the petty cash, old chap, and I'll settle up later.'

'Okay,' Duncan said, rather wearily, 'get me a hundred pounds from the petty cash please, Richard.'

After the other three had gone I explained to Duncan the serious doubts I harboured regarding both the professional qualifications of our builders, and the sanity of our senior partner.

'If they're only charging three hundred pounds they can't possibly do a decent job – and no plans!'

'Ours not to reason why, Richard.'

'Where did he find them, anyway?'

'Where do you think?' Duncan said. 'The locals' bar of The Devonshire Arms. Both fully qualified though. Ryan used to be a jockey, and Rankin was a navvy on the roads. Then they met up and became master builders.'

'But why have anything to do with it?' I asked, 'it's bound to be a disaster.'

'Exactly,' he said, tapping the side of his nose with his finger, 'and once we've got holes in the walls and the floors are up, Anthony will have to spend some money on a proper builder to sort it all out. Smart, eh?'

'Too clever by half,' I said, 'it's bound to go wrong.'

'Nonsense! You really can be the most appalling old woman sometimes, Richard.'

In all the excitement about the alterations, I'd forgotten to ask Duncan if he'd brought in the promised suit. In fact, he'd done better than that. He'd brought two, and one of them turned out to be a remarkably good fit. It was, perhaps, a trifle more generous in cut than it might have been, but it really wasn't bad. To complement the suit there was a dress shirt, a cummerbund, and a clip-on bow tie.

'I thought the clip-on was the best idea,' Duncan commented, 'unless you're used to tying the real thing they're enough to break your heart. I've used this one myself in emergencies before now. It just clips onto your shirt behind the top button – absolutely idiot-proof.'

I thanked Duncan profusely. At least I was going to look the part.

Our builders eventually arrived at three o'clock the following Thursday. There was very little evidence of materials; instead, a strong waft of booze seemed to follow them into the building. I glanced at the collection of tools they brought with them, and became even more confident we were heading for disaster. You can usually judge a workman by his tools, and on the strength of what I saw, Bernie and Ray would have been found guilty as charged. Everything they had was old, broken or rusty, and occasionally all three. However, despite their obvious lack of knowledge of even the most rudimentary building principles, or perhaps because of it, Bernie and Ray were compulsive viewing.

'Roight, Ray, let's have dat wall down,' Bernie Ryan proposed, handing his partner a club hammer and cold-chisel. 'Go at it, moy son!'

Jason and I were both too intrigued to do any work, so we seated ourselves on a refectory table in the middle of the gallery to watch the show.

'Oi'd move back a bit dere if Oi was you, gentleman – moy man's an animal once he get's goin'.'

'In that case, shouldn't you have some dust-sheets down?' I asked.

'Dust-sheets? Ah, dust-sheets – no, dat won't be necessary at all. He may be an animal, but he's terrible-well house-trained. Go at it, moy Ray!'

Ray went at it. The initial couple of blows sent plaster spraying in all directions, then very little else seemed to happen. After a dozen or so blows, Ray stopped and took a long, close look at the resistant brickwork.

'It's like bleedin' granite,' he said, eventually.

'Ah, sure, it can't be dat bad,' Bernie said, 'give me de hammer and chisel.'

Ray handed them over willingly, and Bernie Ryan set about the wall some eighteen inches lower than Ray's abortive effort. He did make more progress than Ray, but not a lot more.

'See what I mean?' Ray sniffed, as he rolled himself a cigarette. 'Just like bleedin' granite.'

'Sure, it's not as bad as dat, Ray. It jus' needs a little perseverance.'

'Yeah, well you can persevere 'ere, an' I'll see if I can make any more sense of it next door.'

'Good t'inkin', Ray. You try to belt your way t'rough from de udder soide.'

Jason and I watched spellbound as The Galleries vibrated to the rythmic thumping of steel on brick.

'You realise, of course,' Jason said, quietly, 'that if Ray is directly opposite Bernie on the other side of that wall, and he breaks through, the first brick he knocks out will land on Bernie's head.'

'It had crossed my mind,' I said.

'Do you think we should warn him?'

'Ah, Oi don't t'ink we should be interferin' wid professionals,' I said.

'You're probably right an' all an' all,' Jason agreed.

In the event, Bernard Ryan's skull was preserved intact, for it was the diminutive ex-jockey and not his lanky colleague who broke through first. He pushed the pieces of broken brick out of the way and peered through the small opening.

'Ray! Ray! Where are you, Ray?' Some sort of muffled reply came from the other side of the wall, then Bernie stepped back. 'Holy Mudder of God! Oi can see his feet! Ray's feet are level wid me head! How can dat be?' he appealed, turning to us.

166

'Perhaps he's hanged himself,' I suggested, 'he was looking pretty depressed when he went next door.'

'Could be doing handstands, I suppose,' Jason offered as an alternative.

'Oh, very droll, very droll indeed. What a pair of comedians. You should both be on de stage,' Bernie muttered, as he returned to his hole in the wall. 'Ray! Ray! Oi can see your feet, but where de hell's de rest of you?'

Another muffled reply came from the other side of the wall.

'Oh, dis is terrible,' Bernie said, turning to us again and shaking his head, 'der's foive foot difference between de floor levels. What de hell do we do now?'

'Put in a big step? I suggested.

Bernie and Ray went into immediate conference over the unforeseen structural problems confronting them. Then they confronted Duncan.

'De t'ing is,' Bernie began, 'we'll be needin' to put in de steps, an' we hadn't budgeted for de steps, d'you see?'

Duncan said he appreciated and sympathised with their problem.

'Ah, dat's good,' Bernie Ryan went on, obviously heartened by Duncan's response, 'so you'll be appreciatin' dat it'll be costin' a bit more now?'

'Oh, yes, I appreciate it,' Duncan said, 'but I doubt Mr Wilson will, and he's the man you've got to break the news to.'

'But we wouldn't be wantin' to worry him . . .' Bernie, protested.

'See you later,' Duncan said, as he held the street door open for them.

'But if you could jus' give him a liddle ring an' explain . . .'

'Bye, bye,' Duncan said, as Messrs Ryan and Rankin trudged miserably out to their van.

'And that will probably be the last we'll ever see of Bernie and Ray,' he said, as they drove off. 'Pity, really, they haven't done as much damage as I'd hoped. I thought they'd last longer than one afternoon.'

*

It was almost a quarter to eight when I drove past the little lodge cottage and up the drive to the Cartwright's house. Antonia answered the door. She wore a rich burgundy velvet gown with a plunging neckline. Her hair was up, and a pair of ruby and diamond earrings and a matching pendant sparkled in the half-light. I was speechless.

'Hello, Richard,' she said, giving me an unexpected kiss on the cheek, 'I'm really glad you could come. Come through and meet the others.'

Shooting a sideways glance at the big mirror in the hall, I checked my appearance. I was quite surprised to find that I really didn't look too bad at all.

My fellow diners were on the terrace taking advantage of the warm evening and the magnificent view. There were only six of us altogether. I said hello to Hugh Cartwright, then Antonia introduced me to the other guests: her aunt, Helen, and two old friends, Giles and Belinda Morris. They were brother and sister. She was pretty and bubbly whilst he was tall, goodlooking and self assured. He had that slightly scruffy look about him that suggested he went to so many black tie functions he didn't trouble too much about them any more. Rather more importantly, he seemed to have an interest in Antonia which was not entirely platonic, remaining close by her as I chatted with her aunt. On several occasions, Antonia's laugh rang out loudly – Giles was obviously entertaining company. I immediately developed a deep-rooted dislike of the man.

'Why don't you work in London?' he asked, as we sat around the table, waiting for the first course.

'I don't really think I'd like it,' I said. 'I prefer the country.'

'I would have thought that if you really wanted to get on you'd have to get a job with Sotheby's or Christie's. An old friend of mine's with Christie's, he says it's the only company to be with. How is it the two companies are supposed to differ? You know – there's some amusing little thing they say about them.'

'Christie's are gentlemen trying to be auctioneers,' I said, 'and Sotheby's are auctioneers trying to be gentlemen.'

'Yes, that's it. Well, which are you, Richard – an auctioneer or a gentleman?'

'Leave him alone, Giles,' Belinda intervened as she and Antonia came in with the food, 'you really are a bully sometimes.'

'Just a bit of fun,' he said, smiling. 'You don't mind do you, Richard?'

'No, I don't mind.'

'Oh, delicious,' Antonia's aunt said, changing the subject as Giles and I eyed each other coldly, 'pasta – my favourite starter.'

'Just as well,' Antonia replied, 'it's an all Italian evening this evening. Help yourselves to parmesan.'

As the small bowl of finely grated cheese was passed around, Giles renewed his probing. 'Where were you at school, Richard?' he asked. 'I can't quite place your accent.'

'Giles!' Antonia said. 'Don't be so rude.'

'A local grammar school,' I replied.

'Oh, never mind,' Giles said, smiling even more sweetly, 'I understand some of them were really quite good – as far as state schools go, that is.'

'More wine, Richard,' Hugh Cartwright asked, indicating I should help myself.

'Do you hunt or shoot?' Giles continued his interrogation.

'No.'

'Oh, I say, you're not anti blood sports are you?'

'No, it's just that I don't ride and I don't particularly enjoy killing things, but rest assured, Giles, should any pheasant ever loose off a couple of barrels at me, I won't hesitate to shoot back.'

A modest ripple of mirth greeted my comment, and I had just noticed that Giles hadn't joined in when, quite suddenly, he collapsed in hysterical laughter. In a moment everybody else was reduced to a smiliar condition. It was too good an audience reaction for what I'd said – the joke had been all right, but not that good. No, something else had happened, but what was it? It wasn't until Antonia, gasping for breath, pointed at my plate, that I looked down and saw my bow tie sitting squarely in my pasta. The wretched thing had come unclipped and must have spiralled down like a wounded butterfly.

'I say, old boy,' Giles managed to splutter between

guffaws as he wiped his eyes, 'you really must tell us – is that some sort of grammar school ritual?'

'I must say, old chap,' Hugh Cartwright said, as he riffled through the chest of drawers in his dressing room, 'you don't seem to have a lot of luck with neckwear. Perhaps you should become a member of the cloth, you wouldn't have to worry about it then. Ah, this one will do the trick.' He produced another bow tie. 'I'll tie it, then we can just adjust the neckband to fit you,' he said.

A few minutes later I was fully dressed again.

'You know you've got the beating of that idiot Morris, don't you, Richard?' he said, as we went to go back downstairs.

'I'm sorry?' I said.

'The boy's a fool and a snob. It's a pity because Belinda is jolly good news, but he really is the most appalling prat.'

'Yes . . . I mean . . . well, I mean I wouldn't want to cause any trouble,' I protested, 'I'm a guest of Antonia's and so is he . . .'

'Take my word for it, young man, nobody would be more delighted to see Giles put in his place than Antonia – other then me that is.'

'But I assumed they were close friends,' I said.

'If you take no other word of advice, Richard,' he said, when we reached the bottom of the stairs, 'take this one: never assume anything about women, and that applies double-strength for my daughter. Now get back in there and sort him out.'

I really didn't know what to make of Hugh Cartwright's prompting to 'sort out' Giles. I watched Giles and Antonia throughout the rest of the candlelit meal, and I failed to spot any sign of animosity between them. If anything, she seemed to hang on his every word. It was very confusing.

'And what are you doing with yourself these days, Giles?' Hugh Cartwright asked as Antonia dispensed the coffee. 'Still in advertising?'

'Yes, Sir, but I'm thinking of going into the City.'

'Really? As what?'

'A stockbroker. Father's sorting out something for me.'

'Just what the country needs,' I said, 'another stock-broker.' I'd been thinking out loud rather than trying to upset Giles, but it didn't matter, the result was the same.

'What do you mean by that?' he snapped, evidently very upset. 'Come on, what do you mean?'

'It's just that sometimes I feel as though the whole country's being taken over by lawyers, accountants and stockbrokers.'

'So what if it is, at least they know how to make money.'

'No, what they know about is pushing around other people's money while taking a slice of it themselves. They don't actually *make* anything.'

'Christ! That's rich coming from an auctioneer!' Giles said, snatching up the sugar bowl.

'Oh, I know I'm a middle man too,' I replied, 'and it concerns me. That's the whole point – it doesn't worry you one bit, does it, Giles?'

'No it doesn't,' he said, spooning half the contents of the sugar bowl into his cup as he glared at me, 'and why should it, pray?'

'Because, one day we're going to wake up and we're going to find there's not a single person left in the country who actually, physically, makes anything anymore. Whose money will you push around then, Giles?'

'Who cares!' Giles said, stirring away furiously at his coffee. 'It won't upset me if every factory in the country closes.'

'Really? You already seem a bit upset.'

'Upset? What do you mean – upset?' he sneered at me across the table. 'What makes you think I'm upset?'

'Oh, nothing really. It's only that you've just stirred three heaped teaspoons of grated parmesan cheese into your coffee – but, perhaps it's just some sort of public school ritual?'

Giles failed to make a recovery from the cheese in the coffee incident. It quickly became evident that his temperament was not suited to being the butt of a joke. He was accustomed to laughing at others, not to being laughed at. He stayed for about half an hour after the meal and then left, saying he had to be in London early the next morning for an important meeting. His sister was dragged off with him, and I thought the time had probably come for me to make my own excuses. However, Hugh Cartwright had other ideas.

'Why don't you take the Armagnac down to your cottage, darling,' he said to his daughter, 'then you and Richard can leave us two old codgers to vegetate.'

'What about clearing up?'

'Tomorrow – go on, hop it!'

I drove the car back down the gravel drive to the cottage. Antonia walked ahead with the Armagnac, and was unlocking the door by the time I'd parked the car on the grass opposite the little lodge. The front door opened straight into a small, cosy sitting room with a large brick fireplace. The ceiling was low and oak beamed. A small dining table and four chairs stood in a square window bay.

'It's very compact,' she said, 'just this room, a bedroom, a minute bathroom and an even smaller kitchen.' She took two brandy balloons from a cupboard near the fireplace and poured the Armagnac. 'Dad and I get on very well really,' she said, handing me one of the glasses, 'but this arrangement allows us both a little more personal space. Cheers!'

'Cheers!'

As she sipped her drink, she started to laugh.

'I trust my bow tie hasn't fallen off again,' I said.

'No, you can relax, it's still firmly in place. I was just thinking of Giles and the parmesan – I did enjoy it so, he was so angry.'

'He did seem to suffer a bit of a sense of humour failure,' I remarked.

'Oh yes, Giles is not accustomed to being laughed at. I don't think he'll ever forgive you. Do you mind?'

'Not really. I'm not likely to bump into him again in a hurry. I don't move in quite the same social circles as Giles Morris, you know.'

'Well, you could always change that if you wanted to.'

I sat and looked at Antonia as she smiled at me from her chair on the opposite side of the fireplace. Her eyes were steady and fixed on mine.

'I'd very much like to see you again, Antonia,' I said, almost without realising I was saying it.

'When?'

'Soon.'

'How soon?'

'Any night but tomorrow.'

'Fine, what about tomorrow?' she said.

'I'll pick you up at eight.'

As I got into my car, Antonia stood in the doorway of her cottage, silhouetted against the lights of the sitting room.

'Promise me something, Richard,' she called out.

'What?'

'That we'll go somewhere tomorrow where you don't have to wear a tie.'

'It's a deal,' I said.

Chapter 16

Duncan was wrong about Bernie and Ray. Along with miscellaneous pieces of timber, they were waiting outside The Galleries when I arrived the following morning.

'Negotiated a new price then?' I asked as I opened up the place.

'Oh, yes. No trouble at all,' Bernie replied, as confident as ever, 'Mr Wilson's a very understandin' man, he is. It's a quality job he's after an' he's prepared to pay de goin' rate for it.'

I made no comment and went to put the kettle on.

By ten past nine, Bernie and Ray were at it again with their hammers and chisels, filling Gallery Two with noise and brickdust. I retreated to my office to have a look at the morning's post.

'How long's this dreadful racket going on?' Kate asked, as the steady hammering shook the building from end to end.

'Until the place falls down I would think,' I said.

The telephone rang, and Kate, handicapped by the din, answered it with some difficulty. 'I think it's Bob Parker,' she said, 'but I can hardly hear him above this noise.'

Bob was a regular contact who was with a local firm of estate agents. He put quite a lot of work my way and had a good eye, so his calls were seldom a waste of time.

'Hello, Bob,' I bawled.

'Hello, Richard. I've got a job for you which I think you'll like. The only thing is it's a bit of a rush.'

'What, where and when?'

'A complete contents, Burwood and sometime today.'

'It shall be done,' I said. 'I need an excuse to get out of here.'

'Yes,' Bob said, 'what is all that noise? Are they knocking the place down at last?'

'Don't joke, Bob, you may be more right than you could ever imagine.'

I arranged to meet him for a beer and a sandwich in The White Hart at Burwood at one o'clock, then I decided the best thing to do until then was to catalogue some of the silver for the next sale. The sole advantage of that job being that Kate and I could station ourselves in the strongroom – the only place in the building that approached being soundproof. It did have its disadvantages, however. To begin with, whatever the weather, it was cold damp and smelled, but even having taken those faults into consideration, we still decided it was the best place to be.

'I'll do a couple more lots, then I'd better get going,' I said shortly after midday.

It had been quite a productive morning and we'd managed to catalogue the bulk of the pieces which had accumulated over the previous weeks.

'A set of six George III silver fiddle and thread pattern forks – London – 1792 – maker . . .' My dictation was halted by an explosion which could be heard even in our inner sanctum. At the same time we were plunged into inky blackness. Kate shrieked and grabbed hold of my arm in the darkness.

'What's happened?' she asked.

'At a guess,' I said, 'Messrs Ryan and Rankin have just severed a mains cable, and if they did it with a hammer and cold chisel, it's quite likely their partnership's been dissolved as well.'

I groped my way to the door and heaved it open. There was an unpleasant, tangy, burning smell in the air. Hurrying through to Gallery Two, I could hear Margaret's voice asking repeatedly if somebody was all right.

'Ah, Jeez, but sure Oi'm all right. It was just a little tickle Oi keep tellin' you.'

Bernie Ryan was sitting amidst a jumble of upturned furniture some twenty feet from where he'd been bashing away at the wall. He picked himself up, still clutching his hammer, and looked around him. 'Where's me chisel? Can none of you see me chisel?' he demanded.

Jason, who, along with Margaret, had been one of the first on the scene, fished underneath a nearby table and produced what remained of Bernie's cold chisel. The cutting end had been melted and split by the voltage that had gone through it.

'Jeez!' Bernie said again, as he looked at the twisted piece of metal and, for the first time, appeared to realise just how close he'd come to being fried to a crisp. 'It was a good job Oi was wearin' me wellies!'

He was probably right, because even with that basic, and in a fine art auction rooms, rather incongruous form of insulation, Bernie had been blown halfway across the gallery. If he'd been wearing his hobnails, we could have just swept his remains under the carpet. As I left for Burwood, Bernie and Ray were locked in animated argument about who should break the news to Anthony Wilson; where the door should go now; and how they were going to pay for the electrician.

At The White Hart, Bob Parker was waiting for me at a table in the garden. Over a pint of bitter and a ploughman's lunch, he told me about the job in hand. The house was a tumbledown Victorian villa called The Limes and our client – Andrew Williams – was the nephew of the owner, Miss Amelia Morant.

'She's in her eighties and just can't cope anymore,' Bob said, 'so Mr Williams has got power of attorney and he's planning to sell everything to pay for her to go into a home.'

I always felt that 'going into a home' was often little better than a euphemism for being buried alive. As a result, I held strongly to the view that it was generally much better for a person to be allowed to live or die in his or her own home, almost regardless of how squalid the home might have become.

'Yes, Richard, I know all about your views on putting people into homes,' Bob said, finishing off his cheese and pickle, 'but when you see The Limes I think even you'll agree the nephew's right.'

I was less convinced. Quite a lot of our business resulted

from this sort of situation and I'd seldom heard the evacuee say what a wonderful idea it was.

I left my car at The White Hart and travelled with Bob Parker the mile and a bit to The Limes.

'I'm warning you, Richard, you've never seen anything like this place. It's like . . . like . . .' he seemed temporarily stumped for a suitable comparison, 'like that woman in *Great Expectations*.'

'Miss Havisham,' I said.

'Yes, just like that. You'll see.'

Bob went on to tell me Amelia Morant had lived in the sizeable house with her sister for many years. The place had been built by their father, a prosperous local doctor, sometime in the 1870s. The two unmarried daughters had moved in there when their father had died and the family home was sold.

'They must have been quite well off when they started,' he continued, 'but any capital they had has long since been swallowed by inflation.'

'When did the sister die?'

'Sister Annie fell off the trolley just over three years ago,' he said, 'and Amelia started to become very reclusive after that. Now she never sets foot outside the house.'

'What does she do for food?'

'WRVS Meals-on-Wheels, and the vicar's wife does a bit of shopping for her. It was the vicar who contacted the nephew.'

The Limes was a very ordinary looking house. It stood back from the road and was approachable only on foot. A flight of a dozen worn brick steps led up the steep grassy bank from the lane to the dilapidated garden gate. The house had a slate roof with a row of three dormer windows set into it. The rendered walls were covered in lichen, and in places the rendering had come away to expose raw patches of crumbling, frost-damaged brickwork. There didn't seem to be a lick of paint on any of the rotting window sashes, and the curtains were drawn in every window at the front of the house.

A narrow cinder path cut its way through the garden jungle where overgrown ramblers and roses fought with the brambles for supremacy. A few woody old apple trees suggested where an orchard might once have been, and the bleached skeleton of a greenhouse rose out of the undergrowth in one corner.

'We have to use the back door as you can see,' Bob said, pointing to the front porch where a large buddleia was flourishing. Having contrived to root itself between the paving bricks, it had obviously been permitted to grow there without hindrance so that its twisted branches now completely obstructed the door. We made our way around the side of the house to the back door where my companion paused for a moment before knocking.

'I'll introduce you, but don't expect any reponse. I've been here three times now and she's only ever spoken to me once – then she called me Mr Dobson.'

'Who's Mr Dobson?' I asked.

'The last vicar of Burwood but one,' Bob said, as he tapped smartly on the door.

Without waiting for an answer he opened the door and we stepped into a little scullery. It was equipped only with some old painted cupboards which reached from the brick-paved floor to the ceiling, and an earthenware shallow sink serviced by a single cold-water tap. Even on that warm summer afternoon it was cold, damp and musty.

Bob led on, through a doorway draped with a heavy brown curtain which appeared to have been made from an old blanket. I followed him into a kitchen-cum-parlour where a fire burned in an old-fashioned range, and there was a heavy residual smell of mince, cabbage and paraffin. A dark green painted wooden dado ran around the room. Above that, the walls were covered in an embossed brown wallpaper and hung with a number of Victorian engravings in heavy gilt frames. The ceiling was greasy and blackened, presumably by the two oil lamps that stood, extinguished, on the marble-topped sideboard. A dark, stained pine table, covered with a very old oil cloth, stood in the middle of the room with three kitchen chairs arranged around it. A plaid rug was draped over a Victorian chaise-longue standing against the wall opposite the window, while a matching armchair was set to one side of the range. In the armchair sat the frail form of Miss Amelia Morant. She was tiny, with thin straight white hair, and hollow cheeks that betrayed the absence of not only her own teeth but also her dentures. Her eyes were steel grey, clear but vacant, and fixed on some non-existent point a few feet in front of her. The only real sign of life was in her hands. They fiddled continually with an embroidered handkerchief which lay on her lap.

'Good afternoon, Miss Amelia,' Bob said in the quiet, soothing tone he reserved for his elderly clients, 'this is Mr Harton who I told you about.'

Miss Amelia gave no flicker of recognition, only continuing to stare straight ahead, twisting and untwisting her handkerchief.

'Fine,' Bob went on, 'I'll just show him round then.'

Still no response.

He signalled for me to follow him, and led the way out of the parlour into a long hallway.

'See what I mean?' he said, referring to Miss Morant, once he'd closed the door to the parlour, 'lights are on but nobody's at home I'm afraid.'

The hallway was thick with dust and the floor bore the impression of two sets of footprints.

'It doesn't look as though anybody has set foot in here for years,' I said.

'Until Andrew Williams and I walked round the place yesterday, they hadn't. Where do you want to start – upstairs as usual?' Bob Parker was used to how I worked. I always started at the top of a house and worked my way down. The rooms on each floor were taken clockwise – first door on the left, second on the left and so on. Inside each room, I inspected everything by again working my way around clockwise. It was as good a way as any to avoid missing things, although I did once omit a huge chandelier from a valuation because it was hanging smack in the centre of the ceiling. Using my method I circumnavigated it with ease, and left the room without giving it a thought. However, allowing for the occasional aberration, the system generally proved pretty well fool-proof.

As we climbed the two main flights of stairs, drawing back the dusty, brittle old curtains as we went, the fabric of the building became noticeably shabbier the higher we got. On the second floor, most of the wallpaper hung off the walls in strips or lay amongst the dirt on the floor.

'You know this is the original paper,' I said, looking at it.

'You ain't seen nothing yet,' Bob replied.

We climbed the final narrow staircase to the attic and servants' quarters, where three identical doors faced us. Like every other door we'd passed on the way up, each lock held a rusting key.

Bob Parker turned the key in the first door, pushed it open and stood back for me to go in. I crossed the threshold and in one stride went back in time a hundred years. The room was furnished as it would have been when the house was built. There was a brass and iron bedstead and a suite of pine furniture, the latter, as the fashion of the day had demanded, was 'grained' to look like oak. With wardrobe, washstand and all the other bits and pieces, the room had everything a cook or housekeeper in the last quarter of the nineteenth century would have expected.

If the timeless quality of the room was remarkable, so was its condition – it was dreadful. Not only was everything covered in thick grey dust, the cane seats of the side chairs hung in tatters, and the upholstery and springs of the solitary armchair lay on the floor where they had fallen when the fabric rotted and the tacks rusted away. The rusty spring mesh of the bedstead had also collapsed to the floor along with the remains of the hair-stuffed mattress, and the petrified fibres of the old red and blue Turkey rug crackled under my feet as I walked.

'Tell me the whole house isn't like this, Bob,' I pleaded.

'The whole house isn't like this, Richard – some of it's worse.'

'Oh wonderful!'

The problem was that the two old ladies had slowly retreated through the house, closing off rooms as they went and never giving them a second thought. The top floor had been surrendered along with the servants, then they'd just worked their way down from there.

'As far as the nephew and I could make out,' Bob explained, 'the two of them started using just the parlour about two years before Annie died. They slept, washed and ate there, and never set foot in the rest of the house again. The only other part of the property in use is the outside privy which, mercifully for you, you don't need to see.'

The condition of the furniture in the other two attic rooms was much the same as in the first, and as we went back downstairs to the second floor I wondered what we'd find next.

'Is it going to be worth anything?' Bob asked. 'Or is it just bonfire time?'

'Oh, it's worth something,' I said, 'just don't ask me how much.'

The second floor turned out to be another collection of bedrooms and an antique bathroom. The bedrooms were as comprehensively furnished as the attic rooms, but this time with substantial mahogany suites rather than the cheap pine that had been considered adequate for the servants. It was all in poor condition but basically sound, and as such was saleable though pretty unexciting.

There were only two doors awaiting us on the first floor. My companion stopped outside the first and turned to me.

'Lord knows what you're going to make of this one, Richard,' he said, 'it's the drawing room. Either it will make the whole job worthwhile or we'll have to have a bonfire after all.' He turned the key, opened the door and led the way into the darkened room.

It wasn't until he'd drawn back the faded, balding, blue velvet curtains that I could see what he meant. The room was elegantly proportioned and, beneath its shroud of thick grey dust, equally elegantly furnished. The seat furniture dated from the 1850s and 1860s when sweeping lines and delicate cabriole legs had been the vogue. The tables, bookcases and side cabinets all appeared to be of the highest quality. A large gilt-framed overmantel mirror above the ornate marble fireplace dominated the room.

It was different to all the other rooms I'd seen, and the thing that set it apart was that it was still fully furnished. The bedrooms had had all their original furniture all right, but that was all. There had been no ornaments, no knick-knacks, none of the bits and pieces that human beings accumulate in the course of living their everyday lives. The drawing room appeared to be intact. It was land-locked Burwood's version of the *Marie Celeste*. Yellowing invitations still leaned against the tarnished glass of the overmantel; vases of flowers, the contents looking more like faded paper copies than nature's originals, dotted the room; a book, complete with bookmark, lay on one of the tables, and ashes from the last fire were still heaped beneath the grate. Bob was right, it was straight out of *Great Expectations*.

'What do you think?' he asked.

'I think we have a problem,' I replied.

'I know,' he said. 'I picked up that little chair the other day.' The chair he referred to was part of a lovely nine-piece salon suite which formed the nucleus of the drawing room's furnishings. There was an impressive settee, two armchairs and six matching side chairs. Their elaborately carved and scrolled frames were all made of walnut, and that was the problem.

'It just came off in my hand,' Bob said, as he showed me the six inch length that had broken away from the middle of the chair's top rail. It was hardly surprising. All that remained of the wood was a fine honeycomb of thousands and thousands of tiny holes – it was riddled with worm.

Woodworm loves walnut. Whereas it will usually turn up its mandibles at mahogany or rosewood, it can rarely resist the temptation of walnut. It had certainly succumbed to the tempting juicy morsels on offer in the drawing room at the The Limes; the salon suite was little more than an empty shell.

'The rest of the stuff doesn't look too bad,' Bob went on, 'but the chairs and settee are just crumbling to dust. Why is that? Why's it just them?'

I explained the problem was that the seat furniture was made from solid walnut, the other furniture was just veneered.

'It's all good quality stuff,' I said, 'so most of it's probably walnut veneer on an oak carcass. Oak's too hard for the common furniture beetle, so the veneered things get left alone.'

He went to a small veneered display cabinet that was clearly badly infested. 'What about that then?' he asked.

'Pine carcass, I expect,' I said, 'though they don't really like pine, it's too resinous – they prefer beech.'

'I'll try to remember that next time I have a couple of them coming to lunch,' he muttered as he surveyed the damage.

Both the morning room and the dining room yielded up more substantial, solid Victorian mahogany. There was no doubt the best thing in the house was the devastated nine-piece suite, the only question was whether it was still worth anything anymore. 'The answer is, Bob,' I said, 'I just don't know. I know they can pump wormed timber full of artificial resin to give it strength again, but it must be very expensive. I don't know if anybody will want to take the risk. I don't even know if we can get it all back to The Galleries without having it crumble to dust.'

'Give it a try, Richard,' he pressed, 'the poor old biddy needs every penny she can get.'

The poor old biddy was still sitting in her chair fumbling with her handkerchief when we re-entered the parlour. She neither turned nor looked up. She just continued to behave as though we weren't there.

'Mr Harton and I will be off now, Miss Morant,' Bob cooed. 'He'll be making all the arrangements to sell everything, won't you, Richard?'

'Yes, I will, Bob,' I said, unconciously dropping into idiot-speak.

'And he thinks it's all going to sell very well and make you lots and lots of money,' he went on.

'Yes,' I took up the baton again, 'I'm sure that once it's all over you'll wonder why you didn't do it before.'

As before there was no response from Amelia Morant. We were halfway through the scullery door before she spoke. Even then she didn't redirect her gaze as she uttered the simple but expressive two word response to all we had said.

'Sod off!' she snapped.

'Have you ever had a client tell you to do that before?' Bob asked as we made our way back down the narrow garden path.

'Not before I'd actually told them what I thought their things were worth,' I said.

To this day I still don't know if Miss Morant's comment was

really directed at Bob Parker and me or whether it was just random words plucked from the depths of her blank, insulated mind. I never saw her again as she was shipped into the nursing home within a couple of days of my visit. Whatever the truth, I prefer to think that, for a split second, the confused clouds had cleared and the real Amelia Morant had spoken. It was certainly a perfectly reasonable reply to the rubbish we had been speaking.

The Galleries was still without power when I arrived back, and Duncan and Bernie were having a heated conversation about its absence.

'Oi would t'ink de electrician would be along any toime now,' Bernie said with all the authority he could muster.

'Mr Ryan,' Duncan said, rather menacingly, 'I don't really care what you t'ink, I just want the power on, and I want it on *now*!'

'Well, Jeez, aren't Oi doin' me best for you? Aren't Oi goin' to pay for de work out me own pocket? Aren't Oi de one what's arrangin' it all?'

'Yes, you are, and the reason you are, in case it's slipped your mind, is because you're the one that cut the power off in the first bloody place!'

Bernie Ryan gave Duncan a hurt look, as though the mention of the incident was some sort of dreadful social gaffe.

'Well, Oi haff to say dat Oi'm terrible disappointed in you, Mr Parkes.'

Duncan stooped down so that his face was level with the ex-jockey's. 'Not half as disappointed as I am with you,' he said, his teeth showing in a threatening smile. 'In fact, I'm so disappointed with you that I'm only going to give you until five o'clock to get the electricity on and this mess cleared up, or as far as this job is concerned, you are finished.'

They stood glaring at one another for a few minutes, then the street door behind me opened and a man in overalls sauntered in.

'This the place with no power then?' he asked.

'Der now!' Bernie said, his face lighting up. 'Didn't Oi say he'd be here any toime?'

Despite the fact that it was still a bright, sunny afternoon outside, twilight came early in some parts of Wilson's

184

Auction Galleries. By half past four, Duncan and I were peering at each other through the gloom as we went through the monthly accounts in my office.

'This reminds me of the miners' strike,' he said, I knew what he meant.

When Ted Heath brought in the three-day week in response to the falling coal stocks, we like everybody else were told when we'd be on and off power. Armed with as many gas and paraffin lamps as we could lay our hands on, we determined to battle on; and battle on we did. To start with, we planned it so we could do all the cataloguing during the hours when we had electricity. It was a good idea in theory but a dismal failure in practice. Constant interruptions wrecked our carefully plotted schedules and resulted in our spending as much time trying to identify things in the dark as we ever did in the hours of government approved light. The identification of silver hallmarks was the greatest lottery of all, especially when it came to Gothic date letters.

'1762,' Duncan said, on one typical occasion, as he dictated a description.

I took the piece from him and glanced at the date letter. 'It's 1769,' I said, 'it's an "O" not a "G".'

'Are you sure?' Duncan asked. 'I was certain it was a "G".'

'Certain – it's an "O".'

'Well, your eyes are better than mine – make that 1769 then, Margaret.'

Margaret duly obliterated the first date and typed in the second.

'May I see it?' Jason asked.

I handed him the piece. He angled it to catch the flickering gaslight and stared at it from a range of about three inches.

'It's a "Q",' he said.

Duncan and I both protested and explained to Jason he was talking nonsense. Then we looked at the item again.

'He could be right, you know,' Duncan said, handing it over to me.

'I suppose so,' I replied rather reluctantly, as I examined it a second time. 'Here, Margaret, what do you think?'

She took a long look at it, then looked up at the three of us. '1760,' she said, confidently, 'it's an "E".'

The other problem was the ambient temperature. As I've mentioned before, it was never particularly friendly, but during the three-day week it was positively hostile. Although there were gas heaters in each gallery, they were all antiquated and desperately inefficient. We had long relied on electric heaters as a back-up and booster to the gas ones. We went for days without taking off our overcoats, and Margaret wore mittens the whole time.

View days were a security nightmare. We had no choice but to rely on the dim, wavering light of gas lamps and candles to enable us to spot our known, regular, sticky-fingered deviants at work. As it was, we only lost one thing during the whole period, although that was particularly annoying because it was a nice piece – a George II silver salver about six inches in diameter. It was stolen from under Jason's nose while the thief's companion created a diversion by knocking over a piece of furniture at the other end of the gallery. Duncan deduced the thief had slid the salver down the front of his trousers in the split second available. Duncan was so convinced about his theory that he was going through an action replay when the lights came back on again. As a result, at least one lady viewer left The Galleries rather shocked and perplexed, having witnessed Duncan produce, with a flourish, a piece of Georgian silver from his Y-fronts.

I was brought back to the present by the neon tube in my office suddenly flickering back to life.

'What's the time?' I asked.

'Five minutes to five,' Duncan replied, looking at his watch, 'the luck of the Irish!'

Bernie Ryan's luck held out. Against all the odds, he and Ray actually finished the job. The standard of construction was generally appalling and the level of finish was worse, but somehow it all hung together and it did only cost Anthony Wilson a few hundred pounds. Duncan had been outsmarted again.

Bernie and Ray weren't the only lucky ones that month. Miss Amelia Morant didn't do too badly either, although I doubt she ever knew it. To start with, Watson's managed, somehow, to transport the salon suite to The Galleries without the whole thing falling apart. I'd certainly harboured serious doubts about their ability to do so, and Arthur Watson had done nothing to allay my concern when he'd arrived at The Limes.

'Cor blimey, Dicky,' he'd bellowed, 'you don't want us, you want bleedin' livestock carriers, boy. I tell you what, if you took a little time, you could train that lot to walk to Kington on its own!'

I was quite prepared for the suite to disintegrate completely but it just didn't happen. Throughout the two view days I winced every time anyone touched it. Bits broke off it, small piles of honey coloured dust accumulated around and under it, but still, in the main, it held together.

It was like trying to nurse a patient with a terminal illness and then having him recover – and what a recovery. When Duncan brought down the hammer at one thousand three hundred pounds there was a stunned silence in the room, which was followed immediately by a great murmur of disbelief. I know thirteen hundred pounds doesn't sound much now, but if you consider The Limes itself sold for only eighteen thousand pounds, it puts the price into perspective. It was a lot of money for a woodworm colony.

Chapter 17

'What are you thinking?' Antonia asked as we sat over our cappuccino coffee.

I hesitated.

'Come on,' she said, 'and it must be the truth.'

'I was thinking that you could snap your fingers and get any man of your choice, and yet here you are with me in a cheap little trattoria in Langton.'

She smiled and spooned up the froth from her cup. 'If it were true that I could get any man of my choice,' she said, 'why should it be so strange for me to choose you?'

'Well, I wouldn't have thought a penniless auctioneer compared too favourably with the Giles Morrises of this world.'

'Oh, so it's Giles that's worrying you, is it?'

'Not really, but . . .'

'And you have the nerve to suggest I'm only interested in men with money.'

'I didn't mean . . .'

'Oh, yes you did,' she said, reaching out at the same time to touch my hand. 'But you're wrong, Richard. I like you for what you are. It doesn't matter to me whether you have money or not. Can you believe that?'

'Yes.'

'Once more with conviction, please.'

'Yes,' I laughed.

'Wow, a smile! May I have some more coffee please?' I called the waiter and ordered some. 'If you're really worried about Giles Morris,' she went on, 'I can assure you that he is an arrogant, thick, self-opinionated snob. Okay?'

'Okay. It's just that I got the impression that you and that arrogant, self-opinionated snob were rather close.'

'We were, once.'

'Once?'

'Yes, once. Once I thought I was deeply in love with Giles. He was handsome, charming and fun – all the things a girl could ask for.'

'What happened?'

'I found out, when you scratched Giles's surface, there was something rather unpleasant underneath. All the charm and fun is just a veneer, and a thin one at that. Anyway, you should know all about veneers, you're a furniture specialist.'

I nodded. 'And was he in love with you?' I asked.

'Good Lord, no! Giles was already deeply in love with somebody else.'

'Who?'

'Why, Giles, of course. He's passionately devoted to himself. He just doesn't have room for anyone else in his life. Oh, he made a great fuss when I left him, but that was only injured pride. It was just that I'd walked out on him before he could kick me out, that was all.'

The waiter arrived with the coffee, and we sat in silence until he'd gone.

'When did all this happen?' I asked.

'It was just over three years ago that Giles and I shacked-up together. I was only nineteen, Mummy had just died, Daddy and I were fighting like cat and dog – it was the worst time of my life.'

'Was your mother's death sudden?'

'Very. She was only forty-one. She'd complained of feeling tired so Dad persuaded her to go to the doctor. He gave her a blood test, told her she'd got leukaemia, and five weeks later she was dead. I hadn't realised how quick it was going to be. I didn't even say goodbye properly.' I squeezed her hand and she looked up and smiled.

'So then you moved out of The Rectory?' I said.

'Yes, instead of Dad and me being drawn together, we argued even more, and there was Giles waiting in the wings with his flat in London. I'd known him for years because Belinda's my oldest and best friend so, in the end, I packed my bags one weekend and Giles collected me. I was so selfish. Dad was shattered.'

'Perhaps it was for the best really.'

'Yes, I think it probably was as things turned out. I stuck it with Giles for nearly two years, until he started knocking me about, then I came home. It was as if Daddy and I were different people. I suppose we were. Certainly we get on so well no it's difficult to remember what it used to be like.'

'So you've been living back at The Rectory for a year?'

'Yes, Richard. And yes, Richard, you are the first man I've been out with since the dreadful Giles.'

'I'm flattered.'

'So you should be,' she said, 'I'm an amazing catch.'

As we walked back to the car, she slid her arm through mine and leaned against me.

'I think I may become horribly fond of you, Richard.'

'Good, because I think I'm already horribly fond of you.'

'I'm glad,' she said, 'let's go home.'

Chapter 18

I'd never been to Highfield House before, although I'd met its gruff owner, Colonel Sidney Fairbrother, on several occasions at The Galleries. Highfield was a solid and fairly substantial Victorian house standing in a large garden just outside the little village of Fernley. It was an unusually peaceful oasis where, waiting for a moment on the doorstep, I realised the only sound I could hear was birdsong.

It all changed when I pressed the doorbell. Pandemonium broke out on the other side of the front door.

'Hell and damnation!' It was the colonel's voice.

'The colonel's not in!' A woman's voice this time.

'It's that damned vicar again!' said the colonel.

'The colonel's not in!' insisted the woman.

'Hell and damnation!'

'The colonel's not in!'

I wondered what the odds were on Colonel Fairbrother and his housekeeper both having gone insane overnight. It was the only explanation I could think of off-hand.

'The colonel's not in!'

'Answer the phone!'

'Shut up you two – be quiet.'

The door was thrown open and the formidable figure of Colonel Fairbrother stood before me. He was short and square, ruddy faced, with silver-grey hair, bushy eyebrows and moustache en suite. He wore an Hawaian shirt so loud it was deafening, and a pair of khaki shorts that reached down to his knees. On his feet were a pair of espadrilles.

'Ah, Harton, good of you to come,' he said.

'The colonel's not in!'

'Hell and damnation!'

'Shut up you two, damn you!' the colonel shouted over his shoulder.

'It's the birds,' he said, turning back to me. 'Come in man, come in.'

As I stepped into the hallway, he closed the door, and I saw what he meant. There, in a large cage in one corner of the hall, were two mynahs. They hopped from perch to perch, heads first on one side, then the other, looking at me with great curiosity.

'They're a damnable nuisance really,' Colonel Fairbrother said, 'but I got used to having a couple of them around when I was in India, so I always keep a pair.'

'The colonel's not in!'

'Shut up, Tonic!' the old man bellowed at the offending bird. 'That's his name – Tonic. The other one's Gin, of course. Tonic's the best mimic, he's got Mrs Goodley, my housekeeper, off to an absolute tee.'

'Hell and damnation!' commented Gin, in an exact reproduction of his master's voice.

'Yes, well, least said about that one the better,' the colonel muttered. 'Come on, Harton, the stuff I want you to look at's in the garage.'

The stuff Colonel Fairbrother wanted me to look at had come from his late brother's house in Hertfordshire. Brother had died some three months earlier and the colonel had had everything shipped down to Sussex without even weeding out the junk; that was one of things I was now supposed to do.

I can't say I'd been looking forward to it very much. Colonel Sidney Fairbrother was careful with his money to the point of being tight. He lived very well himself, but woe betide anybody trying to do a deal with him; he'd screw them down to the last halfpenny. I knew quite well that agreeing reserves on the contents of his garage was going to be like haggling in an arab souk. He was one of those people who assumed everybody – and that definitely included Charles Wilson and Company – was trying to swindle him. It was pointless explaining that, since our income was a percentage of the eventual selling price of each item, it was obviously in our interests (as well as his own) to sell each piece for as much as we could possibly get. He still gave the impression he was absolutely convinced we'd sell everything cheaply if we got half a chance.

'What about that table, Harton?' he asked, after nearly an hour and three quarters of bitter argument. 'What do you reckon for that?'

'Two or three hundred,' I said.

'Hell and damnation, man! You'll have me 'in the workhouse. I'm not going to cover the cost of transport at this rate.'

'Then the carriers must have seen you coming, Colonel.'

'What?'

'Well, we've already agreed reserves totalling in excess of five thousand pounds, and we're not halfway through yet. If the transport cost more than that . . .'

'Humph!' my client snorted, ran his hand through his hair, then stroked his moustache. 'But, dammit, man, surely that table's got to be worth four hundred. I mean, good God, the most appalling junk makes that sort of money these days.'

'Two to three hundred – reserve one hundred and ninety pounds,' I said, pen poised.

'One hundred and ninety!' he howled. 'Hell and damnation, no, not a penny less than three hundred and fifty.'

'You'd better keep it, then,' I said, 'because it won't sell at three hundred and fifty.'

'Three hundred,' he said.

'Two hundred and twenty.'

'Two hundred and fifty.'

'Two twenty-five,' I said.

'Two hundred and forty.'

'Two twenty-five,' I repeated.

A shudder seemed to run through his frame as if he were fighting some sort of phobia. 'All right, damn you! Two hundred and twenty-five,' he snarled. 'You're a hard man, Harton, a damned hard man.'

'Yes, Colonel.' I noted down the reserve and tied a ticket on the table as Colonel Fairbrother fastidiously recorded the figure in his own notebook.

It took us another hour and a half of uncovering,

unstacking and arguing before we arrived at the real rubbish.

'How much for the kitchen table?'

'Nothing,' I said. 'We wouldn't get a bid for it. And that goes for the refrigerator, cooker and the rest of the kitchen stuff, I'm afraid.'

'What the hell am I supposed to do with it all?' he asked.

'Well, the kitchen chairs are probably worth about twenty pounds, so if you include them in the deal, you might just be able to persuade a secondhand dealer to give you a few pounds and take the whole lot off your hands.'

He grunted with dissatisfaction, then pointed into the far corner of the garage. 'What about the safe, is that worth anything?'

'Not really,' I said, looking at the rusty Victorian relic, 'have you got the key?'

'No, no sign of one. I don't think my brother ever used it. It just used to hold up one end of the workbench in his garden shed.'

'It's only worth scrap value then. Get whoever buys the rest to take that as well.'

'God dammit, I wish I'd left the damned stuff in Hertfordshire, Harton.'

'That, Colonel Fairbrother, is precisely what you should have done,' I replied.

'Humph!' he said.

Kevin Prattley was an occasional visitor to Wilson's. I suppose he could best be catagorised as a 'lovable rogue' or 'rough diamond', though neither begins to encompass adequately his diverse talents. I don't know how Kevin used to describe his occupation on his income tax returns (if indeed he'd ever stumbled across such a form or, come to that, heard of such a tax) but it should probably have read 'entrepreneur-cum-scrap-merchant'. He lived by his wits on a council estate in Kington, and somehow managed to stay just one step ahead of the law and the bailiffs. What's more, he seemed to thrive on it.

'Good Lord, Kevin,' Duncan said, 'who drove you here? Securicor?'

'Nah, Mr Parkes, I came in me pick-up as usual. Why?'

'I just thought you were taking a bit of a chance, Kevin. There's more gold on you today than you'd find in Fort Knox.'

'Dun you worry 'bout me, Mr Parkes, they'd 'ave to cut me bleedin' fingers off before I'd let 'em get away wiv this lot.' Kevin Prattley looked down with undisguised admiration at his glistening hands. Each of his fingers was adorned with a sovereign or half-sovereign ring, and both wrists were swathed in heavy gold chain-link bracelets. It must have been all he could do to get his hands out of his pockets, after all, Kevin Prattley was not a big man.

'Where did this lot come from then, Kevin?' Duncan asked. 'Have you been holding out on us?'

'Nah, Mr Parkes. I jus' dun a couple a good deals, yer know? So I treated meself to a few presents, like.'

'Good luck to you, my boy. Have you got something for us?'

'Yeah, I 'ave. I've got some good silver for yer, Mr Parkes. Shall I bring it in?'

'Yes, wheel it in, Kevin,' Duncan said.

'There's some nice stuff here, Kevin,' I said, as Duncan and I helped him unpack the boxes.

'Yeah, Dick, I said it was good, did'n' I?'

'You did, Kevin, you did,' Duncan replied.

'Well, I don't know where our Kevin unearthed this lot, and I don't want to know,' Duncan said, after Kevin Prattley had gone, 'but there must be getting on for fifteen hundred pounds worth here.'

'I know,' I said, 'you don't think it could be . . .?'

'No, Richard, no. Young Kevin would happily try to talk his granny out of her pension money, sure enough, but steal – no, he wouldn't do that. It's just not Kevin's style.'

'I expect you're right.'

'I know I am. I've known Kevin since he was knee-high to a grasshopper, and he's not a thief, just a rogue. Get Jason to enter this lot and put it in the strongroom, Richard. We'll catalogue it tomorrow.'

It was late morning by the time I got into The Galleries the next day, and Duncan was busy in the strongroom.

'Were your calls any good?' he asked.

'So, so' I said, picking up a nice George IV mug that had come in with Kevin Prattley's consignment the previous day.

'Nice one, isn't it?' Duncan said.

'Yes, but I was looking at this crest on it. There's something familiar about it.'

'You probably saw it on those two table spoons – they're both crested as well. Nothing else is.'

'No, it wasn't them,' I said. 'I've seen it somewhere else but I can't think where . . . Hold on . . . Yes I can!'

Amongst the things from Colonel Fairbrother's garage were about thirty leatherbound books. None of them were of any great value, but they all contained book-plates bearing the Fairbrother family crest. 'Look, Duncan,' I said, comparing the mug to the book-plate, 'it's the same. This mug and those spoons were Fairbrother silver.'

'The facts would bear that interpretation,' Duncan said, looking from book-plate to mug and back to book-plate again, 'but how the devil did Kevin Prattley get hold of Fairbrother silver?'

We got the answer to Duncan's question later that day and the source, rather surprisingly, was none other than Anthony Wilson.

'Thought I'd better pop in and warn you chaps that there's a spot of bother on the way.'

'What sort of bother?' Duncan asked.

'Legal bother, about some silver we're selling for young Prattley.'

Duncan and I glanced at each other. Something obviously was wrong if our senior partner was aware of Kevin's consignment. It wasn't the sort of thing Mr Anthony would normally know about. He sat himself down and gave us the full story.

The previous Saturday, Kevin Prattley had been celebrating in the locals' bar of The Devonshire Arms. Like anything else he did, Kevin celebrated both enthusiastically and to excess. By the time last orders were called he was unconscious, but prior to that, on three separate occasions, he'd regaled the whole bar with an account of his latest dealing coup and financed drinks all round out of the anticipated profits.

According to Kevin, he had been invited to buy some things out at Fernley. After almost an hour's haggling he'd agreed ten pounds for the lot. He wasn't very happy about it either. The only decent thing was a set of chairs, but the owner insisted he take everything or nothing. So, Kevin was landed with a load of junk, including an old safe which he'd only seen at the last minute. Because he couldn't move the safe on his own, he'd had to drive into Kington, flush a couple of his impecunious mates out of the pubs, and then drive back to Fernley again. The time involved and the cost of his hired labour was obviously seriously going to erode any profit he was likely to make, so by the time he got back home he was not in the best frame of mind. The last thing they unloaded was the safe. They simply pushed it off the back of the truck and let it fall to the ground. It was then that one of Kevin's temporary staff said he thought he'd heard something rattling inside the safe. Kevin had been rudely dismissive of the suggestion but was eventually persuaded to smash the thing open.

'According to Prattley, it was full of silver, all black as your hat – must have been there for years. He sold some of it in Langton the following day, covered himself in gold, then brought the rest here,' Anthony Wilson concluded.

'Where do the legal problems arise?' Duncan asked. 'It seems to me that Kevin bought the stuff fair and square.'

'Not as straightforward as that,' Mr Anthony said. 'To begin with, the original owner, a chap called Fairbriar . . .'

'Fairbrother,' I said.

'What? Oh, yes, yes, you're right, Fairbrother . . . I say! How do you know his name?'

'Doesn't matter,' Duncan said, 'go on, Anthony.'

'Well, this chap, Fairbrother, has a housekeeper, a woman called Godley . . .'

'Goodley,' I said.

'What? . . . Oh, yes, Goodley . . . but I don't understand!'

'Go on, Anthony, we'll explain later,' Duncan said, impatiently.

'Right . . . Where was I?'

'Mrs Goodley,' I said.

'Ah, yes. This woman, Goodley, has a son who just happened to be in The Devonshire Arms when young Prattley was making such a fool of himself. It seems he went straight to his mother and told her all about it. She didn't waste any time at all in spilling the beans to Fairbrother, and the next thing, he's onto his solicitor demanding injunctions.'

'How do you know that?' Duncan asked.

'Because his solicitor's Francis Ridley, and he telephoned me this morning asking me to arrange for the silver to be held safely pending further action.'

'That's all very well, Anthony,' Duncan said, 'but is Ridley sure of his ground? It seems to me that young Kevin's got good title to this silver. I don't see that we have any right to take instructions from Ridley rather than Prattley.'

'Francis said there was no valid contract of sale. Neither Fairbrother nor Prattley knew of the existence of the stuff, so they couldn't possibly have agreed to buy or sell it.' Duncan frowned. 'No, no,' Mr Anthony continued, 'my advice to you is to put it away in the strongroom and don't let Prattley near it until you've heard from Francis or this Fairbrother chap. By the way, Richard, how do you know these people?'

Duncan sat brooding after Anthony Wilson had left us for the estate office.

'Damn it!' he said, at length, 'they're going to take young Kevin to the cleaners. It's probably the first bit of luck he's ever had in his life, and they're going to take it away from him.'

'I don't see there's much we can do about it,' I said.

'No, but we can make sure the silly young so-and-so knows what's going on,' he said, jumping up from his chair and heading for his office.

'What are you going to do?'

'Leave a message with Kevin's mother for him to come and see me urgently,' he said.

Kevin arrived at five o'clock. 'Wha's the problem, Mr Parkes?' he asked.

Duncan explained.

'I 'eard that Tiddly Ridley was afta me,' Kevin said, when Duncan had finished, 'an' I fought that must be what it was about.'

'Well, the first thing you should do is get yourself a solicitor, Kevin,' Duncan said. 'Ridley may be three sheets to the wind most of the time, but he's still a piranha when it comes to money.'

'I can't afford one of them legal geezers, Mr Parkes. They cost too bleedin' much for the likes of me.'

'You're going to have to do something, Kevin.'

'Yeah, well, what if I say I'll meet ol' Tiddly 'ere an' discuss it?'

'He'll eat you alive,' Duncan said.

'P'raps he will,' Kevin Prattley replied with a gap-toothed smile, 'but sometimes us ol' Sussex boys can be a bit tough to swallow, Mr Parkes.'

Two days later, Duncan received a letter from Messrs Couchman, Bainforth and Ridley, informing him that Mr Ridley and his client, Colonel Fairbrother, wished to inspect silver recently consigned for sale by one Kevin Prattley. It further informed him that Mr Prattley would be present. The date provisionally agreed with Mr Prattley was that of the following Thursday – six days time – and Messrs Couchman, Bainforth and Ridley trusted that would be convenient for Mr Parkes.

'Tell Jason to make sure it's all laid out in order on the table in Gallery Four in good time next Thursday,' Duncan said. 'I don't want any hitches on our part.'

The following Thursday, one hour before the meeting was due to start, Duncan and I inspected the hoard as Jason checked off the last items on his list.

'All present and correct,' he said, 'including the mug Kevin borrowed for a couple of days.'

Duncan and I looked at one another. 'What do you mean, "borrowed"?' Duncan asked.

'Well, he rushed in on Monday, said he'd got to show it to somebody and that he'd bring it back the next day – which he did. He even insisted on giving me a temporary receipt for it when he took it.'

Duncan and I looked at one another again. 'What's he up to?' Duncan said, picking up the mug. He turned the piece round and round in his hands, then passed it to me. 'Spot the difference?'

'My god, the crest's gone.'

'Right in one, Richard. He's had it polished out, but I still don't see what he's up to; the pair of spoons are still crested. Why didn't he have those polished out as well?'

Colonel Sidney Fairbrother and his legal advisor arrived at twenty-five minutes past two. They were accompanied by a strong whiff of cognac, and their complexions suggested a good lunch had been had by all. Kevin Prattley arrived at two thirty looking as though he hadn't eaten for a week. His bleached blonde hair hung in rat-tails, his eyes were sunken and his complexion was waxy pale. There were no rings on his fingers now. His finger nails were bitten and his clothes were scruffy.

The opposing parties took their seats opposite each other, and Francis Ridley opened proceedings: 'It is my client's contention that items of silver were present in a safe which, with certain other effects, you recently purchased from him. My client was unaware of the presence of the silver in the safe, and it was therefore plainly never his intention that such items should have formed any part of any contract between you. He therefore requests that you acknowledge his title to the items concerned.'

'Yeah, sounds fair enough,' Kevin said, nodding.

Colonel Fairbrother glanced uneasily at his solicitor, but Ridley fixed his gaze on Kevin. 'You agree?' the lawyer said, unable to control a note of suspicion in his voice.

'Yeah.'

'In that case,' Mr Ridley went on, still holding Kevin in his watery-eyed, gimlet gaze, 'I will draft a short letter which you can sign, recognising my client's good title to the pieces concerned.'

'Okay,' Kevin said.

'And we must have some sort of schedule of the items concerned, of course,' the solicitor continued.

'Yeah, well it's only them spoons of course,' Kevin said, with all the innocence of a cathedral choirboy, as he reached

200

over and picked up the pair of table spoons.

For a moment, the silence in the gallery was suffocating, then Francis Ridley cleared his throat. 'Mr Prattley, you are not seriously suggesting that the only items of silver in the safe were those two spoons?'

'Yeah, guv. Scout's 'onour.'

'But Mr Prattley, we have witnesses who will confirm that you boasted openly that the safe was *full* of silver.'

'Yeah, I know, but I was Brahms, wasn't I?'

'I beg your pardon?'

'Legless, guv! Widdled as a rat! Paralysed! You know what I mean. I mean we all get a bit daft when we're like that, don't we? I 'spect you do too.'

For a moment it looked as though Colonel Fairbrother was about to have a seizure. He opened his mouth to speak but Mr Ridley, still outwardly cool, pressed on. 'So you're saying only those two spoons came from the safe, and the rest of this considerable collection originated from elsewhere.'

'Yeah.'

'Where.'

'All over. I got it from loadsa different places, like.'

'You bought it?'

'Yeah.'

'So,' Ridley said, taking the time to turn and smile at his client, 'you will have no trouble in producing receipts for all these purchases.'

'No,' Kevin said, standing up and hauling a bundle of disgusting looking, dog-eared scraps of paper from the back pocket of his jeans, 'I've got 'em all 'ere as it 'appens.'

'Game, set and match, Prattley,' Duncan whispered.

'You, Kevin Prattley, are a cheeky young scoundrel,' Duncan said, after the colonel and his solicitor had gone.

'I dunno wha' you mean, Mr Parkes.'

'I mean, having the crest polished out of that mug, that's what I mean. What sort of position do you think that put us in? If Ridley or Colonel Fairbrother had asked us, we would have had to have told them the mug was originally crested.'

'Nah, nah, Mr Parkes, you're gettin' confused. Tha' mug

201

never 'ad no crest on it. Just the spoons, an' I gave 'em back, din' I?'

'Yes, Kevin,' Duncan said, 'you gave them back all right. You gave them back because they were only worth twenty pounds while the mug's worth a hundred and twenty.'

Kevin Prattley looked hurt. 'Mr Parkes,' he said, 'you got me all wrong, I got witnesses wot ud testify tha' tha' mug never 'ad no crest on it.'

'I don't doubt it, Kevin. Nor do I doubt they'd be the same impartial gentlemen who produced that collection of receipts for you.'

'Mr Parkes,' Kevin said, grave-faced, 'you ain't 'alf got an 'orrible suspicious mind.'

Almost six months passed by before I had cause to visit Colonel Sidney Fairbrother again. Once again, I pressed the doorbell.

'Hell and damnation!'

'The Colonel's not in!'

'Bloody Prattley! Bloody Prattley!'

Chapter 19

Duncan and I were having coffee when Patrick arrived with a dozen pieces for the next sale. While Kate went to get him a cup, he stood eyeing me up and down with a look of concern.

'I think Richard's looking a bit peaky, Mr Parkes,' he said, eventually.

'Really?' Duncan replied, scrutinising me as well, 'he looks all right to me.'

'No,' Patrick was adamant, 'he's definitely looking peaky.' I couldn't work out what was coming, but I was sure that he was building up to something. 'He's doing too much overtime,' Patrick went on, 'that's the problem, DP. You're making the lad do too many early morning calls.'

I began to get a sneaking suspicion as to what this was all about.

'Early morning calls? You haven't had to do any early calls have you, Richard?' Duncan said.

'No,' I said.

'He's too modest to tell you,' Patrick went on, 'but I know he's been seeing clients early in the morning . . .'

'Thank you, Pat,' I said, 'haven't you got to be going somewhere?'

'. . . because, only this morning,' he went on, 'we drove past the Cartwrights at seven o'clock, on our way to Southbourne and Richard's car was already parked outside the cottage by the gate.'

'Really!' Duncan said, smirking at me.

'Yes, Mr Parkes, Richard was already at it at seven o'clock this morning – no wonder he looks so tired.'

'Mmmm,' Duncan replied, 'the man's absolutely selfless

203

when it comes to furthering the ends of the company.'

'Time I was gone,' I said, gulping down the remainder of my coffee, and grabbing my briefcase. 'Come on, Kate, we're off.'

Patrick was quite right of course. He had spotted my car outside Antonia's cottage that morning, but then it was there most mornings. I spent more time there than at home, and bit by bit my clothes, books and a lot of other possessions had taken up residence there as well. The permanence of our relationship was unplanned and largely unremarked upon by either of us. By a sort of unspoken agreement we never discussed anything more distant than the next week or next month. We satisfied ourselves with the present, and as far as I was concerned, very satisfactory the present was.

'What have we got today, apart from the probate valuation?' Kate asked, as we motored towards Southbourne.

'Just three calls,' I said, 'but they'll drag on if we're not careful.'

I didn't often take Kate with me on calls but, as usual, we were running late with the next catalogue, and having her to take notes for me on the valuation would save a lot of time. Once I'd dealt with that, the other three appointments were with regular Southbourne clients. Unfortunately, they were all ladies who tended to treat my visits as social occasions, and although I always tried to give them as much time as possible, there was a limit. I just couldn't spend all afternoon drinking tea with them, even if they did always produce something for sale.

'Don't you feel guilty, milking the poor old dears of their heirlooms?' Kate went on as she rolled herself a cigarette.

'Milking!' I replied, genuinely indignant. 'I don't milk them. They call me in, I tell them what an item will fetch, then they decide whether or not they want me to sell it. That's not milking!'

'Oh, come on,' she said, striking a Swan Vesta and cupping it in her hands as she lit the wafer-thin cigarette, 'half the time they don't really want to sell anything at all – they just want "nice Mr Harton" to come along for a chat.'

'If they don't want to sell anything they don't have to sell anything,' I said.

'No, of course they don't. But just how many times would you visit them without getting something for sale before you started to be "out" when they phoned?'

'Why don't you get on with your *Grauniad,*' I said.

'Ah, ha – that touched a nerve, didn't it?' she cried in triumph. 'You're just as bad as Duncan – money, money, money!'

I didn't reply. I was feeling a little bruised by her taunts. I'd always looked upon myself privately as part auctioneer, part social worker. The trouble was, Kate was right: if the supply of goods dried up at any particular source, we soon lost contact with that source. It was basic commerce and there was no getting away from it.

The probate valuation was in the old part of Southbourne. The deceased, a Miss Bartlett, had been in her late eighties, and we were to meet her executrix, Mrs Doris Campbell, at the old lady's flat.

'Now remember,' I told Kate, 'I want to get in and out of here as soon as possible, so try not to encourage Mrs Campbell to chatter.'

'My lips are sealed,' she said, as we drew up opposite a large Victorian terraced house just off the front. There was a middle-aged woman in a tweed coat standing on the steps, evidently waiting for us. A stiff sea breeze gusted up the street as we got out of the car and crossed the road.

'Mrs Campbell?'

'Yes,' she said, 'come in.'

Once inside we introduced ourselves.

'It's the top flat,' Mrs Campbell said, with a slight Scottish lilt, 'be careful, I'm afraid the stair rail isn't in the best of repair. The landlord doesn't bother to maintain the building at all. All he thinks about is money, money, money.'

'Dreadful, isn't it?' Kate contributed. 'I noticed when we came in that the basement railings were broken.'

'Oh yes,' Mrs Campbell said, as we trudged onward and upward, 'there's a dreadful story attached to that.'

'Oh dear, what happened?' Kate asked, totally ignoring my grimaced, silent instructions to shut up.

'Well, my dear friend, Miss Bartlett, was walking her little terrier late one evening, and on her return she fell through that gap in the railings, dropped eight feet into the basement and lay there all night with a broken hip. Her little dog sat on the doorstep and howled and howled but nobody took any notice. She wasn't found until the milkman came the next morning.'

'That's awful,' Kate said, 'what an unnecessary way to die.'

'Oh, she didn't die,' Mrs Campbell said, 'she made a complete recovery.'

We continued the ascent in silence, eventually reaching Miss Barlett's flat on the fourth floor. Mrs Campbell produced a bundle of keys, dealt with the Yale and mortice locks, and let us in. As was usually the case with probate valuations, the place was absolutely freezing. I discovered that wasn't the only thing the flat had in common with a lot of other probate valuations – it also had fleas.

Whenever I walked into an empty home that had contained a cat or dog, it was always the same: within a couple of minutes of setting foot in the place I'd get bitten. Soon, from ankle to knee, my legs would bear witness to the fact that I'd served as a mobile snack bar for the little brutes. Short of wearing bicycle clips I just had to suffer in silence while, most annoying of all, everybody else seemed to escape unmolested. On that occasion, Kate and Mrs Campbell were plainly oblivious to the concerted attack I was trying to fend off.

'If you could just show us round, Mrs Campbell,' I said, trying to resist the irrestible temptation to scratch the affected parts of my anatomy, 'then we'll make a start.'

'Richard,' Kate whispered, as Mrs Campbell led us from room to room, 'why do you keep hopping about? You look as though you've got St Vitus's Dance.'

'Fleas,' I said.

'Ergh – how disgusting!' she said out loud, stepping away from me.

'I'm sorry?' Mrs Campbell said, turning to us as we entered the main bedroom.

'It needs dusting,' Kate blurted, as inane grin spreading from ear to ear.

I groaned inwardly. It was going to be another of those days.

'Yes, well, it has been empty for several weeks now,' Mrs Campbell intoned, 'and of course there is the dust from the hole in the ceiling.'

Kate and I looked up, and sure enough, there was a hole in the ceiling. Not a little hole, not a round hole, but a great big person-shaped hole. It was like something straight out of a Tom and Jerry cartoon. Clearly, somebody rather than something had fallen through the ceiling of the late Miss Bartlett's bedroom.

'Good Lord!' I said.

'Crikey!' Kate added.

'Yes,' Mrs Campbell continued, looking up into the gaping black void, 'my dear friend was trying to repair the roof when she missed her footing and fell between the rafters, crashing to the floor below.'

'That is awful,' Kate said, 'was she killed instantly?'

'Oh, no, she wasn't killed at all. She only suffered a few minor cuts and abrasions and was back on her feet in a couple of days.'

A silence descended on us as we all stood looking up at the stark evidence of Miss Bartlett's tenacious hold on life. I knew what Kate was going to ask. With all the telepathic powers at my disposal I willed her not to, but it was a waste of effort and energy.

'Er,' she hesitated, then surrendered to her overwhelming curiosity. 'What *did* Miss Bartlett die of, Mrs Campbell?' she asked.

'Oh, she went into hospital for a routine check-up and died of pneumonia.'

I remained grave-faced, and concentrated my mind on appalling visual images of disasters and horrors both real and imagined. Kate must have done the same, for not even the faintest hint of a smile was detectable when I eventually plucked up enough courage to take a sidelong glance at her.

'Awful,' I said, 'really awful.'

'Yes,' Kate said, 'really awful.'

By the time Mrs Campbell left us to get on with the valuation we were both ready to explode. There wasn't anything funny about poor Miss Bartlett's demise, of course; it was just the irony of her being killed by a routine National Health check-up when she'd shrugged off two horrific death plunges as though they were no more than trivial inconveniences. I have never since underestimated the dangers inherent in the indiscriminate use of cold stethoscopes.

Once we'd come to terms with Miss Bartlett's demise, Kate and I set about the valuation. It was very straightforward and Doris Campbell was an ideal client: she left us alone. One of the worst afflictions for any valuer is to have the client at your elbow when you're working. It's just not possible to value a house contents and discuss each individual item at the same time. The owner's absence is even more vital when you are dictating the descriptions rather than just writing them down yourself. When you're writing, you can at least cover your notes like a schoolboy in a class of cheats, but when you're dictating, every word can be picked up and debated:

'A Victorian rosewood . . .'

'Victorian? I always understood it was Georgian.'

'No, it's Victorian . . . A Victorian rosewood tea table . . .'

'It's a card table, surely?'

'No, if it was a card table it would be baize-lined. This has a polished top . . . A Victorian rosewood tea table raised on turned pillar . . .'

'Now, I'm interested that you call it rosewood, because a friend of mine who knows quite a lot about antiques told me he was ninety per cent certain the wood was padouk, and that meant it probably came from Australia.'

'It isn't and it didn't.'

'Really? You're certain about that, are you?'

'Yes.'

'Oh, well, I'm sure you're right . . . It's just that my friend really is very good on that sort of thing . . .'

'Aaaaah!'

Next stop, after Miss Florence Edith Bartlett deceased, was Mrs Joan Flowers. Mrs Flowers could sometimes be real trouble. It just depended on whether she'd started drinking before or after breakfast. She was a well preserved and comfortably wealthy woman in her mid-fifties. She'd moved to Southbourne with her husband on his early retirement as chairman of an engineering group in the north of England. His aim was to indulge his passion for sailing. Instead, within a year, he was dead from his first and last coronary, leaving his widow grieving in an eighteenth-floor luxury flat high above a town in which she was a stranger. It was a depressingly familiar story which I saw repeated time and time again with only minor variations. Joan Flowers had the sort of material advantages that most people only dream of, but she was still one of the unhappiest women I'd ever met.

'What's she want to sell?' Kate asked as we went up in the lift.

'Probably nothing,' I said, 'most of our encounters just turn out to be counselling sessions.'

'But?'

'But she's got some very nice things and every now and then she sells one.'

'Why? She's not running out of money, is she?'

I said I thought not. I was pretty convinced that she only sold the odd piece to keep me interested.

'Makes you sound like a gigolo,' Kate remarked.

'Don't joke about it,' I said as the mirrored lift came to a stop on the eighteenth floor, 'she's made a vague pass at me before now.'

'Who's joking?' she sniffed.

The doors of the lift slid quietly open, unveiling the deep pile carpeted landing of the eighteenth floor. I was prepared for the worst. The hall porter had had terrible trouble on the house telephone making Mrs Flowers understand who it was who'd come to see her, and that usually meant she was already smashed. If that was the case, she was almost certainly in the middle of a four or five day binge and our visit would be a complete waste of time.

As the lift doors closed behind us, the door to Mrs Flowers flat opened. She looked dreadful. She was flushed, her eyes were half closed and her make-up looked as though it had been applied by a blind apprentice plasterer.

'Mr Harton,' she said, gripping hold of the door with one

hand and the doorframe with the other, 'what a pleasant surprise, you should have let me know you were coming.'

There was obviously no point in telling her she'd telephoned me the previous week, asking me to come and see her. However, I thought I should make it clear that I hadn't just popped in out of the blue.

'Actually, we did have an appointment for eleven thirty, Mrs Flowers,' I said, 'we confirmed it in writing, but perhaps the letter went astray.'

'Oh, it would have been them,' she said, lowering her voice and pointing mysteriously at the floor.

'Them?' Kate said.

'In the hall – the porters – they open my mail, you know. They spy on me.'

'This is my secretary, Kate Bentley,' I said, changing the subject before we got too heavily involved in Joan Flowers' latest paranoia.

'How nice,' she said, trying to focus on Kate, 'and what unusual clothes. Do come in, do come in.'

We filed through into the huge L-shaped sitting room. It was panelled in some variety of South American hardwood, and one entire wall was a vast window overlooking the channel.

'What an amazing view!' Kate said, walking over to the window.

'View? View? Oh, that! Yes, the view.' Plainly, the breathtaking panorama meant nothing at all to Mrs Flowers. She was so familiar with it she'd stopped noticing it was there. For all the benefit she drew from it she might as well have had the window bricked up.

'Would you like a drink?' she asked.

'No thank you, we had coffee at our last call,' I lied.

'Right. Well, I think I may have a little something myself,' she went on. 'I find coffee gives me palpitations these days so I'll just have a little of this.'

She picked out the vodka from the collection of bottles on a George III sideboard and tried twice to unscrew the top. As she made a third attempt at it she finally noticed the top was already off. Snorting through her nose at her own mistake, she half-filled a heavy cut glass tumbler and raised it. 'Cheers! The first today,' she said, probably half-believing the old untruth.

The flat was an incongruous mixture of ancient and modern. All the furniture, with the exception of two expensive looking settees and a smoked glass coffee table about six feet square, was antique. There was some very good Queen Anne and George I walnut, and a lot of George III mahogany. The combination of the woods doesn't often work too well, but when set against the red-brown of the modern panelling in the sitting room, the resulting effect was unspeakably horrible. The unintended overall impression was that of tasteless ostentation – Dallas comes to Southbourne. There were really only two things Mrs Flowers could do to cure the problem: either she had to completely redecorate the flat, or she had to sell the furniture and buy modern. In the end it was academic really, since in her sober moments she always seemed perfectly happy with the decor, and while she was drunk she didn't give a damn about anything anyway.

'I've decided to sell everything,' she said suddenly, after her third swig from the tumbler, 'every last bit and piece, every last jot and tittle. What do you think of that, Mr Harton?'

Mr Harton thought she'd finally had one vodka too many, but once again, there seemed little point in mentioning it. 'Well, it's entirely up to you, Mrs Flowers,' I said, 'but would you mind if I asked what's brought you to this decision?'

'What's brought me to this decision?' she said, swaying slightly. 'I'll tell you what's brought me to this decision. I've been brought to this decision by the fact that I hate this bloody flat, I hate bloody antiques, I hate bloody Southbourne and most of all I hate bloody England. That's what's brought me to this decision, Mr Harton. Does that answer your question?'

As she finished speaking, she staggered backwards a couple of steps and flopped onto a settee. 'Whoops!' she said.

Before I could say a word, Kate barged past me and sat down opposite Mrs Flowers.

'You mustn't do it,' Kate said, 'you're not well and you mustn't make decisions like that when you're not well.'

Joan Flowers looked even more vacant than usual. She didn't say a word, instead she just sat, clutching her glass,

211

looking at Kate with a faint, lop-sided smile. If she had tried to say anything it would have been to no avail anyway, Kate was in full flood.

'You must get well first, then if you still want to sell everything, that's fine, but you never know, things may look different then and you might decide that you don't want to sell anything. At the moment I think you'd just be running away, and you can't really run away from your illness because wherever you go it'll follow you, and you'll just end up being miserable there instead of being miserable here, and that's no good. No, what you've got to do is concentrate on getting well. Anyway . . . that's what I think . . .'

As her voice faded away into an embarrassed silence, the only sound to be heard in the room was the steady thudding tick of the walnut longcase clock by the door.

'What a sweet child, a sweet child,' Mrs Flowers said, putting down her glass on the coffee table and reaching out to take Kate's hands in her own, 'I think I shall take your advice my dear. I really think I shall take your advice.'

Kate and I travelled down in the lift in silence. In fact, we didn't speak until we'd got in the car.

'You're angry, aren't you?' she said.

'Angry, why should I be angry? All you've done is to convince one of our clients that she shouldn't sell an extremely valuable collection of furniture through us. In fact, you seem to have convinced her never to sell it at all. Why should I be angry? We only make our living out of selling things.'

'I knew it,' she said, looking straight ahead and fiddling with her coat buttons; 'you are angry.'

'As it happens,' I said, starting the car, 'I'm not. Believe it or not – and I'm sure you won't – I would have tried to talk her out of it myself, if I'd been able to get a word in edgeways, that is.'

'Really?'

'Yes, really. And don't sound so surprised. What do you think I am – some sort of vampire?'

'I don't know,' she said thoughtfully, 'but you're definitely not as bad as I thought you were.'

The next call produced half a dozen pieces of porcelain for

sale and almost an entire new wardrobe for Kate. She had casually remarked to the elderly lady owner that she liked a cardigan which was lying on top of a pile of clothing in the hall. It was immediately explained the clothing was destined for a jumble sale, and if Kate wanted any of it she should help herself. For fifteen minutes my assistant and my septuagenarian client crawled happily around the floor making fresh piles of the garments. When they eventually finished, the jumble sale was about fifty per cent worse off than it had been when we arrived.

The final call of the day was on a pair of old regulars: Mrs Leach and Mrs Farrow. At The Galleries they were popularly known – when they weren't in earshot – as Winnie and Minnie. They were sisters, both in their seventies and both widowed. Originating from Yorkshire, they still retained that county's accent, keeping it as polished and bright as any medal. Both were wizened little creatures; Winnie bearing a striking resemblance to Olivier's Richard III, while Minnie was so small and slight she looked as though a stiff sea breeze would carry her off inland. I can't recall ever having seen one without the other. Winnie's stooped figure was always to the fore on every expedition, dragging behind her a wheeled shopping basket. Behind that would follow Minnie, as inevitably as night follows day.

It wasn't just the convoys that Winnie led, she also originated all their conversation. Minnie's role was that of underwriter and echo. Like some diminutive, portable alpine peak, she bounced back almost every word that Winnie said. Having a conversation with them was like listening to a faulty stereophonic record player. One heard exactly the same thing twice, but with a confusing built-in delay.

'Hello, Mr Harton,' Winnie said as she opened the door to their austere little flat.

'. . . Mr Harton,' Minnie said from behind her sister.

'Hello, Mrs Leach, Mrs Farrow. This is my secretary – Kate Bentley.'

'Hello, nice to meet you,' said Winnie.

'. . . to meet you,' said Minnie.

'What have you got for me today?' I asked.

'A Victorian walnut whatnot.'
'. . . walnut whatnot.'
'Fine, lead on,' I said.
'This way, it's in the lounge.'
'. . . in the lounge.'
The two bent and frail little figures made their way down a
short but depressingly dismal corridor with Kate and me
bringing up the rear.
The whatnot – a sort of open display unit with several
different tiers on which ornaments and bric-a-brac can be
displayed – stood in one corner of the room looking very out
of place. I could see why they wanted to sell it – it wasn't a
particularly nice one, nor did it fit in with the rest of their
furniture.
'What do you think?' Winnie enquired, as I made a closer
inspection than the piece deserved.
'. . . do you think,' Minnie echoed from just behind
Winnie's right shoulder.
'Well, it's about 1860 . . .'
'Oh, 1850, I think.'
'. . . 1850, I think.'
'No certainly not that early,' I said. I'd known from the
beginning they'd contest everything I said – they always did.
They looked upon me as a rather poor substitute for
Duncan, and made a point of asking for him every time they
telephoned The Galleries. He made an equally strong point
of always getting Margaret to transfer the call to me, so I was
used to them by now.
'1860, walnut,' I continued, 'inlaid with boxwood . . .'
'Satinwood, not boxwood, satinwood.'
'. . . not boxwood, satinwood.'
'I can assure you, it is boxwood, ladies, and as to price . . .
I would think . . . somewhere in the region of . . .' Their
red-rimmed little eyes were fixed on me without the slightest
movement, just like the eyes of birds of prey. I could almost
feel an electrical charge in the air, their anticipation was
palpable. '. . . a hundred and fifty pounds,' I concluded.
'Oh no! Much more. Much more.'
'. . . Much more. Much more.'
'All right, you tell me,' I said.

214

'Oh no, you're the expert, Mr Harton.'

'. . . you're the expert.'

'Well, I've told you what I think it'll make – how much do you want for it?'

'Well, we were thinking . . .'

'. . . we were thinking . . .'

'. . . we were thinking . . . Three hundred and fifty pounds.'

'. . . three hundred and fifty pounds.'

'Absolutely no chance,' I said. 'It's just possible, I suppose, that it could make two hundred, but certainly no more than that.'

'So you don't think it's worth trying?' Winnie persisted.

'. . . worth trying?' Minnie said.

'Not at three hundred and fifty – it would be a complete waste of time.'

'How did you get on?' Duncan asked, when we got back to The Galleries.

'I don't really know how to rate it,' I replied. 'The probate was all right – apart from the client having fallen through the ceiling – but two of the calls were a complete waste of time.'

'What about that Flowers woman? Didn't she have anything for sale?'

'Oh, yes, she wanted to sell everything. No need to worry though, Kate talked her out of it.'

Duncan looked nonplussed, then he raised one eyebrow. 'Patrick's right,' he said, 'you're doing too many early morning calls.'

Chapter 20

There was always something that triggered it off. Normally it was almost impossible to get Duncan to sit down for half an hour and go through the accounts, but once every six months or so, when something had gone wrong in his life, I was expected to drop everything and produce up-to-the-minute figures. This time he'd just learned that a good collection of silver was going to London for sale rather than coming to us. He vented his frustration by demanding a full set of figures, including – and this was always the real showstopper – a schedule of outstanding accounts.

In theory, we didn't pay the vendor of an item until the purchaser had paid us. In practice, it was so hopelessly unworkable that, except in the case of very expensive lots, everybody was paid regardless of whether we'd got the money or not. Twice a year Duncan turned his back on normal practices and demanded a return to the rulebook.

'It's preposterous, that's what it is,' Duncan said, as he attempted to pace up and down his small, crowded office. 'We're auctioneers, not bankers. If these characters want to borrow money they can go to their bank managers, not to us . . . Who put all this junk in here? I can hardly move.'

'You did,' said Margaret.

'Well . . . get Jason to get rid of it . . . It's supposed to be an office not a store.' He picked his way through the clutter and sat down at his desk again. 'I mean, look at some of these amounts,' he said. 'Fifteen hundred, two thousand, five and a half thousand! . . . Who's that? . . . Who the devil owes us five and a half thousand?'

I ran down the column of names on the schedule. 'Bill

216

Grigson,' I said, and waited for the usual reaction. I wasn't to be disappointed.

'William Grigson! William Grigson! Another of your friends! Typical! Well, you'll just have to go over to Ashley Park and get a cheque out of him, won't you?'

It was an accepted thing that whenever any regulars brought in decent pieces for sale they were Duncan's clients, but when they were tardy in paying they became my, or Jason's, or Margaret's 'friends' – as yet, Kate wasn't held culpable for that sort of thing.

'I'll give him a ring,' I said.

'Never mind about giving him a ring. You give him a shock. Go over there and stick your foot in the door tonight.'

'Antonia and I are going out tonight.'

'Tomorrow then.'

'I'll see what I can do.'

'It's no good putting it off, Richard,' Duncan said, oozing self-righteousness. 'You may as well get it over with.'

The words came more easily than the deed. Duncan knew just as well as I did what was entailed in extracting money from Bill Grigson. That was precisely why it had become one of my duties.

Whether or not Bill had any real friends I never knew, but he certainly didn't lead a wild social life. The only time he and his wife went out together was when they went sea fishing. The prospect of standing on a breakwater in a gale at midnight, armed only with a thermos flask and two packs of sandwiches doesn't appeal to everybody, but for Bill and Elizabeth Grigson it was the high spot of the week.

Elizabeth had little to do with Bill's compulsive collecting despite the several attempts he'd made to get her interested. The only evidence of her forays into the art market was a cabinet full of Crown Derby in the main drawing room. He hated the stuff, but despite Elizabeth having long since lost interest in collecting it, she wouldn't let him sell it; and if Elizabeth Grigson told her husband not to do something, he didn't do it. I think she was the only person in the world Bill was frightened of. She was barely five feet four, slight, and spoke so rarely and so softly that her presence in a room

217

could easily pass unnoticed. To her husband, however, she was the boss. What was more, while she was indifferent to Bill's first passion – collecting – she was positively bored stiff by his second – snooker. He loved the game and never missed any opportunity to play it. That was why Duncan was more than happy for me to go debt collecting. He disliked the game almost as much as Elizabeth did, and he knew that anyone going near Ashley Park in the evening would have to play three or four frames before they'd stand a chance of getting the cheque.

'And who's this?' Duncan snarled, as he continued down the list. 'Four thousand eight hundred and twenty-seven pounds! Who's that?'

'Mr Turner-Parr,' I replied, having checked the schedule again.

'Oh,' he said, inhaling deeply the smoke from his cigarette, and exhaling it slowly through his nose.

There was no denying that Mr Turner-Parr was an important client, perhaps, potentially our *most* important client, but there was also no doubt that he knew it. He had fine collections of furniture and works of art, and he bought and sold through us regularly. Whenever he set foot in The Galleries he was accorded VIP treatment and always received personal attention from Duncan. Most importantly, he had made it quite clear on several occasions that his collections were to be sold by Wilson's on his death. It would certainly be a sale worth having, and Arthur Turner-Parr knew that as well. Duncan cosseted him like no other client. He gave huge amounts of his private time to him, took him here and there, stayed up until the early hours chatting with him, and was generally on call twenty-four hours a day. There was no doubt that Duncan genuinely liked him. However, I was pretty certain he hadn't expected their relationship to be quite as longlasting as it had been. For when they first met, Mr Turner-Parr was already seventy-five years old; now he was ninety-four and still looking good for another twenty years or so.

'Have you sent him reminders?' Duncan asked, casting around for excuses.

'Every month, on the thirtieth of the month, without fail.'

'Well, I expect he's just forgotten. You should have told me. I'll pop in and see him tomorrow and get a cheque. I'm quite sure he doesn't realise he owes us anything.'

I was equally sure he did. The sly old devil was never less than four thousand in debt to us and often more. He had a foolproof system which would come into play when Duncan went to see him the following day. To begin with, there was absolutely no chance whatsoever of Duncan weedling a cheque out of him. In all my years at The Galleries I'd never seen a cheque with Arthur Turner-Parr's name on it, except when we took cheques made payable to him by third parties, presumably because he was indulging in the old and ancient art of tax evasion. No, Duncan wouldn't get a cheque. What he would get would be a consignment of things for sale, and very nice things they'd be too. So, we'd illustrate them in the catalogue without making the usual charge, we'd charge him a reduced rate of commission for selling them, and we would provide him with extra catalogues, reserved seats in the front row and refreshments in the office at lunchtime. In return we'd get to keep the proceeds of sale so, at last, the outstanding account would be cleared. The only flaw in the process was that Mr Turner-Parr was never just a passive observer at sales. By the end of a three-day sale he would be certain to have spent at least another four or five thousand pounds, so the whole cycle would start again.

'And this eleven hundred pounds that's been outstanding for two months,' Duncan went on down the schedule, 'who the hell's that?'

'Mrs Partridge,' I said, bracing myself.

'Mrs Partridge!' Duncan began to change colour. 'Mrs Partridge! That bloody woman again. Have we still got the goods?'

'Yes, she just did her usual trick of coming in, bidding for things and disappearing again.'

'Right. Put all the things back in the next sale to get some of the money back on the account, and from henceforth she is banned.'

'Okay,' I said, 'but I hope you'll write to her this time to let her know. It's bound to be me on the rostrum when she comes through the door again.'

'That wretched woman will never set foot in these Galleries again,' Duncan said, lighting yet another cigarette, 'I'll see to that.'

'That's two frames each then,' Bill Grigson said as I potted the black ball into one of the middle pockets. 'We'll have to play a decider.'

'I'd love to, Bill, but I really don't have the time, it's getting on for eleven now,' I said, well aware that he'd let me take the last frame so he'd have an excuse for one more.

'The night is yet young, Dick. What's yer rush?'

'Well, apart from anything else, I did tell Antonia I wouldn't be late.'

'You're not late, Dick. That's what I'm tryin' to tell yer – eleven o'clock ain't late, my son. I fink you're beginnin' to get 'en-pecked, boy.'

'I'm not hen-pecked, Bill, but I am tired. We're not all like you, you know. Some of us need more than a couple of hours sleep each night. Now, where's the cheque?'

'I'm disappointed in yer, Dick. I fought yer was a real go-getter.'

'I am, Bill,' I said, 'only the day before yesterday, Duncan said, "Go and get a cheque for five and a half thousand from William Grigson", and here I am. Give me the cheque, Bill. Please!'

'Yeah, yeah, all right. 'Old on! Where's me cheque book?' As he spoke, he ran his hands through the pockets of his cardigan.

'It's where it always is – in the top right hand drawer of the desk in the drawing room.'

'Yer don't say?'

'I'd be prepared to put money on it.'

'That's more than yer'd do wiv the snooker, yer cheapskate.'

'I may be naive, but I'm not completely stupid,' I said, as I went to the door and opened it. 'After you.'

'Miserable sod,' he said, as he finally put his cue back in the rack.

It was almost eleven thirty when I eventually wrested a correctly signed and dated cheque from Bill Grigson's grasp.

220

At last, I could go home. At least, I could have gone home if, just at that moment, I hadn't opened my big mouth.

'What on earth's that doing in here?' I asked.

'So that's where it is. I wondered where the 'ell I'd put it.' It wasn't the sort of thing one could easily misplace, like a pen or a cufflink. Nor was it the sort of thing that readily blended into the furnishings of an elegantly appointed drawing room. It was a seven foot long punt gun and it was leaning incongruously against the fireplace.

'I must 'ave brought it in 'ere earlier on the way to the museum an' then forgot abat it.'

'It's joining the collection, then?'

'Nah, not really. I bought it in a job lot off a dealer in Langton. I 'spect I'll flog it off – ain't the sort of fing I want in the museum.'

It was understandable. It was neither rare nor beautiful, just big. Punt guns were much used in the nineteenth century by wildfowlers and were formidable weapons. The gun would be mounted on a short tripod in the front of the punt with the wildfowler lying down behind it. When he discharged it, there was enough shot and powder in the thing to take out an entire flotilla of ducks in one blast. They were strictly utilitarian pieces and had absolutely no style.

'Bet it used to make one hell of a bang when it went off,' I commented.

Bill didn't reply, but when I glanced at him there was a manic twinkle in his eye. 'Stay right where you are,' he said, 'I won't be a minute.' He was out of the door and gone before I could say a word. I couldn't be certain, but I had a horrible feeling something unpleasant was on the way.'

If not in one minute, Bill was certainly back within five. He was carrying a coil of rope, a ball of string, and his pockets were full of twelve bore cartridges. He piled them onto a nice sofa table which I always admired, and laid an old clasp knife next to them.

'Open 'em up, Dick, an' get the shot an' powder out,' he instructed.

'Bill,' I said, 'if you're thinking of doing what I think you're thinking of doing, you mustn't do it.'

'Don't be such an old woman, Dick – get on wiv it, Boy!'

'Bill,' I continued to protest, 'the charges in these cartridges are no good for this. You know you've got to use black powder for guns of this age.'

'Yeah, yeah, I know. But look at the barrel on the fing – the metal's a quarter of an inch fick. It's like a bleedin' howitzer. You get them cartridges apart, my son.'

I could have just left him to it; I *should* have just left him to it; but I didn't. Instead of going straight home, I stood there carefully opening the cartridges and separating the charge from the shot. Bill tipped all the charge down the barrel then tore up his handkerchief to use as wadding. Once he'd rammed it down, in went the shot, along with some extra he'd discovered somewhere; again, more handkerchief was ripped up and rammed down after it.

'That'll do the trick, boy. Now get them French winda's open an' give me an 'and wiv the sofa table.'

'What on earth are you going to do with the sofa table?' I asked as I unbolted and opened the French windows.

'You'll see.'

The cold night air flooded in, and the wind billowed out the heavy damask curtains as I fastened back the windows. The sofa table was about four feet long and fitted with castors. Bill piled three cushions from the settee on it, then carefully laid the punt gun on top of the cushions.

'Wheel it to the window, Dick, then I'll rope her on.'

'You're mad, Bill. You know that, don't you?' I said.

'Oh, yeah,' he replied, while he wound the rope round and round both gun and table, 'I know that.' He tied off the rope, checked the gun was held firmly in place, then tossed me the ball of string. 'Unwind that to the door,' he said.

'Why?'

'Well, I may be bleedin' mad, Dick, but I ain't goin' to stand anywhere near this old sow when she goes off. Course, you can stand 'ere an' pull the trigger if yer want to.'

'No, no,' I said, quickly unravelling the string, 'remote control will be just fine, thank you.'

He tied the string onto the trigger, gave the whole contraption one last shake to make sure all was secure, then fine tuned the alignment of the fowling piece as it stuck out of the window into the darkness. Finally, he cocked the hammer and placed a tiny percussion cap on the nipple.

'All set, Dick. Let's go,' he said, like an excited child with a new experimental toy.

We both stood in the corridor with the drawing room door just fractionally ajar.

'Five . . . four . . . three . . . two . . . one . . .' we counted together, '. . . FIRE!'

Bill yanked at the string. For a split second there was absolute silence, then an incredible explosion split the night. Before the reverbations of the blast had died away there was the sound of shattering glass followed by another noise, more difficult to identify. It was a sort of rhythmic rumbling and it was coming towards us. Just as it seemed about to burst through the door, it stopped. Once again there was the sound of breaking glass, another split second's silence, then the most appalling crash I'd ever heard. The silence following that final, awesome cacophony of destruction, was so deep and intense it had an almost spiritual quality.

'Bloody 'ell, Dick,' Bill said, at length, 'what do yer reckon that was?'

'I want to go home,' I said, shaking my head.

'We're in this one togever, my son. Nobody does a runner now.'

He pushed open the door and we both peered round it into the room. It had changed quite a lot. To begin with, it smelt strongly of discharged cordite and a smoky blue haze hung in the air like a layer of light cloud. Directly ahead of us, one of the French windows hung from its top hinge, twisted and stricken, like the broken wing of a bird. Its companion was nowhere to be seen. The doorframe to which it had been attached was splintered to matchwood and a large amount of plaster was missing from the wall next to it. The damask curtain flapped in tatters in the wind, like regimental colours after battle, but there was no sign of either punt gun or table. We found both when we looked behind the door. Remarkably, the gun was still tied to the sofa table although it was a lot shorter than it had been. The barrel had exploded, flared out, twisted and curled back like a banana skin. Considering what the table had been through, it was in remarkably good shape. The richochet

223

from the blast had obviously propelled it across the room at some speed, and it had been its castors on the polished floor that we'd heard coming towards us. Just at the last minute, it must have veered to the left of the door and crashed into a display cabinet which had been hidden away in the corner. The cabinet, in turn, crashed to the floor, where it now lay face down guarding its shattered contents from prying eyes.

'Oh, my Gawd!' Bill Grigson said, a look of horror spreading over his face. 'The bleedin' Crown Derby, Dick. It's written orf the bleedin' Crown Derby. She'll kill me!'

No sooner had he spoken than a great commotion started up in the corridor outside. As it got closer two voices were distinguishable. One was the excited gabble of Mario, the caretaker, while the other was a shrill twitter I'd never heard before. Bill Grigson gripped hold of my forearm in something very close to blind panic.

'It's 'er!' he whispered, as beads of perspiration formed on his brow, 'it's 'er – I'm done for, Dick. Gawd 'elp me, I'm done for, boy.'

An instant later, Mario and Elizabeth Grigson burst into the room. Both had obviously come straight from their beds and wore dressing gowns and slippers.

'I a tella you so! I a tella you so!' Mario howled, as soon as his eyes took in the scene, 'itsa all blowed off! Everythinsa all blowed off!'

Mrs Grigson surveyed the damage in silence, ignoring Mario's hysteria, then she spotted the prostrate display cabinet.

'Where is he?' she demanded of me in the same shrill voice I'd heard coming down the corridor. It wasn't her voice. Her voice was no more than an inoffensive little whisper. I didn't know whose voice it was, but I wished it would go away and find whoever it belonged to.

'Where is he?' the voice repeated. I looked round at Bill, and there he was – gone. His grip on my arm had been so tight it felt as though he was still holding on to it, but he wasn't. He was gone. Gone into the dark, wet, windy night, just like the missing left hand door to the French windows. Across the terrace, over the lawn, out among the trees somewhere, Bill Grigson was skulking like a hunted animal.

I opened my mouth to reply to Elizabeth Grigson's repeated enquiry but no intelligible sound came out. Realising I wasn't going to be any help, the miniature Medusa, complete with curlers rather than writhing serpents, picked her way through the debris in the room and stepped out onto the glass strewn terrace.

'You come back here, Bill Grigson,' she screeched out into the night, the glass splinters crunching and powdering beneath the rubber soles of her woolly slippers, 'you come back here at once, or you'll wish you'd never been born.'

'Did he come back?' Antonia asked.

'Not while I was there,' I replied, 'but then I didn't hang about very long once Mrs G. had arrived on the scene.'

'I don't know, all you men are just overgrown schoolboys really.'

'What do you mean? It was an important scientific experiment.'

'It was an excuse to stay out until one o'clock in the morning playing childish games.'

'Yes, all right, but as excuses go, I don't think it'll be good enough to save Bill Grigson when his wife gets her hands on him. I really think she is going to kill him.'

'He won't be alone if you don't stop burbling and come to bed at once.'

'Yes, Mrs Grigson,' I replied.

Chapter 21

Antonia sat on the edge of the dining table.

'Well, turn around,' she said.

I did.

'And the other way.'

I rotated slowly back again.

'Not bad at all – for off-the-peg. It's the shirt that does it, of course.'

From the very beginning, Antonia had made it quite clear she thought my taste in clothes was awful. I had watched a steady procession of treasured, trendy, high fashion items travel from the wardrobe to the dustbin as they were replaced by things either chosen or officially approved by Antonia. Generally speaking I hadn't protested, although the sudden and unheralded demise of a particular velvet jacket had caused a temporary silent rift in our relationship.

'How much did it cost?' I asked, looking down at the crisp, striped shirt front.

'It's a gift – you shouldn't ask how much gifts cost.'

'I'm sure it must have been very expensive.'

'Jermyn Street shirts have never been known for being cheap, my sweet! Anyway, do you like it?'

'Oh, yes,' I said, 'no doubt about me being the smartest man on the rostrum today. Talking of which, I must go.'

The morning of any sale is always chaotic. The telephones go non-stop, either with last minute reserves from dithering or panic-stricken owners, or with last minute bids from would-be buyers who suddenly find they're going to be late or can't make it to the sale at all. People are in and out of the offices the whole time with countless last minute questions –

what? where? when? how much? – and there are always last minute complaints.

'There's an old geezer outside . . .' Patrick stopped in mid-sentence as he stuck his head round the office door, 'blimey, you're a bit posh this morning, mate. New whistle?'

'Yes, new shirt as well,' Kate said. 'You're supposed to notice the shirt, it's a present from Antonia.'

'Oh, I did, I did – absolutely 'squisite – not Mark-Parky I take it.'

'No, definitely not Marks and Sparks,' Kate confirmed.

'Well, this is one of the advantages of being shacked-up with a rich bird. Anyway, coming back to why I'm here: I've got this old geezer outside who's driving me bleedin' crazy.'

'What's his problem?' I asked.

'A broom.'

'A broom?'

'A broom – it's missing from the lot of gardening tools from that place on the Langton road.'

The job Patrick was referring to had been handled by Duncan. It was a sizeable house clearance and there'd been two or three lawn mowers and a whole heap of garden tools among the outside effects.

'I don't know whether there was ever a broom there,' I said.

'Nor do I, but the old boy keeps on and on about it, and Jim and I are trying to get the line ready for sale, and if you don't get him off our backs one of us is going to kill him.'

Patrick's and Jim's tormentor turned out to be an elderly little man in an old overcoat and open necked shirt. A battered brown trilby hat sat on the back of his head, and white stubble frosted his jaw.

'Can I help you?' I asked.

'Me broom's gorn.'

'I don't quite understand,' I said, 'you say *your* broom's gone.'

'Yeah, me broom's gorn.'

'What broom is this?'

'Moine – I keep tellin' yer. It's gorn.' He continued to rummage through the lot of garden tools, his false teeth clicking together furiously each time he spoke. Every now and then he raised his bottom plate with the tip of his tongue before dropping it back into position with a loud 'clack'. It was like standing next to a crazed flamenco dancer.

'But this lot of tools has come from a house on the way to Langton,' I said to his back, 'they're not yours, Sir.'

'Course they be moine! Who else's they gonna be?'

'They've come in from a house on the Langton road,' I repeated, 'they're part of a deceased's estate – the owner's dead, Sir.'

'Oi know's that,' he said, turning around, his teeth still chattering away independently, 'ol' Miss Donaldson's they was. Oi know she be dead. Oi bain't daft young'un. Wha' Oi wanna know now is – where's me broom?'

Suddenly, the truth dawned on me. 'You were Miss Donaldson's gardener,' I said.

'Oi knows that an' all,' he retorted, impatiently, 'an Oi still wanna know wha' you've done wi' me broom.'

I should have guessed earlier that he'd been the old lady's gardener. Of course, technically, the tools belonged to the estate but, quite naturally, the old chap regarded them as his own. It struck me, considering it was December, we could play Father Christmas for once.

'As it happens,' I said, 'I know the executor of the estate very well, and I'm sure he'd agree to withdraw these tools from the sale if you'd like them.'

'Loike 'em?'

'Yes, if you would like to have them, I'm sure I can arrange to have them withdrawn from the sale. There wouldn't be any charge.'

He stared at me with a mystified expression on his face. For a moment he seemed quite overcome by my act of spontaneous generosity. 'Oi shouldn't think there would be neither,' he said at length, shattering my illusions, as his bottom plate clacked back into position again, 'they be a load of ol' rubbish. She'd ne'er spen' no money on new 'uns – tight ol' bird she were – so I used to take me own tools roun' there to work with, an' that's the problem, Oi'd lef' me broom in the shed an' you buggers come along an' 'ad it.'

'I see,' I said, rather deflated and beginning to suspect I was on a hiding to nothing. I glanced at my watch, there was only half an hour to go before the start of the sale. 'Well, I don't really know what to suggest. All I can do is ask around, but if it was in the shed it should be in that lot.'

'Wha' you mean, *if* it were in the shed. Course it were in the shed. It were in the shed an' one o' you buggers 'as 'ad it – that's wha's 'appened.'

'That's certainly *not* what's happened,' I insisted, 'but there's always a chance it's been misplaced . . .'

'Yeah, misplaced in one o' yourn garden sheds Oi reckon.'

'. . . misplaced,' I continued, determined not to be drawn by his repeated accusations, 'So I'll speak to the carriers and the other staff here. It would probably be best if you could call back later today or tomorrow. Now, if you'll excuse me.'

As I walked off I could feel his eyes following me while his teeth continued to clatter away like castanets. 'Oi'll be back alright!' he shouted after me.

I didn't doubt it for a moment.

The unmistakably foul aroma of one of Tom Jeffrey's cheroots greeted me as I opened my office door. He was sitting talking to Kate.

'It's a pain in the backside, that's . . .' he stopped as I walked in and eyed me up and down. 'Well, I know you haven't had a pay rise, so you must have won the pools.'

'Antonia bought him the shirt,' Kate said. 'Apparently, it's Jermyn Street.'

'You don't say,' Tom said, re-lighting the stub of the cheroot, 'what it is to have rich friends.'

No doubt about it, it was beginning to become tiresome. The only person who'd made no observation on my dress sense that morning was the old man with the remote controlled teeth, and that was probably only because he was preoccupied with his missing broom.

'So what were you moaning about just then, Tom?' I asked, changing the subject.

'DP and his sodding credit crack-down,' he replied, stubbing out the final half inch of cigar into my ashtray, 'you know what it's going to be like, don't you?'

'Yes, I know what it's going to be like.'

It was going to be mayhem, that was what it was going to be like. As was customary on such occasions, Duncan had

229

given strict instructions that absolutely nobody could clear their lots without settling their bills in full. No problem in theory, but a recipe for disaster in practice. Every time Duncan outlawed credit it was the same. The small, but influential group of buyers who always kept us waiting for our money created hell in the sure and certain knowledge that Duncan would relent. That was the daft thing about it: he always did relent, but not until the staff had endured a barrage of complaints.

He'd been just the same the previous sale when it came to viewing on the morning of the auction. Strictly speaking, viewing was not allowed on sale day mornings, but in practice that was when a lot of the trade had their one and only look at the goods on offer.

'Richard, Gallery Three is absolutely heaving with people,' his tone was that of shocked disappointment. 'I want them all out at once or they'll strip the place bare like vultures on a carcass. You know there's no viewing on sale day mornings. I want them all out and the door locked.'

He turned to go without waiting for a reply, then stopped in the doorway and turned wearily to me again. 'I mean, you are supposed to be in charge of this sort of thing. I shouldn't have to tell you about it, Richard.'

I didn't bother to argue; there was no point. I went straight to Gallery Three and, as instructed, threw them all out and locked the door. The people who put up the biggest fight were half a dozen London rug dealers. We'd ended up having a full and frank exchange of views which was terminated when I strode off.

'If we're not allowed to view, we won't bid,' one of them had shouted after me. 'We'll see Mr Parkes about this.'

'Best of luck,' I'd replied.

Ten minutes later Duncan was pacing up and down my office again, his brow drawn up in a frown.

'. . . it's taken me twenty five years to build up this business, Richard. I'm not going to stand by and watch it destroyed by foolish, thoughtless acts like yours.'

'But you said you wanted everyone out and the gallery locked,' I protested.

'I didn't mean the carpet boys. Surely it was obvious I

didn't mean the carpet boys. You know they always view on sale days.'

'But you told me to *lock the door*. Don't tell me you wanted me to lock them in there?'

'Now you're just being ridiculous, Richard. I assumed you would have realised I was speaking metaphorically when I said "lock the door".'

'Metaphorical! How can "lock the door" ever be metaphorical.'

'Easily, and that was plainly what it was – purely metaphorical.'

The worst thing about Duncan's latest credit squeeze was its timing. The December sale was when the porters got their best tips of the year, and regular customers who'd just been upset at the cashier's desk tended to be a bit short on Christmas spirit when it came to dipping into their pockets.

'There'll be blood on the floor out there before the day's done,' Tom commented gloomily, as he got up to go, 'you mark my words – blood on the floor.'

As he wandered out of the office, Duncan erupted into it. 'Have you heard the news?'

'Mafekin relieved?' I suggested.

'What?'

'Nothing – no I haven't heard the news.'

'Arson attacks in Kington!'

'In Kington? Are you sure? Who's been burnt out?'

'Nobody yet, but it's only a matter of time. We must take precautions.'

'What had you in mind?' I asked, ready for almost anything from the installation of a sprinkler system to a permanently manned stirrup pump.

'Not sure yet,' Duncan replied, 'you see, they've been dropping rook scarers through letter boxes all over the town.'

'Sounds like pranksters rather than arsonists.'

'Doesn't matter what they are. Think what would happen here; this place would go up like a tinderbox. No, we must think of something.'

'What about a sandtray under the letter box,' Kate offered.

'Good thinking,' Duncan said, 'we'll work on that – that's a smart shirt you're wearing, Richard.'

'Antonia bought it for him,' Kate said, 'it's from Jermyn Street.'

'Really? What it is to have rich friends, eh! Never mind Kate, you and I'll keep Oxfam going.'

Duncan left as abruptly as he'd arrived.

'Kate, you don't have to tell everyone that my clothes are bought for me by Antonia, you know,' I remarked after Duncan had gone.

'I know, but it's very good for you – stops you getting pompous,' she replied with a giggle.

'Pompous!'

'Yes – pompous.'

'I'm not pom . . .' I was interrupted by Margaret. She was laden with auctioneers books, catalogues, bidding slips and notebooks.

'He's ready, Richard; let's go!'

The first part of the morning session went off without incident, and as arranged I took over from Duncan to sell the metalware – everything from seventeenth-century firedogs to twentieth-century ormolu light brackets. I'd sold about fifty lots when it became evident that somebody was experiencing difficulty getting into The Galleries. A figure was just visible through the frosted glass of the main door, and whoever it was was clearly having problems with the handle. Since, as far as I knew, there was nothing wrong with the handle, I concluded any fault must be with the phantom figure. At that moment the door finally swung open and my worst suspicions were confirmed: silhouetted against the winter sunshine though she was, it was still unmistakably Mrs Partridge. For one thing she was carrying a wicker shopping basket with a dog in it. That, among our customers at least, was a habit unique to Mrs Partridge. Her poodle, Popsy, accompanied her everywhere and, to the best of my knowledge, was never required to set foot on terra firma. I have no idea why. I certainly can't imagine the dog could have been unsteadier on its feet than its devoted owner was on hers.

The lady concerned launched forth into the gallery leaving

the door behind her wide open. She weaved her way through the thirty or forty people standing at the back of the room and, presumably by luck rather than design, avoided falling over any of them. Then she made her way down the wide central aisle which led directly to the rostrum and divided the crowded seating into two separate groups.

'. . . at fifty pounds . . .' I said, trying to concentrate on the bidding but finding my eyes drawn to Mrs Partridge like iron filings to a magnet, '. . . fifty-five . . . sixty . . .' I continued, '. . . sixty-five . . . All done at sixty-five pounds? . . . Last time at sixty-five pou . . .'

'A sheat!' Mrs Partridge demanded of me in the same way you'd order your fifth or sixth dry martini from a cocktail waiter. 'I must have a seat – my doctor says I must not shhhtand for prolonged periodsh.'

'. . . Last time at sixty-five . . . Wade – sixty-five pounds,' I said, bringing my hammer down, still trying to ignore the swaying form of Mrs Partridge. '. . . Lot 368 – a helmet-shaped copper coal scuttle, bid me twenty pounds . . .'

Seeing she was going to get no assistance from me, Mrs Partridge looked both right and left in search of an empty chair. Somehow, her fuzzy vision identified a vacant one at the far end of the second row on my right. She aimed herself at it and began the hazardous journey towards it. It wasn't that it was particularly dangerous for Mrs Partridge; it was everybody else who was in peril. As she barged her way into the row of seated bidders she seemed to trample on every foot available. Her victims' reactions varied from the silent wince or involuntary gasp of pain to the full-blooded yelp of agony.

'. . . twenty-two . . . twenty-five . . . twenty-eight . . .' I went on.

Mrs Partridge's progress set off a sort of chain reaction which ran through the people around her. In her own row, one by one, they leapt to their feet as she trod all over them, then they slid back into their seats again, glaring after her as she forged onwards to the beckoning chair. Those unfortunates in the front row behaved rather differently. As Popsy's wicker basket caught them solidly in the backs of

their necks, or knocked their hats over their eyes, suddenly
plunging them into darkness, they jerked forward and
doubled-up like tin ducks going down in a fairground rifle
range.

'. . . at twenty-eight pounds then . . . Any further bids at
twenty-eight pounds? . . .'

'Thirty!'

It was inevitable, of course. There was never really any
chance that Mrs Partridge would have been happy merely
disrupting proceedings; she always had to participate as
well. I leant over the side of the rostrum and whispered to
Margaret:

'I suppose it's too much to expect of Duncan that he's
actually written to her and informed her that her bids are no
longer acceptable here?'

'Oh, ye of little faith,' Margaret replied, 'he wrote the
same day he had his last credit purge. Mrs Partridge is an
official non-person within these walls.'

'Oh, well, that's something I suppose; not a lot, but
something.'

I sat up in the rostrum again, and looked towards the back
of the room where the twenty-eight-pound bid had come
from, and brought the hammer down. 'Dawson –
twenty-eight pounds . . . Lot 369 – a Dutch-style five-branch
chandelier . . .'

'I bid thirty! Thirty! I bid thirty!'

'I took the gentleman's bid of twenty-eight, Mrs
Partridge . . .'

'I bid thirty, you stupid man! Thirty!'

'I'm sorry, madam, I am instructed not to accept your
bids . . .'

'Thish is outrageoush – I shall see Mr Parkes forthwith.'
With that, Mrs Eleanor Partridge gathered up herself and
Popsy and retraced her footsteps in, for those in the front
two rows at least, the long and painful journey back to the
centre aisle. The front row seemed to come off worst on the
return trip as they were once again viciously beaten about
the ears with Popsy's chosen mode of transport. Once back
in the aisle, Mrs Partridge turned, gave me a boss-eyed look
which I assumed was supposed to be withering, and

zig-zagged her way towards Duncan's office. And that would have been the end of it – a text book handling of a drunken bidder at auction – had not Mrs Partridge's misted eyes lit upon lot 284. It was a rather nice mahogany-cased baby grand piano by Broadwood which had been sold earlier, and it was standing away in one corner. Mrs Partridge and Popsy weaved over to it. Popsy was parked, in her basket, on top of the instrument and Mrs Partridge immediately vamped out a few chords. No sooner had she touched the keys than Popsy threw back her head and let out a blood curdling howl.

'Mrs Partridge! . . .' I remonstrated.

'Mummy will play Popsy's favourite song,' Mrs Partridge said, addressing the wailing beast and completely ignoring me.

'Mrs Partridge! I must insist . . .'

'Howwww much is that doggy in the window?
The one with the waggily tail . . .'

I looked down at Margaret. She shrugged her shoulders and buried her face in her hands.

'Howwwww much is that doggy in the window?' Mrs Partridge enquired again of the balefully howling poodle, 'I do hope that doggy's for shale.'

The room was in a state of hysteria. Dealers who'd never been known to smile, let alone laugh, were falling about unable to catch their breath, while normally severe matrons were publicly reduced to tears.

Drawn from his office by the commotion, it took Duncan several minutes to entice Mrs Partridge into his sanctum, where she applied herself to the gin while he called for a taxi to take her home. As he led her away, she received a considerable ovation which she acknowledged graciously with that special upturned wave so favoured by the Queen Mother.

'There'll be no charge for the cabaret,' I said, 'but bid me fifty for the chandelier . . . fifty I'm bid . . . fifty-five . . .'

If I'd had a rough morning, Tom Jeffreys had had a rough day. No rougher than he'd anticipated, but still rough.

'I'll give you a hand,' I said, joining him in the claustrophobic little cupboard behind the cashier's desk.

235

'Thanks, but the worst is over. Most of the big guns have already refused to pay.'

'What happened?'

'Oh, same as usual: I told them they had to; they bitched to DP, and he said it'd be all right if we got their cheques first post tomorrow. It's alway's the same – complete bloody waste of time.'

'Never mind,' I said, 'there won't be many more clearing lots today, it's gone six o'clock. I'll start to balance up the money – where's the cash?'

'There's a couple of thousand in the drawer and another fifteen grand in the safe in DP's office . . . watch out, here comes real trouble!'

The object of Tom Jeffrey's warning was a dumpy little man in a black overcoat and black Homburg hat. His face was round and yet strangely long at the same time, and as he approached the cashier's desk his expression alternated between beaming benevolence and bleak lugubriousness. It was the inimitable Arthur Turner-Parr.

'What's he owe?' I asked.

'Three thousand nine hundred,' Tom hissed as the old man arrived at the desk and went into lugubrious mode. 'Good evening, Sir – you'd like to pay?'

Mr Turner-Parr switched to beaming benevolence and raised his hat to us without replying to Tom's question. It was true he was slightly hard of hearing in one ear, but any mention of settling our accounts always seemed to make him profoundly deaf.

'Would you like to pay, Sir?' Tom shouted.

'Isn't it,' Arthur Turner-Parr replied, still beaming.

'I swear the old bugger can hear every word I say,' Tom whispered in an aside to me, then leaning across the desk and right through the hatch into the gallery, he bellowed, 'WOULD YOU LIKE TO PAY?'

'No,' replied the instantly mournful Mr Turner-Parr, 'I wish to contra.'

Tom glanced at me and I nodded. 'That'll be fine, Sir,' he said.

The verb, 'to contra', had been invented by Duncan and was the product of a half-grasped piece of accounting jargon.

As far as Duncan was concerned, it meant customers offsetting the cost of their purchases against what we owed them for things we'd sold on their behalf. In the case of Arthur Turner-Parr, we'd sold a little over ten thousand pounds worth that sale.

'I've just checked your account, Mr Turner-Parr,' I said, 'and after commission and other deductions we owe you eight thousand, seven hundred and eighty-nine pounds nett.' The beam returned; no trouble with his hearing now. 'So that's eight thousand, seven hundred and eighty-nine, less three thousand, nine hundred pounds for this sale . . .' I paused to give extra effect to what I was going to say next, '. . . and . . . four thousand, eight hundred and twenty-seven pounds for the previous sale . . .'

I paused again. There was no reaction at all. The old chap just stood there silent and beaming. It wasn't what I'd expected at all. Normally he'd have gone straight up the wall and then given us a dozen reasons why we couldn't deduct both amounts from his sale proceeds, but today, not a word of protest. '. . . WHICH LEAVES JUST SIXTY-TWO POUNDS,' I concluded, loudly, just in case he hadn't heard me.

'Sixty-two pounds,' he concurred, still smiling. Tom stamped his bill 'PAID' and handed it to him. 'Thank you so much, and a very Merry Christmas to you both, good evening,' and with that, he raised his Homburg once more and waddled off.

'Sorry to interrupt, Duncan,' I said, 'but could you get the cash out of your safe so that Tom and I can finish balancing-up.'

Duncan was draped in an armchair in Gallery Two, talking to Jim, Patrick and Jason. 'Yes, of course,' he said, getting up. 'Patrick was just asking what you and Tom did to Arthur this evening.'

'Why? What was wrong with him?'

'He gave me a tip,' Patrick said.

'Good Lord! How much?'

'Oh, only ten pence, but that's ten pence more than he's ever given me before.'

'Well, I suppose it is nearly Christmas,' I said.

'There we are,' Duncan said, handing me a fat manilla envelope, 'twelve thousand in cash and a voucher for the cash that Arthur drew on account.'

'The what?' Tom and I asked together.

'The cash Arthur drew on account. I worked out that we owed him about nine thousand for this sale, less the four thousand nine hundred he's owed us for however long it is, leaves about four thousand, so I gave him three on account when he asked for it – why? What's the matter?'

'What about the three thousand nine hundred he spent this sale?' I asked.

'He's paid for that separately, surely? Hasn't he?' Tom and I shook our heads. 'But he said he was going to pay for that by cheque. He'd got his cheque book and fountain pen out of his pocket before he'd walked out of my office!'

'He'd put them both away again by the time he'd reached the cashier's desk,' Tom remarked.

'You mean he just didn't pay.'

'We mean,' I said, 'that he collected three grand in cash from you, and then came out here and offset eight thousand, seven hundred and twenty-seven pounds of purchases against eight thousand, seven hundred and eighty-nine pounds of sales, thus putting himself back into debt to the tune of two thousand, nine hundred and thirty-eight pounds.'

'No wonder he gave Patrick that ten pence tip,' Tom added.

Duncan looked confused. He stood stroking his chin, looking at the floor, sorting out the mathematics of what I'd just said, then he glanced up and grinned. 'The old sod,' he said, 'you've got to give it to him, though – he never misses a trick.'

By eight o'clock, we were at last ready to go.

'Well, that should do it,' Duncan said as he looked with obvious pride on his home-made anti-arson device.

It comprised a large wooden tray of wet sand, in the centre of which stood a battered red fire bucket full of water.

'If anybody puts a rook scarer through the letter box tonight,' Duncan continued, 'it'll either drop straight into the bucket or it'll fall into the sand, either way it's not going to do any damage.'

'What's the idea of the sand all over the floor?' Jason enquired.

'Oh, that's just where I spilled it. I was going to sweep it up, but I'm not sure whether we've still got a broom.'

'There was one in your office this morning,' Jason said, 'I noticed it because I wondered what it was doing there.'

'Well, it's not there anymore,' Duncan replied, giving his invention one last admiring glance as he opened the street door, 'I meant to tell you about it – quite extraordinary.'

As Margaret set the burglar alarm, we filed out into the dark street and Duncan told us about the strange case of the vanishing broom.

'It was when I helped that awful Partridge woman to her taxi,' he said, watching Margaret lock the door, 'she was so pickled that she'd brought her glass out to the cab with her, then she tried to give it to me and, of course, dropped it. Being the public-spirited chap I am, I went inside and got the broom to sweep up the broken glass. I'd just about finished when this scruffy little old man appeared from nowhere and just snatched the broom out of my hands.'

'Snatched it?'

'Yes, just walked up to me, grabbed the broom, called me "a thievin' sod" and walked off with the thing.'

'Didn't you try to stop him?' Margaret asked.

'How could I? Short of using physical force, there wasn't really much I could do. I can see it in the local paper now: "Respected Auctioneer Assaults Geriatric Vagrant – he stole my broom, claims Parkes". No, no, it wouldn't do at all. Anyway, I'd just had the better part of half an hour with Eleanor Partridge, and a man can only take so much in one day. All the same, it was very odd – perhaps the old boy had some sort of broom fetish!'

The Galleries seemed to possess some of the qualities of a laundry when I arrived the following morning; pieces of damp, steaming paper decorated every piece of heating apparatus we had, and Duncan was dashing around, turning them, flattening them, and occasionally holding them up to the light.

'What on earth's going on?' I asked.

'It's all a matter of good news and bad news, really,' he answered, as he brushed past me on his way to the heater in my office.

'Good news and bad news?' I said, following in his wake.

'Yes,' he continued, 'for instance: a lot of the London trade were good to their word and put cheques in the post yesterday afternoon – that's good news.'

'Yes.'

'And nobody put rook scarers through the letter box last night – that's good news.'

'Yes.'

'And the post arrived early this morning.'

'Well, that's good news,' I said.

'Not exactly,' Duncan said, holding a small rectangle of apparently blank paper up to the light, 'you see, it arrived so early, neither Margaret nor I had arrived.'

'You mean . . .'

'Yes, the bad news is the whole lot ended in your anti-arson device.'

'*My* anti-arson device!'

'All right, *our* anti-arson device.'

'Did everything go into the bucket?'

'No, as far as I can tell, Murphy's law came into play.'

'What do you mean?'

'Well, it would seem that all the cheques for small amounts were written in ballpoint, and they all landed in the sand; whereas all the cheques for large amounts were written in fountain pen, and they all went straight into the water.'

'Oh, great!' I said, slumping into my chair.

'Yes, I'm afraid that you and Kate are going to have to make a few phone calls this morning to sort this lot out.'

'Just wonderful – exactly how I'd wanted to spend my morning.'

'Never mind,' Duncan said, as he peered at another piece of discoloured scrap paper, 'look on the bright side – at least we haven't lost a cheque from Arthur Turner-Parr.'

Chapter 22

I had first seen the pendant back in October on the day James Browning had bought it. It was Edwardian, diamond and sapphire, very beautiful and very expensive. Fortunately, James was a very understanding man. He took pity on me, agreed a price which was a steal, and said he would keep it for me until Christmas. By Christmas Eve I'd just about scraped together enough money to buy it, so I hurried along Kington High Street to his shop.

James Browning specialised in silver and jewellery and had particularly nice premises to work from. On that cold, damp morning, the inside of his shop looked even more inviting than usual through the small, square panes of the old bow window. The window display was laid out as immaculately as ever, and the silver, gold and gem stones sparkled and twinkled under the sharp white beams of the spotlights. The buzzer sounded loudly in the back room as I opened the door. Before I had closed it, the proprietor was in his place behind the counter.

'Hello, Richard. Not changed your mind then?'

'No, James, I've just about managed to raise the money, as promised.'

'Well done, it's a good buy anyway. I could have sold it a dozen times over since I promised it to you. I'll just pop out to the back and get it – won't be a minute.'

While he was gone I glanced around his shop. It was a million miles removed from the dirt, dust and general chaos of The Galleries. The steady tick of a mahogany bracket clock added to the general impression of somnolence which belied the growing business James Browning presided over. Although he specialised in silver and jewellery he usually had a few pieces of furniture for sale as well. They were

241

always strictly utilitarian items for the shop – display tables, hanging shelves, pairs of elegant chairs and so on. He would put a big price on them and if somebody bought them, all well and good; if they didn't sell, James didn't mind. On this occasion, one particular piece caught my eye. It was a Victorian walnut whatnot, and not a very nice one at that. I had a look at the price tag. It was marked at three hundred pounds. I handed James the cheque for the pendant and slipped the box into my overcoat pocket. 'James.'

'Yes.'

'That whatnot – where did you buy it?'

'That thing – I remember it well. I picked it up at auction in Langton and I wish I'd never seen it. I hate it more with each passing day, but unfortunately everybody else hates it even more than I do. I'm afraid it'll probably end up with Wilson's Auction Galleries in the New Year.'

'You can't have had it long, surely?' I said.

'Not long! I've had that dreadful thing for a year or more. It haunts me like Marley's ghost, every day reminding me what an idiot I can be when I start buying furniture. Anyway, why all the questions?'

'It's just that I saw it about three months ago in a flat in Southbourne.'

'Not possible, Richard,' he said, emphatically, 'I told you, I've had the misfortune of owning the thing for a year now . . .' he paused, then gave me a quizzical look.

'. . . Hold on a minute,' he said, 'you say you saw it in Southbourne?'

'Yes.'

'Was the flat concerned owned by two elderly ladies by any chance?'

'Yes.'

'Not the Mistresses Leach and Farrow?'

'Yes.'

James shook his head slowly and smiled. 'You know, it's supposed to be us dealers who are the cunning ones, but we're just amateurs compared with certain members of the great British public.'

'Are you going to explain this to me or do I have to guess?' I asked.

242

'Well, those two old birds come into the shop quite regularly – every month or so, I suppose. They rarely buy anything and when they do it's usually cheap and nasty, but that's up to them. Anyway, one day they say they like the whatnot and they start to try to beat me down on the price. It went on for hours, and in the end I told them they could have it for two hundred and fifty, just to get rid of them. It didn't work. Instead, they went into a huddle and umm-ed and ahh-ed about it for another quarter of an hour. The upshot was they said they were very nearly certain they wanted it, but could they just try it on appro for a week to see if it fitted in with their decor. I should have chucked them out then and there but they'd worn me down so I agreed. Then they asked me if I'd mind dropping it over to them the next time I was going to Southbourne, so like an idiot I agreed to that as well. I carted the damned lump all the way over there and didn't hear another word for three weeks, so I sent them a bill. Next thing, I got a telephone call asking me to collect the bloody thing because it "just didn't fit in".'

I couldn't help laughing at poor old James's tale of woe. Before they finally admitted defeat, Winnie and Minnie had probably had every dealer and auctioneer in Sussex to look at the whatnot to see if they could make a profit on it. If nothing else, they were thorough.

Christmas Eve was a day of time-honoured ritual at Wilson's. It was the day Duncan entertained the staff to Christmas lunch. It was a lavish affair, with good food and wine in the best old hotel in Kington. I always felt Christmas had begun when we sat in the lounge after the meal, with coffee, brandy, and liqueurs, in front of the blazing log fire. I say I always *felt* it had begun, but whether it had or not depended on Duncan's mood. He was just as likely to announce it was time to go back to get on with the catalogue as he was to wish us Merry Christmas.

One year in particular, we trooped back to The Galleries in mutinous mood, only for him to relent after half an hour, probably as a result of pressure from Margaret. I was out of the door and into the Ford Prefect so fast I must have been a blur. Naturally, things slowed up a little once I was in the car. Consequently, while chugging past The Brickmaker's Arms, I had plenty of time to peer through the customary pall of black smoke and notice the bar lights were still on. Since it was half past three, and since Harry and Elsie were normally back in bed by a quarter to three at the latest, I felt I should investigate.

The car stopped as reluctantly as it had started, but once safely parked I got out of the thing and approached the door to the Brickies public bar. Even before it was opened a rumbling din of conversation and laughter spilled out into the cold street. When I actually turned the handle and pushed on the door, the noise was momentarily overwhelming, then all was quiet in an instant. Exactly one hour after closing time the pub was packed and a sea of suddenly silent faces was turned towards me. Recognition took only a split second though, and the hubbub restarted as though somebody had thrown a switch.

'My dear boy, wonderful to see you,' gushed Harry from his perch behind the bar, 'what will you have? On the house, dear boy, on the house!'

I eased my way through the massed bodies of locals until I got within reach of the bar, 'Half of Guinness please, Harry,' I eventually replied.

'Half? Half?' Elsie's querulous voice rose above the background noise. I glanced in the direction of the voice but there was no sign of the speaker. Then the crowd swayed, tottered and eventually parted like the Red Sea as Elsie rose from a chair in the bar and came towards me.

'Happy Christmas, darling,' she said, planting a huge kiss on my lips, 'no halves today – give him a large malt, Harry.'

Harry stood up, took a bottle down from the shelf behind him and cast around for a spirit measure. 'Can't seem to find anything, old boy,' he giggled, 'it's Elsie, you know, she never puts anything back.'

'It's by your hand, Harry,' Elsie said, 'no, not that hand, the other one.'

Harry pushed his spectacles back onto the top of his head and stared at the work top. 'Remarkable woman,' he said, locating the measure at last, 'eyes like a hawk. Not that I couldn't see it, of course, just that I couldn't decide which one to pick up.'

'There is only one,' I said.

'To you, dear boy, there may indeed be but one spirit measure, but I assure you, to those like myself who have been partaking of true Christmas Spirit since eleven o'clock this morning, there is a choice.' Giggling again, he made a valiant effort to bring bottle and measure together. He failed, and flopping back onto his stool as his spectacles dropped crookedly back onto his nose, he pushed the bottle, measure and glass across the bar towards me.

'You have a go, Richard,' he said, smiling serenely, 'I know when I'm beaten.'

It must have been about half past four when somebody suggested Christmas Carols before we went to our homes. Our resident police sergeant – one of three members of the local constabulary present – said he'd play the piano if anyone could find it. The battle-scarred instrument was eventually located in its usual corner under a mound of coats and an artificial Christmas tree. The tree was an annual feature, and must have started to show signs of old age and wear and tear many years earlier. It was draped with a set of lights which didn't work, and for all any person present could tell, probably never had. Each year Harry got them out of their box, plugged them in and expressed surprise and disappointment at their non-illuminatory properties. At the end of each Christmas they were carefully packed away again for the following year.

The assembled company bawled out one old favourite after another. 'O Come All Ye Faithful', 'Good Christian Men Rejoice' and 'Once in Royal David's City' all came and went, delivered with much enthusiasm if not a lot of skill. Harry made a brave stab at singing the first verse of 'Silent Night' in German. He failed, but that was hardly surprising since by that stage he was experiencing some difficulty in just speaking English. The pianist displayed remarkable concentration and skill throughout the performance. Not only was he locked in open combat with a choir which refused to be restrained or limited by accepted musical tenets, he was also subjected to an insidious form of sabotage by the piano itself. The instrument always had at least three sticking keys, but on that occasion, due perhaps to the cold spell, or just the number of pints tipped into it in the past, it seemed to deliver combinations of notes at random.

'What's the matter with it?' I asked.

'I don't know, Richard,' the pianist replied, 'I'm certain I'm playing all the right notes – the piano seems to be rearranging the order though!'

It was a quarter to six when we at last spilled out onto the street. More kisses, more Merry Christmases and then I was back in my car and on my way. As I drove away, Harry and Elsie were sliding the bolts and turning out the lights. As every other pub in Kington was preparing to open, The Brickmakers' Arms was closing for the night.

'It's beautiful!' Antonia said, as she picked the pendant from its box and laid it on the palm of her hand.

'Do you like it?' I asked.

'Of course I do, Richard, it's beautiful. But it must have cost a fortune.'

'It's a gift, and I'm told it's rude to ask how much gifts cost.'

'Oh, shut up and put it on for me please,' she said, handing it to me.

'Okay, but I think it would look better on you.'

'Richard!'

'All right, all right, just a little joke.'

As she stood in front of me, looking into the mirror, I put the gold chain round her neck and fastened the clasp.

'Whenever I wear this, I shall think of you,' she said, looking at me in the mirror. There was something about the way she said it that made me feel uncomfortable – like reading one's own obituary.

'That's like a line from a B-movie.'

'Don't be so horrible,' she said, turning round and putting her arms around my neck, 'I mean it – it will always remind me of you, of us, of our time together.'

'You make it sound as though it's over.'

'No, no, I don't mean to. It's just that nothing stays the same. Times change. People change. It's wrong to pretend that anything lasts for ever; it doesn't. That's why it's important to enjoy each day and to have good memories. There's nothing wrong with good memories, Richard.'

246

'No, it's just that I'd intended to be around in person for a bit longer, that's all. I hadn't intended the pendant as some sort of *memento mori*.'

'I'm not talking about anybody dying, you idiot. It's just that I'm going to have to think about getting a proper job soon. I've been messing about temping for nearly two years now and my brain's beginning to seize up. And what about you?'

'What about me?'

'Well, are you planning to stay at Wilson's for ever?'

She'd never put the question that directly before. She'd only hinted at it before, and I'd always refused to be drawn. 'Perhaps. Why not?' I replied, with all the sullenness I could muster.

'Oh, you do annoy me when you get like this!' she said, walking over to the fireplace. She stood there, leaning against the mantelpiece, looking down at the flames from the logs in the grate.

'Like what?'

'You know perfectly well,' she said, looking up at me again, 'so stubborn and stuck in your ways. You're too comfortable at Wilson's. You're frustrated, you moan, but you're just too comfortable to move, and that's awful. You're already middle-aged and you're not thirty yet.'

'Thanks very much – what did you get me for Christmas: a wheelchair?'

'It's no good, Richard. It's true, and you know it is.' She turned back to the fire and pushed one of the logs with her foot. As the sparks flew upwards she looked up again. 'Just promise me one thing.'

'What?'

'That you'll think about London.'

'I've told you . . .'

'I know, I know,' she interrupted, 'you wouldn't like it, and you wouldn't be offered a job anyway, and even if you were you'd probably be worse off financially. I know, but next time Bill Grigson offers to introduce you to someone important up there, just think about it. All right?'

'All right. I promise. Now can we get on with Christmas?'

'I wish you would – that champagne's going to be tepid if you don't open it soon.'

Chapter 23

Although the dawn chorus had barely subsided the cottage was already uncomfortably sticky. Despite the windows having been wide open all night, neither of us had slept very well in the un-English summer heat, so we both decided to get up early. It was evident it was going to be another blistering day.

'Are you going to London?' I asked.

'I should, but I can't face it,' Antonia replied, 'it's going to be in the nineties again. Are you at The Galleries or out?'

'Bit of both – why?'

'Oh, I just thought it would be nice if we could have a swim this evening and then go into Langton for a meal.'

'Sounds fine, I shouldn't be late. I've only got two appointments: one probate in the middle of nowhere near Frisham, and yet another visit to the dreaded Mrs Hill in Newbay.'

Mrs Hill was not my favourite client. She was in her late sixties, comfortably well off, fit and healthy. She was also duplicitous and greedy. Some months earlier she had decided to move from an eight-bedroomed house in the country to a three bedroomed house in the popular coastal retirement town of Newbay. As a result, she had a considerable surplus of furniture, pictures, porcelain and everything else. I must have spent hours with her during the three months leading up to the move, while she tried to decide what she was going to keep. At last she made up her mind, and I went ahead and made all the necessary transport arrangements with Watson's.

Three days later she changed her mind again and I was summoned once more. I spent another three hours going through all the values with her, taking items off the list of things for sale and putting others on in their place. I removed our tickets from the bits she no longer wanted to sell, and put tickets onto the new things that were coming to us instead.

Twenty-four hours later she changed her mind again and I went back and put everything back as it was. I could forgive her her indecision; moving house is a traumatic experience at the best of times, and if it's after a long spell in one place the accumulated belongings are awesome. What I couldn't forgive Mrs Hill was her last minute crookery. When Watson's eventually arrived at The Galleries, instead of having a truck full of eighteenth- and nineteenth-century furniture, pictures and china, all they had to offer were five box-based divan beds, some worn fitted carpet and a quantity of old kitchen equipment.

'What the hell's this junk, Pat?' I asked.

'She's decided to keep everything else,' Patrick said, as he collapsed onto the tailboard of the lorry. 'She's had us running round in circles all bleeding day. I swear, I'll never do another job for that old bat as long as I live.'

'But what's she going to do with it all? She can't possibly fit it all into her new place.'

'No, but she's going to have a sodding good try. Jim said there's stuff stacked to the ceiling in almost every room.'

'But what about her dining table and the set of chairs – there were fourteen of them. Don't tell me she's keeping them as well.'

'No, but I thought I'd break that to you gently. Are you sitting comfortably? . . . She's sold them.'

'Sold them!'

'Yeah, to a local dealer. He came and collected them this morning while we were loading up.'

'I'll kill her!'

'After you,' Patrick said.

I didn't attempt to contact Mrs Hill that afternoon. It would have been a mistake. After all, I still wanted to salvage something from what would otherwise turn out to be nothing other than the most monumental waste of time. It was best to allow my temper to cool before I spoke to her, so it wasn't until the next morning that I found myself listening to her twittering excuses.

'It was just that you said the table would make five hundred and the chairs would make fourteen hundred, Mr Harton, and Mr Beale – the dealer – said he would give me eighteen hundred cash, for the lot. I mean, I would have got less than that from you after you'd deducted your commission, wouldn't I?'

'I said the table would make five to seven hundred, and the chairs an absolute minimum of fourteen hundred. I would have expected them to make nearer two thousand, perhaps more.'

There was silence at the other end of the line, then a little whining voice said, 'Have I been terribly silly, Mr Harton?'

Mrs Hill's problem was not so much stupidity as greed. You could reason out everything with her, make all the arrangements for her, then at the last minute a complete stranger could wave a bunch of five pound notes under her nose and off she'd go without a second thought.

Nor was the fiasco of the table and chairs the last of Mrs Hill's woes which resulted from her move to Newbay. About two weeks after Watson's had somehow managed to squeeze her into her new home – a sort of loaves and fishes act in reverse – Patrick popped in to see me.

'It's your friend Mrs Hill,' he said, 'she's been driving us mad for the past two days.'

'What's her problem now,' I asked.

'She can't find her Mason's Ironstone.'

'You're joking – there were about fifty pieces of it. It can't have been lost.'

'Well, she claims she can't find it, and none of our blokes remember it because she'd already packed it before we'd arrived. God knows where she put it.'

I sat back in my chair and rubbed my eyes. I'd got to the stage when just the mention of Mrs Hill's name made me feel tired. 'Have you been over to Newbay to have a look?' I asked.

'Chance would be a fine thing! She says we're a bunch of thieves, she won't have us in the house, and she's going to report us to the police.'

250

'Oh, God! Leave it with me, Pat, I'll see if I can make any sense of the wretched woman.'

It wasn't as if Mrs Hill's Mason's Ironstone was an easy thing to lose. It was a large dinner service which had always been on display in a cabinet in the dining room of her old house. It dated from between 1815 and 1820, and was really quite valuable; now she'd managed to mislay it – all fifty pieces of it.

'I don't know what to do,' she sobbed when I called her.

'Well, I can tell you the first thing to do is drop these preposterous charges you're making against Watson's, or I'm not in the slightest bit interested in helping you.'

'Oooooh . . .' she wailed.

'But if you do that, and if you're really certain the service has gone missing, I'll help you make a claim against your insurance policy – yours, not Watson's; do you understand, Mrs Hill?'

'Yes, Mr Harton,' she sniffed.

'And as a matter of interest, how many dealers did you have look around your old house between my last visit and the time Watson's moved you out?'

'Mmmm?'

'I think you understand the question, Mrs Hill.'

'Well . . . er . . . I suppose . . . er . . .'

'How many, Mrs Hill?'

'. . . er . . . About a dozen . . . Perhaps . . .'

I sighed deeply. The woman was incorrigible. If they'd all been respectable dealers that would have been one thing, but I could well imagine the sort of individuals to whom she'd given guided tours. She might just as well have stacked the boxes of china on the lawn with a notice saying 'Please Take Me' pinned to them.

That had all been over six months ago, and the insurance claim was long settled, so I had been a little surprised when, out of the blue, I received a telephone call from Mrs Hill.

'Hello, Mr Harton,' she said, 'I'd like you to come out to Newbay if you would, to have a look at some pieces I've decided to sell.'

I was very sceptical. 'Surely you haven't still got all the

furniture from your old house, Mrs Hill. I assumed you'd sold it elsewhere.'

'No, Mr Harton, I do admit I sold a few pieces to local dealers, but I don't think I did as well as I would if I'd got you to sell them for me.'

'No, Mrs Hill, I don't expect you did.'

'I know you think I've been very silly, Mr Harton . . .'

'Yes, Mrs Hill, quite frankly, I do.'

'But I've still got my Queen Anne bureau, and my Regency sofa table, and most of my best pieces, and I do so want your advice, Mr Harton. You're the only person I can trust.'

The sea lay flat and still as I drove into Newbay. Although it was barely eight thirty, the promenade was quite busy with people on their way to the beach. Overweight parents with their overweight offspring – each member of the family transporting some piece of equipment vital to beach life – perspired their way along the front in search of the steps that would deliver them down to the sand and cool water. Elderly men with open shirt collars lapped over their blazers, slouched along in buckled leather sandals and grey woollen socks. They bristled with umbrellas, aluminium folding chairs, redundant windbreaks and blankets. Accompanying them, and walking either a few steps ahead or a few steps behind but never alongside, were the spouses. In straw sunhats, printed cotton frocks and surgical stockings, each and every one seemed to be carrying an identical tartan-patterned bag, full, doubtless, of fish paste sandwiches, slices of fruit cake, thermos flasks of tea and half pints of fast curdling milk in plastic containers.

Unable to resist the call, the British were being drawn to the water's edge, and in most cases, no further. It's odd that an island race should look so out of place on a beach, but we do. I suppose it's our normally inhospitable weather that makes us such strangers to sand and spray. At least the climate couldn't be blamed that summer. As I turned off the front and headed up the tree-lined street to Mrs Hill's house, the sun flashed silver off the sea in my rear view mirror while the temperature continued to rise.

252

Mrs Hill was contrition itself. She swore she'd seen the error of her ways and said she'd never be so silly again. As she'd said on the telephone, she still had most of her better pieces crammed into the house, although several nice things, including a good walnut chest on stand, were missing. I shuddered to think how little she'd sold them for.

'I know I behaved stupidly,' she simpered, 'but it was because I'd got so over wrought with the move. I'm sure you understand, Mr Harton.'

'Yes, but I'm afraid there's nothing we can do about that now, Mrs Hill,' I said, without feeling much sympathy, 'what is it you'd like me to look at today?'

'There are three pieces,' she said, apparently untroubled by my brusque manner. 'The thing is, I must make some room. I've just got too much furniture for this house.'

'You don't say,' I said, looking round. Even the entrance hall was packed with furniture; one of the pieces being a large Edwardian mahogany wardrobe. It was heavily inlaid with classical motifs, and couldn't have looked much more out of place. Plainly, Watson's had either been unable to get it up the stairs or they'd simply got tired of Mrs Hill and dumped it.

'Yes, now that's one of the pieces,' she said, 'what did you say you thought that would make when you saw it last time?'

'Three to four hundred pounds.'

'Ah yes,' she said, producing a tiny spiral-bound memo pad and a pen, and carefully noting down the price, 'two to three hundred.'

'No, three to four hundred.'

'Oh, yes, right, three to four hundred,' she said, scribbling out the first entry and writing down the correct figures. 'The other pieces are in the drawing room, Mr Harton. I expect you'll remember them.' I followed her out of the entrance hall. 'Now, the Georgian secretaire really must go, Mr Harton . . . Mr Harton? . . . Mr Harton?'

I wasn't looking at the George III secretaire bookcase; I was looking at the large mahogany display cabinet which used to stand in the dining room of her old home. More to the point, my attention was focused on what I saw in the display cabinet: about fifty pieces of Mason's Ironstone dinnerware. I turned to Mrs Hill. She was scarlet with embarrassment.

'Surely, that's the service you claimed for as missing, isn't it?' I asked.

'Er . . . yes . . . I mean, no . . . I mean it's very similar . . . but not the same . . .' she blustered, in some considerable confusion.

'Not the same?' I said, as I went over to have a closer look. 'You amaze me. It looks identical, right down to the staining on those two plates.'

'Well . . . I can assure you it's not the same one, Mr Harton . . . I bought it with the insurance money to replace the stolen service.'

'Really! Where did you buy it?'

'A dealer in Langton,' she said, shuffling from foot to foot.

'Langton? Now that does surprise me, I wouldn't have thought you'd have found a service like this so quickly in Langton.'

'No . . . er . . . I was very lucky.'

'You certainly were,' I said, smiling at the increasingly uncomfortable Mrs Hill, 'what was his name?'

'What?'

'What was the dealer's name – I probably know him.'

'Er . . . I don't remember . . .'

'You spent a thousand pounds or more with him, and you don't remember his name?'

'No . . . I told you . . . I've been very overwrought . . . Why do you keep asking me all these questions, Mr Harton?'

She was close to breaking, but since I was certain she'd turn on the tears rather than tell me the truth, there seemed little point in pursuing the matter. I was certain in my own mind what had happened. She'd mislaid the service, made the insurance claim with my assistance, banked the insurer's cheque and then discovered the boxes containing the service, probably when she was busy selling some of her furniture to some dealer or other. At that stage she'd had three choices: she could have given her insurers their money back, or she could have given her insurers the service (which was by then technically theirs anyway), or she could have kept them both. The temptation proved too much for her. She kept both money and Mason's and forgot all about it. She even forgot I knew about the reported loss and the subsequent claim.

'It's not the same one,' she said, regaining her composure, 'I can understand you being so convinced it was, though; it's so very like my old service . . . Remarkable, really remarkable. Of course, that's why I bought it.'

'Of course.'

'Anyway, Mr Harton,' she smiled and managed a rather theatrical laugh, 'I'm sure you don't really think I'm a common thief.'

As it happened, that was precisely what I did think she was. She was also the sort of lady who would have happily sat on a magistrate's bench sending others to gaol for stealing half the amount she'd taken. She really was a difficult woman to feel sorry for.

'The secretaire bookcase will make eight to twelve hundred,' I said, leaving Mrs Hill to come to her own conclusions as to my opinion of her. 'What else was it you wanted to sell?'

'The Queen Anne walnut bureau,' she said, taking my arm and leading me to it.

'I think I mentioned, when I saw it at your old house, that it's George II not Queen Anne, Mrs Hill.'

'Oh, whatever! How much?'

'Five to eight hundred.'

'Fine, fine,' she said, noting down that price as she had the other two. She seemed fully recovered from the nasty turn my identification of the dinner service had given her.

'Will you arrange transport for me, Mr Harton?' she asked.

'If you're absolutely certain you want to sell them this time,' I said.

'Oh, absolutely.'

'All right, then, I'll arrange it now if I might use your telephone.'

'Yes, of course. Will it be? . . . Now that was their name? . . . Such nice men . . .'

'Watson's.'

'Yes, that's it. Will it be them?'

255

'No,' I said, firmly, but without explanation, 'I'll be using one of the Newbay firms.'

'Oh, well, I'm sure you know best.'

'Yes,' I said.

As I drove over the Downs towards Frisham, I wondered what Mrs Hill would do this time to wreck the arrangements I'd made for her. Whatever it was going to be, she wasn't going to have much time to organise it; the carriers were going to pick up her three pieces of furniture the following afternoon.

Old House Farm really was in the middle of nowhere. It was about five miles outside Frisham, down a rough track that must have been impassible when it rained or snowed. The track was bordered on one side by a flint wall, and on the other by a rather unruly blackthorn hedge. The two eventually opened out into a sort of funnel shape, providing a rough triangle of grass in front of the house. It was obvious cars didn't go that way often. As I drove up, a dozen or so geese got up reluctantly from the grass and strutted about, honking loudly to announce my arrival. The house was a typical old Sussex farmhouse: oak-framed but clad in brick, flint and faded clay tiles. On either side of the crookedly ajar, blue painted front door, two tiny asymmetrically placed windows overlooked the patch of grass. I picked my way through the goose droppings and knocked at the open door. Somewhere in the house a dog barked, then I heard a woman's voice followed by footsteps.

Miss Beeching was a petite, white-haired, seventy-five-year-old who seemed to be blessed with a naturally happy disposition. That was just as well since her immediate future looked rather bleak. As I sat with her, drinking homemade lemonade, in the surprisingly cool, brick-paved kitchen, she told me all about her problems.

Alice Beeching and Lucy Deniker had lived at Old House Farm for the better part of thirty years. They'd bought it, along with six acres of downland fields, shortly after the war when there was little competition for damp old houses with no mains water, no electricity and no telephone. Miss Deniker had provided most of the money, so house, land, and flint-built outbuildings all went in her name. It had been agreed at the outset that each would will her entire estate to the other, so the survivor could live on at the house for as long as she wished.

It never crossed their minds to stay abreast of changes in tax laws; to be fully conversant with death duties, capital transfer tax and capital gains tax. They'd never discussed with accountants or solicitors the advantages of holding the property in both names or the formation of a trust. And why should they? They'd never had any money in their lives. Admittedly, they'd both received small private incomes, paid to them quarterly by cheques written in the trembling hand of aged trustees, but that was certainly not enough to live on. The bulk of their income had come from the fruits of their labours; from free-range eggs and goat's cheese, before either had become a trendy essential on the shopping lists of Barbour-clad ladies in Range Rovers; from geese, ducks and hens for the table; from bottled fruits and homemade jams. It had always been hard work and there had never been much to spare, but then neither of the ladies had ever wanted much, other than to be allowed to live as they were.

They had had the house connected to mains water and plumbed, and in later years they'd also, with great reluctance, accepted the intrusion of the telephone – just in case of emergencies. The one public utility they'd always spurned was electricity; both of them preferring the kinder light of oil lamps and candles. In this way, and with the added assistance of a single Jersey milk cow and half a dozen sheep, they'd quietly lived their lives at Old House Farm.

The end of their idyll had been foreshadowed by a sudden loss of both appetite and weight on the part of Miss Deniker. Eventually, at her friend's insistence, she had paid a rare visit to her GP who had immediately arranged an appointment with a specialist. She had sat impassively as the doctor had delivered his prognosis, and had reached out just once to squeeze her friend's hand, as though it were Miss Beeching rather than she who was ill. When the doctor had finished, she'd thanked him for his trouble but refused any treatment, although she did ask if she might have some help with the pain at the end. Just eight weeks after seeing her GP, Miss Lucy May Deniker was laid to rest in the cool

257

shadow of the old yew trees in the churchyard at Frisham. It was then that Alice Beeching's problems began.

I can't believe that those politicians and Whitehall mandarins responsible for devising our re-distributive taxes actually set out to ensnare the likes of Miss Beeching when they designed our various inheritance taxes, but that was precisely what they achieved. While the really wealthy take advantage of tax havens, off-shore companies and expensive advice, the Alice Beechings of the world swim blindly into the nets cast to catch bigger fish.

When Lucy Deniker died, Miss Beeching inherited a few hundred pounds in cash, the proceeds of a small life insurance policy intended to provide for funeral expenses (which it almost did), and Old House Farm. It was the latter which was her undoing.

The farm had cost Miss Beeching and her friend just a few thousand pounds. That they'd had to scrape around for the money didn't matter to them; they'd simply fallen in love with the place and wanted to live there, miles from anybody. And why not? They'd both served as nurses during the war and had seen all they wanted to of man's inhumanity to man. So live there they did, with their candles, their livestock, their produce and the changing seasons. Unfortunately, not just the seasons changed; the value of property changed as well. Neither of them gave it a thought. Neither of them dreamed for one moment they might have to sell Old House Farm just to pay the tax on it, but that was exactly the scenario Miss Beeching's solicitor had presented her with.

'It just seems so unfair,' she said to me as she refilled my glass, 'I never asked for our house to suddenly become valuable. All I want to do is go on living here. It doesn't seem right that they can make me leave. It's just not . . . not English, somehow.'

'No, it isn't,' I said. 'I suppose you haven't any cash, or investments you could realise to pay the tax?'

She laughed. 'With what Lucy left me and what I've got in my post office account, I'll have about a thousand pounds in all the world. Apart from that, I have my own little income from father's trust, and my old age pension. I don't think that's going to get me very far.'

She was right, it wasn't.

Anthony Wilson had already valued the house and land, and had called me the previous day to have a chat about Miss Beeching's problems. Despite his rather blimpish exterior he was a decent man, and was concerned about the old lady's plight.

'I've put the house in at the lowest figure I dare,' he'd said. 'In fact, I'm not at all sure the Revenue will swallow it, old boy. The problem is that, even at that level, there will be a tax liability of several thousand pounds, and the old girl just hasn't got the money – no money at all . . . none at all.'

It certainly was a dilemma, and what I saw, as I walked around the house with my notebook and pen, didn't help. Poor Miss Beeching was scrupulously honest about telling me which pieces of furniture had been Miss Deniker's and which were her own. Such honesty tended to be the exception rather than the rule in my experience. It wasn't at all unusual to walk into a room and be confronted with deep impressions in the carpet where fine pieces of furniture had stood, or to encounter large rectangles of clean paintwork, or unfaded wallpaper, where valuable oil paintings had once hung. For some reason, the guilty executors or beneficiaries would almost always hang some horrible print or engraving on the vacant hook. The replacement was usually quarter the size of the original occupant of the space, so it would dangle there, surrounded by a wide border of pristine wall, while family members stood by, self-consciously trying to interest me in something else, anything else, just as long as it was at the other end of the room.

There was no such deceit in Old House Farm – it wouldn't have crossed Alice Beeching's mind.

I still remember it as one of the most perfectly furnished houses I've ever seen. Nothing to do with value, far more to do with everything just looking as though it belonged there. It had all obviously been cherished and cared for over the years. The rich colour of the waxed oak complemented the creamy-white plaster and black-brown beams that constituted the unvarying decoration throughout. The rooms were sparsely furnished and most things were utilitarian. The floors were either brick paved or bleached oak boards and

259

were dotted with worn, but colourful, old rugs. The quietness of the setting, and the lack of electric light fitments, heightened the feeling of going back two hundred and fifty years in time.

'Is any of it worth huge amounts of money?' asked Miss Beeching. 'I do hope not.'

'No, it's not,' I said. 'That's not to say it's not very nice; it is, but you'd have to sell the lot to raise the sort of sum you need, and that would rather defeat the object.'

'Yes, it would.'

'So, unless you've got something hidden away that I haven't seen, I can't really be of much help.'

'No, I'm afraid you've seen it all,' she paused, laughed, then went on, 'except for Cecil's "Strad" that is.'

'Cecil's "Strad"?'

'Yes, my brother's violin. He was killed in the Great War. The last time it was ever played was the last time he came home on leave, in 1917. Lucy always used to scold me about it. She said that keeping a musical instrument and not playing it was like owning a beautiful picture and not looking at it. Still, I always feel close to Cecil when I pick it up.'

'You called it a "Strad",' I said. 'Does it have a Stradivarius label in it?'

'Oh, no, I don't think so – the name was just a joke – I think there is what remains of a label inside it, but I'm sure it doesn't say Stradivarius or anything important like that. Really, the whole thing was only a joke.'

'I'd like to have a look at it anyway, if you don't mind. Obviously it's got nothing to do with Miss Deniker's estate, so it's entirely up to you.'

'Oh, I'm quite happy for you to look at it, Mr Harton. I'll get it now.'

As Miss Beeching disappeared upstairs, I stood looking out of the open sitting room window, across the downland fields, and out towards the sea. The normally distinct colours had begun to fade under the sort of weather usually reserved for the Mediterranean. I was quite certain it would be the end of Alice Beeching if she had to move away, but I was much less sure about how to prevent it.

The violin was a million to one shot; the only thing in it's favour so far was that it didn't have a Stradivarius label – that would have almost certainly meant it was worthless. Another problem was that I knew only marginally more about stringed instruments than I did about wind instruments, and since I knew nothing about wind instruments, that wasn't saying a lot.

'Here we are, Mr Harton,' Miss Beeching said as she reappeared holding out a violin case in front of her.

I took the case and opened it. The violin itself was wrapped in a blue silk scarf, and there were two bows clipped to the inside of the lid of the case. I looked at the bows first. 'Well, one of these is by a good maker, anyway,' I said.

'Is it?' Miss Beeching said. 'I didn't know that bows could be special.'

'Oh, yes. This one's by James Tubbs; he worked in London mainly, from the 1830s until the end of the First World War I think.'

'Goodness, how clever of you to be able to recognise his work.'

'Not really. His name's stamped on it.'

Miss Beeching looked at the bow as I pointed to the stamped signature. 'Well I never! You know I'd never noticed that in all the years I've looked after it. Does that mean it's of some value?'

'Several hundred pounds at least.'

She rolled her eyes heavenwards and sank slowly down onto the settee. 'I don't think the other bow's any good,' I went on, 'but let's have a look at the violin.'

It was a lovely colour and looked beautiful, but that wasn't much help. I looked inside at what remained of the label.

'Something . . . Crem . . . something . . . seventeen-something – that's about all that's left of the label.'

'What do you think it is?' she asked.

'I really don't know, but if it's genuine, "Crem . . ." should be "Cremona" – several good makers worked there so that's hopeful. The date appears to be early eighteenth-century, but I have no idea about attribution. In all honesty, Miss Beeching, I don't know if it's any good or not, but if you'd like me to, I'll take it away and find out.'

'Oh, yes please, Mr Harton. Please do!'

'Amati,' Duncan said, as he stroked the violin.

'Is it?'

'I'll bet you a month's salary on it.'

'No thanks – I'll bow to your superior knowledge,' I said. I was in no position to argue. I'd heard of the Amati family of makers but that was as far as my knowledge went.

'I'm sure it is an Amati, but I don't know how good it is. I'll take it round to Dougie Fox on my way home this evening – he'll know more about it.'

Dougie Fox was a very knowledgeable local dealer in musical instruments, and Wilson's unofficial consultant.

'If it is right, what's it worth?' I asked.

'I'm not sure; certainly not hundreds of thousands, but enough for your Miss Beeching to pay her tax bill and have some change left over.'

Antonia had been unusually quiet all evening. She'd ploughed remorselessly up and down the pool for fifteen minutes when we went swimming, she hadn't said a word during the journey into Langton, and had hardly lifted her eyes from her plate during the meal.

'Are you going to tell me what's wrong?' I asked, 'or shall we just continue to sit here in silence?'

She put down her fork and looked at me. 'I've been offered a job,' she said.

'A good one?'

'Yes, a very good one,' she paused, looked down at her plate again, then back at me. There was a look in her eyes I'd never seen before, 'I've decided to take it,' she said.

'I see. What does it entail?'

'It's in your line of business actually. I'll be working as European P.A. for a big American collector of *art nouveau* and *art deco*. His name's Emile Jerome Junior . . .'

'Good God!'

'Yes, it is a bit unlikely, but he's very nice and absolutely genuine. I met him when I was temping for that picture gallery last year. He offered me a job then but I didn't even

262

consider it, I just thought he was a dirty old . . . well . . . middle-aged man. Then he contacted me again just before Christmas and I got Daddy to check him out. Apparently he's just what he says he is – a stinking rich international businessman and a collector. So, I thought about it, but still decided against it. Last week he telephoned me again – he made me an offer I couldn't turn down, Richard.'

'But why didn't you tell me?'

'Because I knew you'd be upset.'

'Why should I be upset about you getting this fantastic job – no matter how unlikely it might sound.'

'You don't understand, Richard. It means leaving England. I'll be based in Monte Carlo and Paris, but I'll have to travel to and from New York quite a lot. Emile lives in California and he wants to cut down on the amount of travelling he has to do.'

'It all sounds very jet-set,' I said. 'How often will you come back to Sussex?'

'That's the other thing, Richard. Dad's decided to sell up. He's never really been happy at The Rectory since Mummy's death. I think he's only kept it on for me.'

'I see,' I said, beginning to grasp the scale and finality of the changes about to overtake me. 'When do you start?'

'Next week – Wednesday.'

'Next week! Why the hell didn't you tell me what was going on before?'

'I wanted to,' Antonia said, reaching out to touch my hand, 'but I was frightened – I knew how unhappy you'd be.'

'How considerate of you,' I said, throwing some notes from my wallet onto the table as I stood up.

'Aren't you going to finish your meal?'

'I'm suddenly not hungry – I wonder why!'

'Richard!' she called, as I turned my back and walked towards the door. 'Wait! Please wait!'

Chapter 24

'God, you look awful!' Kate said, as she dumped her bag on her desk. 'Have you been here all night?'

'Not quite,' I replied.

'What on earth's the matter?'

I hesitated for a moment, then gave in. I needed to tell somebody. 'Antonia and I are splitting up. She's taking a job abroad, and Hugh's selling The Rectory – end of story.'

'Oh, no! I am sorry, Richard. When did she tell you all this?'

'Last night.'

'And you'd no idea anything was wrong until then?'

'None . . . Well, Antonia had mentioned she wanted to get a proper job, but that was all.'

'You mean she'd tried to talk to you about it and you wouldn't listen.'

'No, I don't, I mean . . .'

'You're a typical man, Richard – an abject coward. As soon as you know there's something nasty on the way, you put your hands over your eyes, stick your fingers in your ears and bury your head in the sand.'

I felt I had to object, if only on the grounds of physical impossibility. 'That's absolute rubbish, I . . .'

'No it's not – you're all the same,' Kate went on. 'This has obviously been coming for months. Antonia must have been desperately miserable.'

'But . . .'

'The important thing now is to be positive. You're bound to feel shattered, but you've got to use this as a fresh start.'

'Really? How easy it all is when you explain it to me,' I said.

264

'Don't be sarcastic, Richard, it doesn't suit you. No, you've got view this as a crossroads in your life, evaluate what you've achieved so far, and decide what you want to achieve next.'

'But . . .'

The telephone on my desk started to ring.

'There we are,' Kate said, with grotesque brightness, 'the first call of the day – probably an unexpected new and exciting opportunity; a call from a stranger that will change your life.' She picked up the telephone, 'Wilson's Auction Galleries . . . Yes, he is . . . May I say who's calling . . . Hold on . . .' she put her hand over the mouthpiece, 'Never mind, I expect the next one will be a new and exciting opportunity.'

'Why, who is it?'

'Mrs Hill, I'm afraid.'

I groaned.

'There you are,' Kate went on, 'you see how wrong you can be?'

'Wrong?'

'Yes, a few moments ago you thought life couldn't get any worse, and it just has.' She grinned, 'I'll make some coffee.'

'Yes, Mrs Hill,' I said, 'what can I do for you?'

'Good morning, Mr Harton. The problem is I'm afraid I'm a little confused.'

'About what, Mrs Hill?'

'Well, how much did you say my Sheraton wardrobe was worth?'

'Nothing – you don't have a Sheraton wardrobe, Mrs Hill.'

'Yes I do – the one in the hall.'

'That's Edwardian, Mrs Hill.'

'Oh, are you sure it couldn't be Sheraton, Mr Harton?'

'Yes, Mrs Hill, I'm sure it couldn't be Sheraton.'

'But couldn't you have made a mistake, Mr Harton?'

'No, Mrs Hill, I couldn't.'

'Really? Oh dear, oh dear,' she said, becoming more and more agitated. 'But how can you be so sure?'

'Because no such piece of furniture existed in the time of Thomas Sheraton, Mrs Hill. The design is much later.'

265

'Oh!'

'What have you done, Mrs Hill?' I asked, with a sigh.

'I think I may have been very silly again, Mr Harton.'

'You don't say.'

'Well . . . you see . . . two men came to my door yesterday afternoon . . .'

I sighed again. I knew exactly what was coming.

'. . . and they said my wardrobe was Sheraton and whoever had valued it at three to four hundred pounds didn't know what he was talking about . . .'

'What did they offer you for it, Mrs Hill?' I asked.

'Three thousand pounds, cash.'

'And what else did they offer to buy?'

'The secretaire and the bureau, but they said you'd overvalued both of those, and that the secretaire was only worth five hundred, and the bureau three hundred.'

'Which was about twelve hundred pounds less than my upper estimates,' I said.

'Yes, but I thought, since I was getting so much more for the wardrobe, that didn't matter.'

'I see. Shall I tell you what happened next, Mrs Hill?'

'I'm sorry, Mr Harton. What?'

'Let me try to guess what happened next, Mrs Hill. I would think they immediately gave you eight hundred cash for the secretaire and bureau and loaded both pieces on their truck, or Volvo, or whatever it was they were driving.'

'Yes, that's right.'

'Then they came up with a reason why they couldn't take the wardrobe straight away.'

'Yes, they said they'd have to get a bigger lorry.'

'Ah, yes, that's a good one. So they said they'd be back first thing this morning, with the three thousand pounds in cash, to collect the thing.'

'Yes, they said they'd be here by eight o'clock at the latest. I've been waiting for them since seven.'

'And you'll go on waiting, Mrs Hill.'

'What?'

'You'll never see them again, Mrs Hill. You've just fallen for the oldest trick in the "knockers'" handbook. You've sold them two thousand pounds worth of furniture for eight hundred and they've made their profit for the week in just one call.'

'Oh . . . Mr Harton,' she wailed, 'what am I going to do?'

'I don't know, Mrs Hill. But whatever you eventually decide upon, you're on your own.'

'I beg your pardon, Mr Harton.'

'I said, you are on your own now, Mrs Hill. I am fed up with wasting hour after hour advising you, just so you can go and give your things away to any Tom, Dick or Harry that knocks on your door. Goodbye, Mrs Hill.'

'But, Mr . . .' She was cut off as I slammed down the receiver.

Kate, who had arrived back with the coffee, grinned as she passed my mug to me. 'Well!' she said. 'That was a good positive start to the first day of the rest of your life. Well done!'

Margaret took a long look at me.

'You look awful,' she said, 'have you got flu or something?'

'He and Antonia have . . .'

'Just a bit under the weather,' I said, before Kate could pour out the whole saga. 'Is Duncan in yet, Margaret?'

'That's why I was coming to see you. He's just called in – apparently his car won't start so he asked if you could cover his appointments for him.'

I groaned again.

'It'll do you good to get out,' Kate chirped. 'No point sitting around here being miserable.'

'Thank you, Kate,' I said. 'How many are there, Margaret?'

'Six – all the details are here.' She handed me a sheaf of notes.

'Cromwelliana?' I said, as I read the last one.

'Yes, I've no idea what the old boy was blathering about, he just kept on and on about "Cromwelliana".'

'Okay. I'd better get going.'

Margaret was almost out of the office when I remembered Cecil's 'Strad'.

'Oh, Margaret, did Duncan mention if he'd seen Dougie Fox?'

'Oh, yes, I almost forgot – I didn't have a clue what he was talking about either, but he said, "Fox gave the fiddle the thumbs up. About ten thousand, and you owe him a month's salary." Does any of that make any sense to you?'

'Yes, yes it does.' I turned to Kate. 'While I'm out, ring Miss Beeching and just say "Cecil's going to pay your tax bill." '

' "Cecil's going to pay your tax bill," ' she repeated as she jotted down the words.

'Everybody's talking in code this morning,' Margaret complained as she turned to go.

'And tell her, I'll call her this afternoon,' I concluded.

Kington shimmered below me as I pondered my future. A huge, noisy bumble bee, liberally dusted with bright yellow pollen, wobbled through the air towards me, then alighted heavily onto an undersized dandelion flower. It rumbled about among the stunted petals for a while before lifting off again in search of a more profitable host. The creature was indefatigable. All that mattered was its work. Nothing else was important. Nothing was permitted to interfere with or disrupt its labours.

'You look better,' Kate said, when I arrived back at The Galleries.

'I am,' I replied, putting my jacket over the back of my chair and loosening my tie.

'Good. May I ask what's brought about this transformation?'

'A bee.'

'A bee?'

'A bee,' I repeated.

'Oh well, if you say so.'

'I do. What's Bill Grigson's number?'

As usual, the telephone at Ashley Park rang for some minutes before it was eventually answered.

'Grigson,' Bill's throaty voice grated out the name.

'Bill, it's Richard Harton.'

"Ello son, 'ow are yer?"

'I'm well. Bill, I want to ask a favour.'

'Ask away, boy.'

'You've mentioned on several occasions that you could give me an introduction to a firm of London auctioneers.'

'No problem.'

'Good. I've decided I'm overdue for a change. It's time I concentrated on where my career's going, and, frankly, if I stay in Sussex, it's probably not going anywhere.'

'I've bin tellin' yer that for two years, Dick.'

'I know. And you're not the only one. So—London here I come!'

A·1